# FUMIHIKO MAKI

## Buildings and Projects

PRINCETON ARCHITECTURAL PRESS

PUBLISHED BY

Princeton Architectural Press
37 East 7th Street
New York, New York 10003
212.995.9620
Call 1.800.722.6657 for a free catalog of books.
www.papress.com

DESIGNER: Kijuro Yahagi
EDITOR: Maki and Associates
Gary Kamemoto, Mark Mulligan,
Tohru Onuma, and Geoffrey Moussas
PRODUCTION EDITOR: Clare Jacobson
COPY EDITOR: Andrew Rubenfeld
LAYOUT: Sara Stemen
COVER PHOTOS: Kijuro Yahagi

SPECIAL THANKS TO: Eugenia Bell, Caroline Green, Therese Kelly,
Mark Lamster, and Annie Nitschke of Princeton
Architectural Press
—KEVIN C. LIPPERT, PUBLISHER

LIBRARY OF CONGRESS CATALOGING-IN-PUBLICATION DATA
Maki, Fumihiko, 1928–
    Fumihiko Maki : buildings and projects.
      p.   cm.
    ISBN 1-56898-108-2 (cloth : alk. paper).
    —ISBN 1-56898-109-0 (pbk. : alk. paper).
    1. Maki, Fumihiko, 1928– —Themes, motives. 2. Architecture—Environ-
mental aspects. 3. Architectural practice, International.
    I. Title.
    NA1559.M24A4 1997
    720'.92—DC21
                                                                97-3063
                                                                  CIP

# CONTENTS

# INTRODUCTION

Last summer in the Event Hall of Hillside Terrace, we held a party to commemorate the thirtieth anniversary of my Tokyo-based architecture firm, Maki and Associates. The dinner was attended by nearly one hundred present and former staff members and collaborators, and the occasion gave me a chance to reflect on the more than one hundred projects produced over those thirty years, the ideas and explorations that led to them, and the collaborations that arose from them.

For this monograph I have selected from those years twenty-five projects—both built and unbuilt—that I feel might provide insight into my thoughts and aspirations as an architect. While the material appears as a series of finite designs and realized works, it is more a continual process of ideas evolving over time than a series of individual architectural conclusions that I hope to emphasize here. Thus I have deliberately avoided presenting projects in a strict chronological order, arranging them instead in thematic groupings in order to clarify certain continuities that appear and reappear in our work over time. Although this approach cannot promise to cover any one theme in its entirety, and though the reader will doubtlessly discern missing links from one project to the next, I hope that through this presentation the gist of some important, overlapping issues will begin to emerge—ideas and theses that constitute a continuous link from the beginning years of my career to my present investigations.

In every project my first concern is the creation of spaces where certain human activities are both physically and mentally enhanced and where a sense of public character may develop. Those spaces then begin to acquire a kind of symbolic presentation in abstract architectural form. Issues of available technology and appropriate building materials are then investigated simultaneously, and the project takes on a dimension of time as it begins to resolve these. The refinement of form and space continues down to precise architectural details which, as primary elements, are essential to the spirit of the whole. For me, more than any question of style, this kind of evolutionary approach to architectural design—layering issues of space, use, form, technology, materials, and detail one over another in sequence—constitutes the essence of modernism and provides fertile ground for my present and future explorations in architecture.

FUMIHIKO MAKI

# SPIRAL

Minato, Tokyo 1985

The Wacoal Media Center, commonly known as the Spiral Building, has become a kind of landmark building not only for our office but also for Japanese urbanism in the 1980s. Incorporating art galleries, a theater space, shops, restaurants, and offices, the Spiral sponsors a multifaceted arts curriculum in an informal, noninstitutional setting. The idea for the building came about in the early eighties when the Wacoal company, a leading manufacturer of women's lingerie, decided to move operations to Tokyo from their base in western Japan. Along with this move, they wished to sponsor a building that would make the company known to Tokyo; this building was not necessarily to be a sales place for their product so much as a place to establish a new corporate image. From their headquarters in Kyoto, Wacoal sent a team to work with us on programming, and after a long period of collaborative investigation, we arrived at a design we felt was appropriate. Since its opening in 1985 the Spiral has become one of the most popular places in Tokyo for performances and exhibitions, owing to the company's continuing efforts to provide a forum for the cutting edge of new art.

The multifaceted nature of the program is reflected in the front facade where overlapping grids of square aluminum panels, cut out windows, and geometric volumes are worked together. This fragmented, collaged composition also echoes the heterogeneous urban context of Tokyo where the juxtaposition of many buildings unrelated in scale and expression borders on the chaotic. Like the city itself, one's understanding of the Spiral Building's facade relies on piecing together selected fragments.

Sharp, precise aluminum panels and thin sash profiles create an abstract texture of pure planes and tautly etched lines. Open joints between the panels and the avoidance of sealant on the facade surface produce these straight, black lines. Set against this silvery gray texture are several geometric solids—a cone, a cube, a piano curve, and, in the roof garden, a pyramid and a hemispherical dome. The collaged solids are white and abstracted, lack the materiality of the aluminum surfaces, and also serve a more symbolic function. At a time when buildings in the United States and other countries were beginning to recycle classical motifs, this building was paying tribute to icons of twentieth-century architecture and the vision of cubist art.

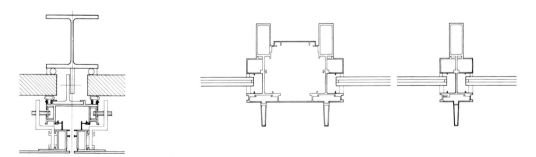

The front facade is made up of several interwoven building skin systems, including open-jointed square aluminum panels (*left*) and thin-profiled extruded aluminum sash (*right*).

*Above:* View of atrium through first floor café

*Right:* Entrance at dusk

The first floor includes spaces for three different but overlapping functions. The entrance lobby facing Aoyama Boulevard provides a space for meeting friends in the city. Beyond the lobby is a café surrounded by galleries displaying continually changing exhibitions. The main gallery space is located at the very back of the first floor in a semicylindrical three-story atrium; a gently sloping ramp leading to the second floor encircles this space and provides views in the round of sculptures and installations. The gallery and its spiraling ramp are flooded with natural light from above and can be seen from the street entrance, looking through the lobby and café.

Visitors may also reach the second floor via a broad esplanade stair at the front of the building, whose ascent is discernible in the facade above the entrance. More than a mere circulation space, the esplanade stair has an inviting, public atmosphere and is frequently used as an extension of the first-floor galleries. A few chairs are placed in front of the window, offering a place for visitors to relax for a moment and watch scenes of street life along Aoyama Boulevard. Our idea was thus to sponsor a kind of public space where an individual would feel free to be alone and yet would be able to participate vicariously in the street life of the city.

The esplanade stair continues up to the third-floor foyer of the Spiral Hall. The hall seats three hundred spectators and is used primarily for fashion shows, concerts, and various theatrical performances. The upper floors are devoted to offices, video studios, a restaurant with a rooftop garden, a costume design center, and the owner's private entertainment spaces in the penthouse.

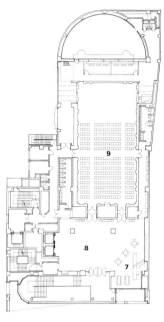

Third floor

Fifth floor

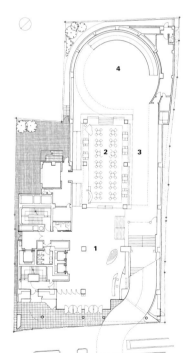

First floor

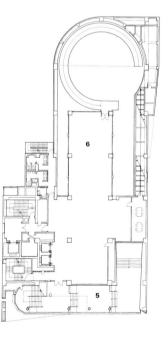

Second floor

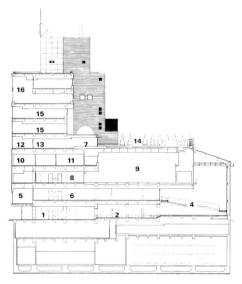

Section

| | |
|---|---|
| 1 entrance hall | 9 Spiral Hall |
| 2 café | 10 office |
| 3 gallery | 11 studio |
| 4 atrium | 12 kitchen |
| 5 esplanade | 13 restaurant |
| 6 shops | 14 roof garden |
| 7 bar | 15 design center |
| 8 foyer | 16 club |

7

Spiral ramp leading to the second-floor shops. The thin profile of the ramp is achieved with a structure of built-up steel plates, and the ramp itself is attached to surrounding walls at only three points. The continuous stainless steel handrail was welded and polished on site to achieve a seamless finish.

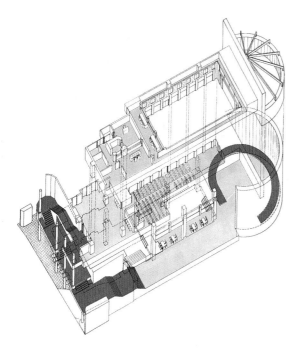

Axonometric drawing showing public circulation between first and third floors

*Above:* View from the first-floor gallery to an art installation in the spiral atrium

*Right:* The atrium is illuminated by a semicircular skylight. The lower wall is articulated as a base in rough-finished marble, with polished horizontal bands set in to give a sense of scale. The stainless steel rings attached at the top of the base can be used to suspend installation materials across the atrium space.

Esplanade stair leading to the Spiral Hall on the third floor

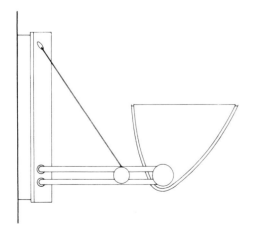

Bracket lamp designed for esplanade stair

The roof garden of restaurant on the fifth floor was conceived as a kind of theatrical landscape, detached from the real world. Abstract forms, such as the fountain's pyramid and the conical cypress trees, are used to create a still, surreal space, seemingly far removed the surrounding city.

When the Spiral Hall is not in use for theatrical and musical events or fashion shows, it occasionally hosts lectures and exhibitions.

The art deco-inspired lobby of the Spiral Hall. A deliberate choice of different architectural vocabularies was made for different floors of the building in an attempt to reflect the eclectic nature of its program.

*Above:* Aerial view—the "fifth facade"

*Facing page:* Aoyama Boulevard elevation

# NATIONAL MUSEUM OF MODERN ART, KYOTO

Sakyo, Kyoto 1986

Perspective with the museum's abstracted volume shown in relation to the Heian Shrine

The new National Museum of Modern Art in Kyoto houses an important collection of modern Japanese ceramics, lacquerware, and *Nihon-ga* (Japanese-style painting) as well as twentieth-century Western-style paintings, prints, and sculpture. Reflecting its importance in the culture of present-day Kyoto, the museum is located adjacent to other museums and cultural facilities in Okazaki Park along the approach road to the Heian Shrine, the ancient city's most important shrine. The entire area is a designated historic/scenic zone, and all buildings within it are limited to 20 meters in height. The museum site is bounded on the southern side by a canal feeding Kyoto's Kamo River, while the remaining three sides face other cultural facilities: to the west, an industrial exhibition hall; to the north, the prefectural library; and to the east, the Kyoto Municipal Art Museum. The main entrance to the National Museum of Modern Art is on the east side, facing the Heian Shrine's great red *torii* gate, which serves as a symbol for the park and its cultural institutions.

As opposed to Tokyo's chaotic sprawl, Kyoto's streets largely follow the patterns of an orthogonal city grid—recalling the city's origin as a new capital, laid out based on models from imperial China. The clarity of this grid provided inspiration for organizing the facade of granite-faced precast panels and a curtain wall system composed of both transparent and translucent glass. For the entrance facade facing the *torii* gate, we felt a certain formality or symmetry was required in keeping with the neoclassical style of surrounding buildings. The side facades, particularly the south facade facing the canal, enjoyed more compositional freedom in relation to interior spaces; still, a hint of classicism can be found in their tripartite division.

The multistory entrance lobby provides a reference point for visitors to the museum; around it are grouped a café, an auditorium, and a side gallery for temporary exhibitions. At the center of the lobby is a skylit promenade stairway leading to the main exhibition galleries on the third and fourth floors.

As a building type, art museums tend to offer a very insular, self-contained environment for appreciating their contents. Against this prevailing view of the museum as an enclosed box, this design deliberately brings circulation paths to the exterior edges of the plan, using stair halls and intermediate vestibules to draw in views of the distant landscape and to make to links between art works and the experience of the city outside.

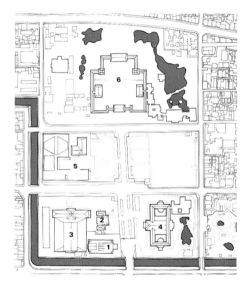

Site plan

1 National Museum of Modern Art
2 Prefectural Library
3 Exhibition Hall
4 Kyoto Municipal Art Museum
5 Kyoto Hall
6 Heian Shrine

South facade along canal

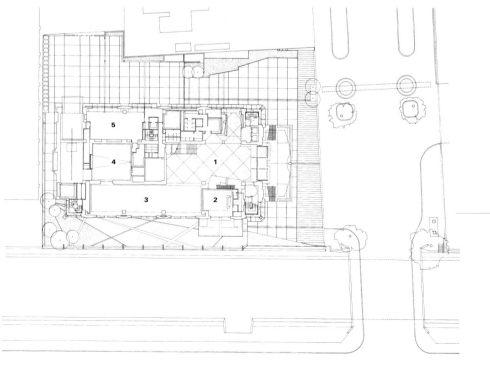

1 entrance lobby
2 café
3 gallery
4 auditorium
5 office

*Above:* First-floor plan

*Facing page:* East facade seen with the Heian Shrine's grand *torii* gate

Main stair leading to exhibition spaces on third floor. The atrium walls are clad in white marble, with geometrical patterns of polished and sandblasted finishes made faintly visible by the reflection of sunlight across their surfaces.

The main stair's mezzanine level can be used for installations related to changing exhibitions.

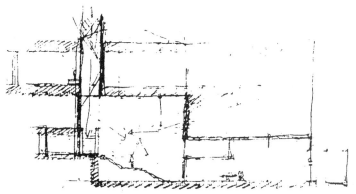

Section of skylit main stair

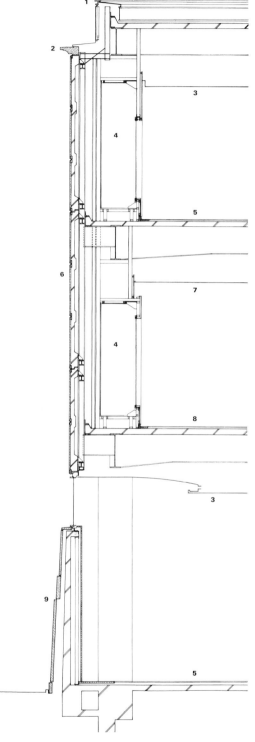

Exterior wall section expressing the tripartite organization of the facade: rusticated granite base, panelized granite middle section, aluminum cornice and roof.

1 aluminum parapet
2 granite cornice
3 plasterboard (12 millimeters x 2)
4 display case
5 carpet (thickness = 15 millimeters)
6 granite-faced precast concrete panels
7 steel-perforated ceiling panels (thickness = 2.3 millimeters)
8 rubber flooring (thickness = 6 millimeters)
9 granite-clad base

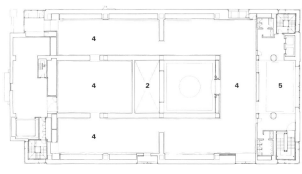

Fourth floor

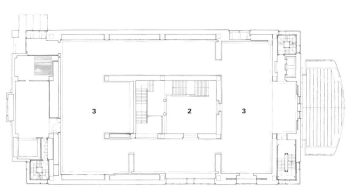

Third floor

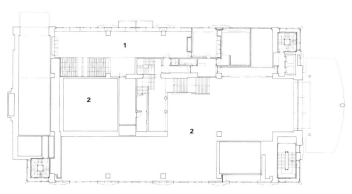

Second floor

1 office
2 void
3 temporary exhibition
4 permanent exhibition
5 lounge

Three kinds of galleries are provided in the museum. The fourth-floor galleries are the most traditional, consisting of a series of rectangular rooms with display boxes incorporated into the perimeter walls. The third-floor galleries employ a system of movable partitions that can be configured freely in response to changing exhibitions. The first-floor gallery—essentially an extension of the entrance hall looking out on the canal—is the most informal, calling for exhibitors to be creative in setting interactive displays.

A lounge at the entrance to the fourth-floor permanent exhibition galleries looks over the city toward the mountains to the east.

# TEPIA

Minato, Tokyo 1989

The 1980s witnessed a period of unprecedented prosperity and optimism in Japan. In the wake of its economic miracle, the country staked out an unparalleled international reputation for cutting-edge technology and industrial precision. What is remarkable about this situation in Japan is that while extremely sophisticated technology was being developed in fields such as computers, video imaging, and robotics, at the same time low-tech industries such as manufacturing and construction, far from being neglected, were experiencing a kind of renaissance as well. It was during this time that an organization affiliated with the Ministry of International Trade and Industry conceived the Tepia Science Pavilion as a place to exhibit the most advanced products of high technology and electronics. The building itself was to utilize and exemplify the latest building technology, while its exhibits were to provide an information exchange between professionals and the public as well as among the experts themselves.

Tepia is located near the center of Tokyo in the Meiji Jingu Park. Although its site is only a short walk away from the Spiral Building, the urban context of the park is quite different. With a floor-area ratio of just over 200% (versus Spiral's 500%), Tepia is surrounded by spacious gardens and walkways. The building consists of four floors above ground and two floors below. A two-story lobby on the ground floor serves to orient visitors to the adjacent exhibitions halls. The video library, small lecture room, and café are located on the second floor; additional exhibition, conference, and seminar rooms are located on the upper floors.

Built five years after the Spiral Building, the facades of Tepia represent a more distilled approach to treating the same materials. Whereas the Spiral's facade is treated as a collage with layers of different patterns and constructions revealing and overlapping one another, the approach to Tepia's exterior is purer and more formally restrained, its inspiration coming from de Stijl architecture. The design emphasizes an apparently weightless composition of points, lines, and planes in modern materials of metal and glass. New means of mobilizing these materials—using, for example, five-millimeter-thick aluminum panels, structural glass, and extruded aluminum solar air heating panels—have been investigated and used from the largest scale of the building to the smallest of details. The building's exterior form combines strict vertical walls and broad horizontal overhangs; at their point of intersection, a tight gap is revealed to heighten the tension between sharp plane edges. Further refinement of the design principles occurs in the interior by utilizing a variety of glass and metal screens to dematerialize the architecture and create a sense of deeply layered space. For example, a wall of perforated panels of aluminum is suspended between the lobby and the front stair by slender cables allowing a vague sense of transparency between these spaces. Conceived as a modern equivalent of the *shoji* screen of traditional architecture, this screen is dematerialized by lines of light showing through the gaps of the slightly separated panels.

Although aluminum, stainless steel, and glass are used as the major finish materials throughout the building, Tepia combines them in new and different ways, adding finishes varying in degree of reflectivity and translucency to create a sensuous ambiance not usually associated with these materials. They are supplemented with granite, marble, rubber sheeting, and specially designed carpets using a diverse palette of whites, grays, silvers, and blacks—occasionally accented by bright hues.

The high standard of technology and craftsmanship maintained by Japan's system of building construction made this design and its details possible. In all likelihood, this level of technology and craftsmanship may not endure indefinitely and, in this sense, Tepia is an unusually revealing testimony to the Japanese society of its day.

A semitransparent screen of perforated aluminum panels provides a layered view to the exterior from the first-floor lobby. Narrow slits between panels create a grid of light.

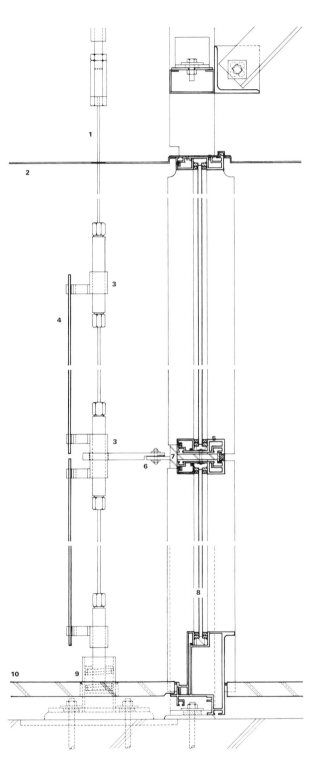

*Top left:* The perforated panels of the screen wall are held tautly in place by connector rods suspended at points along vertical tension wires.

*Bottom left:* Entrance lobby

*Above:* Suspended screen detail

1 tension wire (diameter = 0.5 millimeter)
2 steel-perforated ceiling panel (thickness = 1.6 millimeters)
3 aluminum panel mounting bracket
4 perforated aluminum panel
5 aluminum window sash
6 mounting bracket stabilizing bar
7 steel flat bar
8 single-pane glass (thickness = 10 millimeters)
9 tension wire mounting bracket
10 granite flooring (thickness = 35 millimeters)

The semicylindrical volume of the north entrance is enclosed in white glass block, which softly filters sunlight and catches the afternoon shadows of swaying trees.

Third-floor lounge

Second-floor restaurant

First-floor exhibition gallery

*Facing page:* Marble-paved roof garden courtyard on fourth floor, with rooftop Sol-air panels lined up above. Like the Spiral's roof garden, the intended effect is largely theatrical.

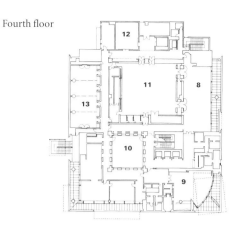

Fourth floor

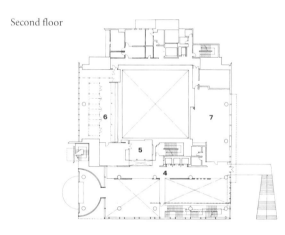

Third floor

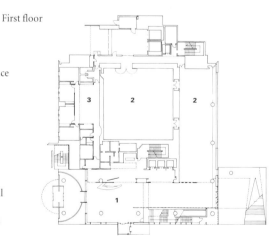

Second floor

First floor

1  entrance hall
2  exhibition space
3  office
4  gallery
5  theater
6  video library
7  restaurant
8  lobby
9  lounge
10  courtyard
11  conference hall
12  kitchen
13  meeting room

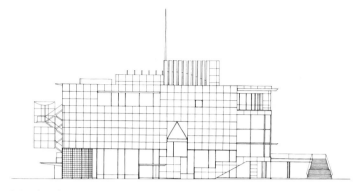

West elevation

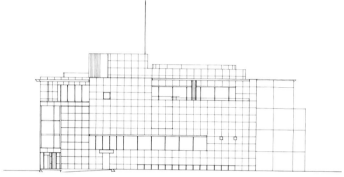

South elevation

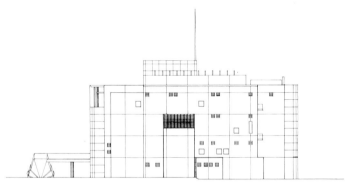

East elevation

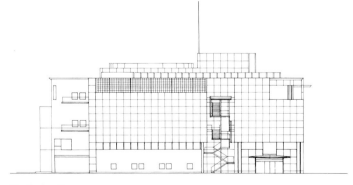

North elevation

*Top right:* View from southwest

*Bottom right:* Corner detail of curtain wall

Garden seen across reflecting pool. The bottom of the pool is finished in black granite and white Neo-pariés, an artificial stone made of glass.

# SALZBURG CONGRESS CENTER

Salzburg, Austria 1992

Austria's importance as a meeting point between Eastern and Western Europe is reflected in the broad range of international conferences and events taking place in its cities. In 1992 the city of Salzburg decided to sponsor a competition for the reconstruction of its Congress Center on a site facing the gardens of the Mirabell Palace. In order to gain financial support for the project, the city proposed a program that would combine the Congress Center with an expansion of the hotel on the adjacent site. The two institutions would be housed on the same site within a single block; functionally, however, they would remain viable separate entities.

An architectural solution had to begin with extremely careful positioning of the program's required spaces: large, medium, and small congress halls, an exhibition gallery, offices, and boutiques belonging to the city; banquet rooms, meeting rooms, a restaurant, a kitchen, offices, and guest rooms belonging to the hotel; and ground floor public areas and underground parking belonging to both. Strategic location and interconnection of all these spaces would ensure an efficient separation of the management functions while allowing direct access between the Congress Center and the hotel at desired points. Simply put, this very difficult program presented itself like a kind of three-dimensional puzzle—a Rubik's Cube.

An even greater challenge facing the design came from the fact that the various parts of the program required an amount of space far exceeding the maximum volume allowed by height restrictions and other zoning, even allowing for subterranean floors. Since the scope of the program had clearly departed from the scale of the surrounding cityscape, the only viable solution seemed to accept the entire program, build higher than the neighbors, and then find ways to minimize the perceived mass—a pragmatic approach, in essence. We proposed to envelop the building mass in an abstract "cube of light" 48 by 48 meters in plan and 36 meters high. The cube is defined by a lightweight skeletal structure against which the layered facades of glass, perforated metal panels, louvered screens, and sculptural voids produce an ephemeral, transparent effect veiling the actual volume of the interior. Thus, while the Congress Center projects the image of a large glowing cube set in the city, we have greatly reduced the apparent volume contained within by consciously eroding the cube at its outer surfaces—in particular matching the height of its rooftop restaurant terrace to the height of surrounding buildings—and introducing gradated areas of transparency between inside and outside.

Within this framework, the resolution of the complex program began to resemble the process of putting together a kind of Chinese magic puzzle box. Beyond the three-dimensional allocation of spaces to separate hotel and center functions within the cube, we faced the additional problem of providing maximum flexibility within these spaces for different kinds of events. We began to conceive interior partitions—particularly those between the halls and foyers—as separate parts in a mechanical assembly, able to move and shift in response to desired combinations of space. During its use as a congress hall, for example, the main hall could function as an enclosed box contained within the larger light box; for large exhibitions or gala events, the box could be used together with adjacent foyers by opening doors and sliding partitions. The elliptical volume of a café and sculptural stairs ascending through a series of foyers are used to animate the space contained within the cubical building membrane.

The Congress Center's cube of light seeks out the optimal, weightless nature of modernism. Its vocabulary of transparent layers and floating screens—both revealing and concealing spaces beyond—represents a further exploration of ideas first tested at Tepia, here rendered almost weightless and more transparent. Set within the context of Salzburg's historical cityscape, the glowing, ephemeral cube provides a clear symbol of the center's public and contemporary character, and, together with the Mirabell Place and adjacent Saint Andrew's Church, completes a trilogy of public architecture evoking the rich character of the city's history.

Figure-ground plan of city, with the new Congress Center, Mirabell Palace, and St. Andrew's Church in red

The new Congress Center—an ephemeral, glowing cube adjacent to Salzburg's historic Mirabell Palace gardens

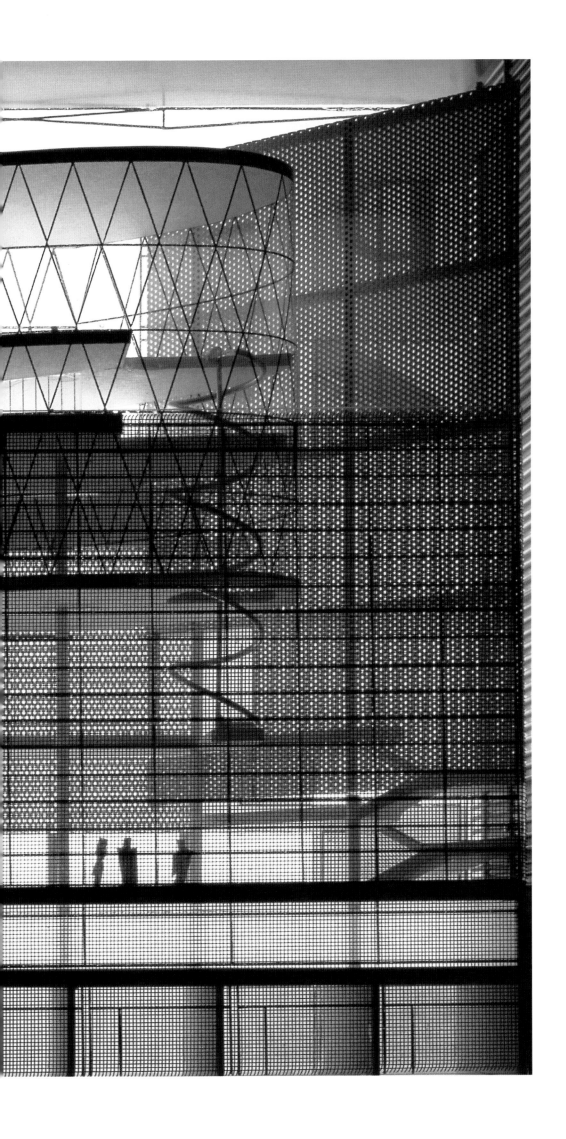

Congress Center foyer

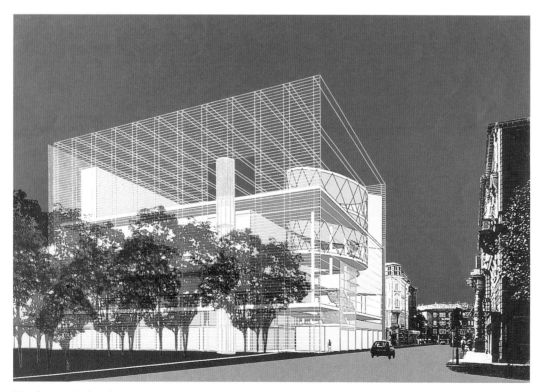

View from south along Rainerstrasse

Model

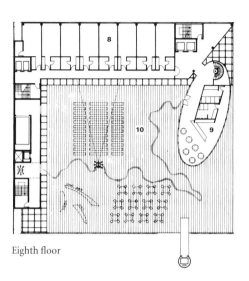

Eighth floor

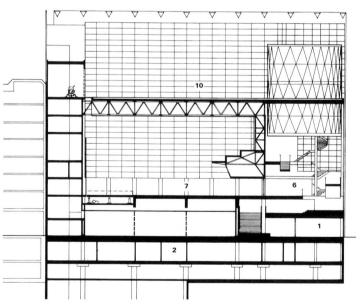

East-west section

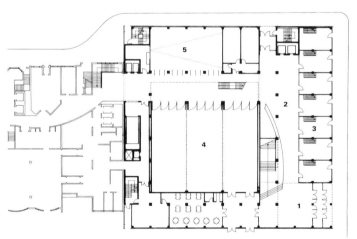

First floor

1  entrance hall
2  lobby
3  shop
4  banquet room
5  meeting room
6  foyer
7  congress hall
8  hotel/guest room
9  bar
10  roof terrace

# CENTER FOR THE ARTS YERBA BUENA GARDENS

San Francisco, California 1993
(in association with Robinson, Mills + Williams)

The Center for the Arts Yerba Buena Gardens, our first building designed in the United States in more than thirty years, is part of a major mixed-use redevelopment complex south of Market Street, aimed at creating a new hub of cultural activities in downtown San Francisco. Its particular mission is to showcase San Francisco's ethnic and cultural diversity through a variety of art disciplines, providing space for changing exhibitions, installations, and performances of an experimental nature. The center's open-ended program, together with the challenge of designing in a very different social context and a charged political environment, provided a completely new set of issues to be addressed in the design.

The Center for the Arts sits at the corner of Mission and Third Streets, at the northern edge of the Yerba Buena Gardens. Although there are several high-rise buildings surrounding the site, the center's height and mass were severely restricted by the fact that it rests not on solid ground, but rather on the posttensioned waffle slab roof of the Moscone Convention Center's underground extension. This massive facility underlying the arts center and its gardens is recognizable at street level only by its emergency stair exits surfacing at several locations around the perimeter of the block. Its influence, however, was immense, not only on the arts center's structure but also on the aboveground positioning of its mechanical and electrical machinery and the location of entrances. Because of the limitations the underground Moscone Convention Center imposed on the site, the Center for the Arts is forced literally to float within its dense urban context.

We chose a steel-frame structure in order to minimize structural loads on the convention center's roof slab, and our search for other lightweight materials for the building skin suggested an aluminum corrugated cladding together with flat aluminum panels and glass. This combination rendered the image of the arts center as an "elegant factory"—paying homage to those artists who, before making the center their new home, had their gallery lofts in disused industrial buildings. The apparent weightlessness of this light, diaphanous metallic building also expresses the temporality and changeability inherent in the center's contemporary art programs, consciously avoiding any suggestion of the monumentality we tend to associate with conventional museums.

On an additional level, the building aspires to recreate another image rooted in the consciousness of San Francisco and its origins as a port town: its low-profile horizontality, metallic skin, and sculptural elements such as light steel stairs, handrails, and flagpoles all suggest the image of a ship harbored in the gardens, gleaming in the California sunlight.

Aerial view

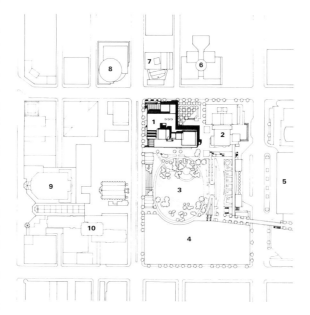

Site plan

1 Center for the Arts
  Maki and Associates/ Robinson,
  Mills + Williams
2 Center for the Arts Theater
  James Stewart Polshek & Partners
3 Yerba Buena Gardens Esplanade
  MGA Partners Architects
4 Future development
  (entertainment/retail)
5 George R. Moscone Convention
  Center
  Hellmuth, Obata & Kassabaum
6 San Francisco Museum of Modern
  Art
  Mario Botta/Hellmuth, Obata &
  Kassabaum
7 Future development (office)
8 Office Building
  Pei Cobb Freed & Partners
9 Office Building
  Cesar Pelli & Partners
10 Marriott Hotel
  Daniel Mann Johnson &
  Mendenhall

*Facing page:* Entrance hall. Visitors gather for an informal string quintet performance.

Gallery 1 features adjustable skylights.

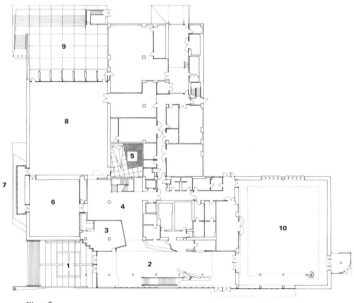

First floor

| | | |
|---|---|---|
| 1 entry plaza | 7 vestibule | 13 Gallery 3 |
| 2 entrance lobby | 8 Gallery 2 | 14 café |
| 3 gift shop | 9 sculpture court | 15 void |
| 4 anteroom | 10 Forum | 16 conference |
| 5 courtyard | 11 media lobby | 17 office |
| 6 Gallery 1 | 12 screening room | |

Second floor

# A MODERN BUILDING FOR POSTMODERN ART

Paolo Polledri

When the Center for the Arts Yerba Buena Gardens opened in October 1993, it seemed destined to take a difficult course toward an uncertain purpose. The first building designed by Fumihiko Maki for San Francisco, it is also the first he has completed in the United States in more than thirty years. The center's mission is to celebrate multiculturalism, a current, much discussed term that refers to the convergence of established and marginal cultures and proposes an equitable approach to the numerous ethnic and social groups and means of expression that coexist in the Bay Area. This is art as it should be—a transmitter, not a servant, of updated political ideals of democracy and human dignity.

The center is not a museum, a place reserved for the art and artists that are validated by the public and critics. It is an agency that pursues an enthusiastic, inclusive approach to artistic programs and experimental, anticanonical ideas. Ignoring the conventional medium-bound categories of painting and sculpture, the center opts for a multidisciplinary program and views itself as an evolving institution in step with or even ahead of changes in the world. Since its opening it has accommodated shows ranging from the traditional to the arcane—exhibitions, installations, performances, and numerous indefinable events. If there is still room for the avant-garde, this is where one would expect to find it.

This is a worthwhile but vague and sometimes contradictory agenda. A building designed accordingly would have to be everything at once: open-ended, impossibly large and flexible, and unrealistically expensive for a publicly supported institution. It would also run counter to the ethos of architecture, which, unlike art, is built methodically, with a clearly stated program and well-defined goals. But a building designed for the display of contemporary art must be neither at odds with its contents nor an inert container. It must neither be overpowering nor overpowered by art. It may offer opportunities, and sometimes challenges. Art will respond. The building's space will react with that of art to yield a new, unexplored territory.

The relationship that art establishes with its surroundings is crucial. For a painting, wall proportions and the viewer's position are essential considerations. With sculpture, spatial demands are all the more obvious. Less traditional media such as video and installations often have even more precise requirements. Even a building designed specifically to accommodate change must be aware of these circumstances.

How has Maki expressed the mixture of defiance and ecumenism that is at the core of the center's artistic ideal? It is to be found in the complexity of the building's spatial qualities, internal volumes, textures and light conditions, sequence of galleries and ancillary spaces, intense concentration on all scale of details, lack of ostentation, and pursuit of lucidity. But this complexity is not obvious from the outside. On the surface this seems like a straightforward, practical building, clad with aluminum, interrupted by windows and glazed surfaces, surmounted by light monitors, its roof littered with sheds for climate-control and lifting machinery. The structure adapts to its setting with factorylike eagerness. Pure practical reason, rather than aesthetics, seems to govern its design.

In the setting of Yerba Buena Gardens—the latest and grandest addition to San Francisco—the center could have been more self-consciously imposing. Over forty years of planning have gone into this section of San Francisco. In the optimistic mood of the post-World War II years, the idea emerged as a very ambitious redevelopment effort involving a much larger urban area—eleven hundred acres against the current twenty-five. During the mid-1960s an international team of architects and planners, including Kenzo Tange, proposed a megastructure covering several city blocks.

Anteroom to Galleries 1 and 2. A small courtyard garden is visible beyond a screen of glass block.

When the city attempted to implement this proposal, it encountered overwhelming opposition from neighborhood activists. In the end the project was shelved. It left an enduring legacy, however, in the concept of an underground convention facility. In the following years only part of the convention area was built, and not until the 1980s, after much negotiation, were the remaining six blocks developed. In addition to Maki's Center for the Arts, this area includes the Center for the Arts Theater designed by James Stewart Polshek, Mario Botta's new building for the San Francisco Museum of Modern Art, Romaldo Giurgola's large Esplanade, a hotel, and several other amenities and cultural facilities still in the design stage.

Maki seems to have decided that the ordinary is more appropriate than the monumental to express the center's goals. He does not overplay his hand. In appearance the building recalls the factories and old warehouses clad with corrugated metal that can still be found in the area. Like them it has a self-effacing, almost ephemeral quality. But there is no ironic appropriation of the past. Its forms are too charged with energy; they establish historical distance, not proximity, with their models. The polished granite base signals solidity and durability, not impermanence. The details communicate a rigor and an uncommon sense of refinement, not simply a functional response to need.

The fractional mass of the building is partly responsible for this appearance. The center looks as if it had been built over a period of years, with parts added when space became available. Additions are second thoughts to a building, a pragmatic absorption of space and functions that were at first deemed unnecessary. They may also signal a reaching for the aesthetic measure that eluded the initial effort. Additions imply a generational rhythm, as segments do when they spawn off the main body. But in the case of the center, the parts are only effigies of additions. They are

too integral to the body of the building, in both form and function, to imply a change of mind. One of them, a small gallery, protrudes like a veranda or a greenhouse midway between public and private space. But too much care has been given to the materials, the alignment of window mullions, and the calibration of the joints scoring the satin aluminum finish to establish more than a remote connection with the standardized appearance of prefabricated glazing elements.

The largest of these additions seems to cantilever to an implausible extent over the fully transparent space of the entrance. This is a necessary presence in contemporary public buildings, providing a place where visitors can gather and rest. But the entrance also has the centripetal function of unifying the entire building. It is the key fragment of the puzzle, where one can measure the entire vertical and horizontal space of the interior volume. This addition differs from the rest in function and finishes, just as a sky lounge does to the rest of the air terminal. The streamlined forms and geometric compositions of the glazing—symbols of the dynamism, efficiency, and mechanical perfection of the industrial past—map on the facade the contents of the interior. There is nothing tentative about the design; it represents the architectural apogee that can be reached only after a long and disciplined process.

The building's eccentric form was not entirely a matter of design. Some of it was given. The center sits without real foundations on a large platform on top of the underground convention center. It must deal with constraints from below—openings, structural conditions, and ventilation ducts. Its L-shaped footprint was intended to make room for a Chinese garden that never materialized. Surrounded by the city or by the garden, it cannot have a real front or rear, this most basic of architectural hierarchies. Its mechanical equipment or storage rooms could not be hidden in

Gallery 2, with Sculpture Plaza beyond

its basement. Because one of the safety exits from the floor below had previously been positioned at the intersection of two busy streets, Mission and Third, the entrance could not be located in the most important and visible place of the whole site.

During the early design stages, while the rest of the area was under construction, Maki had to proceed in the dark. There were no existing landmarks, neighboring buildings, or strong urban design directions that could prompt visual axes, symmetries, or polarities. The design and construction of other buildings moved on a different schedule, and there was scant coordination. Perhaps more importantly, the center's program and organizational structure changed frequently, and changes in city politics and internal shuffles in the overseeing board of directors provided sporadic leadership for the architect.

Clearly, flexibility was not an option; it was a necessity. Could a strong visual identity coexist with changing requirements? Maki thought of a ship as a means to achieve an overall unity in the building and, at the same time, the independence of individual parts. During the fall and winter of 1987 he abandoned earlier experiments with plans based on regularity and symmetry. The new operative concepts were "elegant factory" and "space depth." Rather than hiding the mechanical equipment in the basement, Maki positioned it on the roof, like a superstructure on a ship deck.

Ships and the proximity of the bay have played a constant role in the history of San Francisco. Few architects, however, have drawn inspiration from this history. Figuratively speaking, the city has turned its back to the water. Ships—or rather the ship metaphor—have also had a relevant part in the history of modern architecture, standing for rationality, efficiency, and self-containment. For Le Corbusier ships and airplanes were the engineering equivalent of the Parthenon. In Maki's case the ship metaphor

had the additional appeal of making the center an immediate part of the historical and urban environment of San Francisco.

The outwardly utilitarian configuration of the center makes the surrounding buildings—high-rises, offices, and cultural facilities—appear stolid. These are dominating structures, ostensibly determined to outlast eternity itself, isolated from one another in their egocentric determination, competing for attention with occasional displays of classical, nearly Vitruvian architectural features, and doing so with widely uneven degrees of success. The center stands out in this context because of its lack of architectural vanity.

Only the flimsiest membrane seems to separate the fen of the surrounding city from the center. It seems unable to withstand the complexity and intensity of this environment. The city intrudes from unexpected openings; internal vistas appear suddenly; volumes flow into one another; spatial and emotive textures overlap constantly—big and small, light and dark, anxiety and serenity, intimacy and openness. In plan the center belies its exterior directness. Instead it conjures up a puzzle—a Casbah-like conglomeration of rooms, all different in dimension, some irregular in shape, adding up to a building with an informal layout. This is the irregularity one finds in traditional Japanese houses. There is no single point of view, no dominant perspective to organize visually the internal space. There are several ways to approach or enter each of the galleries. This excess creates the impression of a deeper and more complex space than actually exists. But intricate as it may look, this plan does not give full credit to the volumetric complexity of the building, more akin to multi-layered urban complexity than to the purely architectural kind.

This disorder is not an accessory to anxiety and frustration. Rather it encourages exploration and rewards curiosity. "One may move freely,"

The Forum serves as a "black-box" theater and performance space as well as hosting receptions and other events. Catwalks around its perimeter and a tension-grid ceiling are provided for flexible lighting and audio/visual configurations.

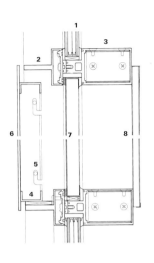

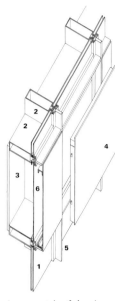

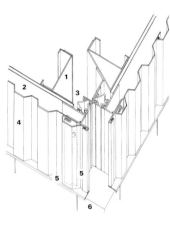

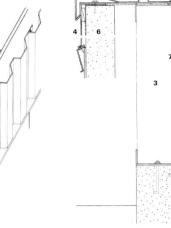

Aluminum panel section

1 glazing
2 aluminum snap-on trim
3 aluminum mullion
4 aluminum extrusion
5 stainless steel drive pin
6 ³/₁₆" aluminum panel
7 metal closure panel
8 gypsum sheathing

Axonometric of aluminum panel

1 glazing
2 aluminum mullion
3 gypsum sheathing
4 ³/₁₆" aluminum panel
5 aluminum snap-on trim
6 metal closure panel

Axonometric of aluminum panel

1 metal stud
2 gypsum sheathing
3 neoprene gasket
4 ribbed metal panel
5 aluminum extrusion
6 corner stone

Corrugated panel section

1 aluminum parapet coping
2 aluminum extrusion
3 metal stud
4 aluminum flashing
5 metal subgirts
6 concrete curb
7 sheathing board
8 ribbed metal panel
9 stone base

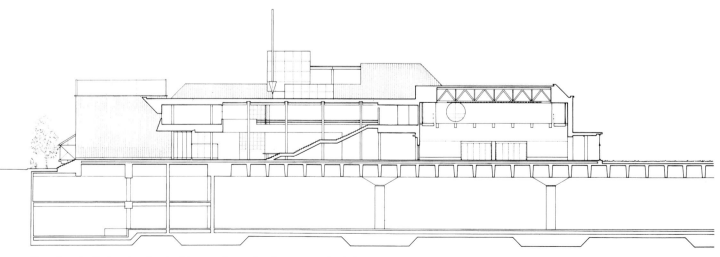

*Above:* Longitudinal section showing Moscone Convention Center expansion below

*Facing page:* Entrance plaza

50

Opening day festivities at Yerba Buena Gardens

Maki writes about this building, "within and between floors without ever turning back." Change invites interaction with the building. Doorways and transitional spaces exert a sort of gravitational pull, provoking anticipation and apprehension. Even the thickness of the wall in the doorways has a function, that of allocating material substance to the transition.

For Maki the disorder of the city is evidence of energy and intensity, not anarchy. His Japanese buildings are nothing if not sympathetic with this environment. One of his most famous Tokyo designs, the Spiral, stands as a metaphor for the creative potential of the city. Its intricate exterior coalesces with the vernacular of the Tokyo street. A labyrinthine interior transliterates the buzzing confusion of the city, so turbulent with historical citations, spatial stimuli, and architectural elements that it can be absorbed only selectively—a decision required at every step. Of course, this is the point. Making decisions, taking responsibility, becoming aware of one's own circumstances—all indispensable ingredients of learning—are the privileged essence and burden of city life. Cities are the locus of culture.

The sequential experience in this building is characteristic of Maki's recent work. He and others have called attention to his aesthetics of fragmentation—no privileged point of view, no classical unity, no typical closure: open-ended architecture. In discussing the relationship between architecture and the city, Maki has referred to the "unstable equilibrium of a cloud." Architectural historian David Stewart, however, has cautioned against pushing this concept too far. Indeed, it would be too easy to view the center's complexity as simply another incarnation of Maki's aesthetics. But this view would belittle its substantial unity and uniqueness. Beyond the multilayered experience, one must recognize here the coherent cadence of intention, place, and materials.

The center is not an endlessly accommodating, architecturally neutral box. Architecture is still very much a part of it; the designer has left traces of his presence. Maki's eye for the minute incident is particularly evident in the interior details. No one is so naive as to think that the sole function of architectural details is to sublimate the process of building. They serve this purpose, but they are also the grace notes, the harmonic devices that simplify our experience of the whole. Each stair or balustrade has a differently designed handrail. It is a subtle difference, insufficient to introduce discontinuity but enough to establish a separate identity. Most are assembled with prefabricated, relatively humble elements, such as small I-beams or thin steel rods, as if the architect had to be imaginative with scrap metal. Nothing is wasted. The results have the alert presence of a live wire.

Maki's assemblies of light-metal components show vestiges of traditional Japanese craft. But the apparently simple elements dissolving into a myriad of prodigiously complex assemblies also display modernist Western influences—Mies van der Rohe and especially Carlo Scarpa.

There are moments of intense lyrical sensibility in Maki's buildings. Even the large buildings, such as the Fujisawa Municipal Gymnasium, offer a sense of intimacy, a reassurance that size will not displace privacy. Even the very large ones, such as the Makuhari Messe, appear delicate against the lesser construction of the industrial hinterland of Tokyo—the driftwood of Japan's economic miracle.

In the center it is arresting to see one of the stairs set against the light from a small outdoor garden. This is less an actual garden than an allegorical representation abstracted to its elemental composition: a reflecting pool, a low triangular pyramid covered with stone, and a few stalks of bamboo. Its view is also reduced by a large opening made of milky white, translucent glass blocks reaching from the ceiling to a point below eye level. Because of this screen it is not possible to see much of the garden; one senses its presence without being able to perceive its confined dimensions. Like traditional Japanese dry gardens, it is surrounded by nearly featureless walls—a symbolic representation of the infinite. Paved with tiles rotated in relation to the direction of the building, it looks like an archaeological fragment from a much larger field still under the building—another emblem of the floating ship. The view of the bamboo through the lightweight steel elements of the stair—the lightness of the two—does not simply set the artificial against the organic. Perhaps more poignantly, it suggests a bridge, a continuity between architecture and nature and between tradition and the present.

The center's galleries are not equally suited for all kinds of art. Each of them has a distinctive character, with particular syntheses of volume, scale, proportions, and light sources. Some respond to three-dimensional works. In some, small works on paper would seem diminished. Others are stately, contemplative spaces, and visitors feel fittingly awed in front of the large-scale works favored by contemporary artists. Other galleries are made for performances or large groups of people and seem incomplete without a live presence.

If all of this does not make the center an open-ended receptacle for all possible art forms, it makes it a suitable place for learning about them. Here we willingly suspend our previously acquired notions and open ourselves to new possibilities. This is not exactly spatial flexibility, but it is the conceptual answer to the demands of the center's unending project. This structure requires time to be assimilated—not the chronological time of a ticking clock but the compression and distention of the tempo of the building, the rhythmic unfolding of a plot.

This is the plot, the structure, not the story. Without art the gallery walls dwarf the rooms; their proportions are skewed, light and textures look lifeless, space itself becomes quiet—the calm of emptiness, not the peace of enlightenment. Nowhere does this absence become more evident than in the area next to the street intersection, the most prominent of the whole site. Instead of another enclosed room, Maki has situated an open, empty space. It is elevated from the street like a podium. A screen of metal louvers, like a mechanical curtain, separates it from the adjacent indoor gallery. A stage without actors, without art, it has a constant air of expectancy. With art, it celebrates the purpose and content of the center in front of the whole city.

*Facing page:* A glazed passage between the two large first-floor galleries provides visitors with a momentary glimpse of the city life outside.

# IWASAKI ART MUSEUM + CRAFT MUSEUM

Ibusuki, Kagoshima 1979 and 1987

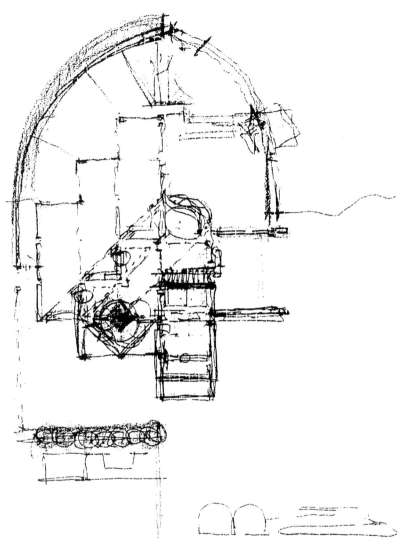

Early sketch for the Iwasaki Art Museum, first phase

Second floor

First floor

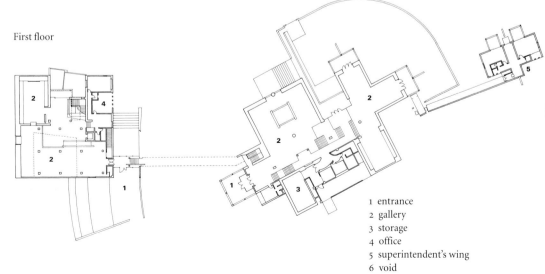

Plan of the original museum (*right*) and its annex (*left*). The two buildings are joined by an underground passage.

1 entrance
2 gallery
3 storage
4 office
5 superintendent's wing
6 void
7 lounge
8 exhibition terrace

Aerial view of the Iwasaki Art Museum (*right*) and its annex, the Craft Museum (*left*)

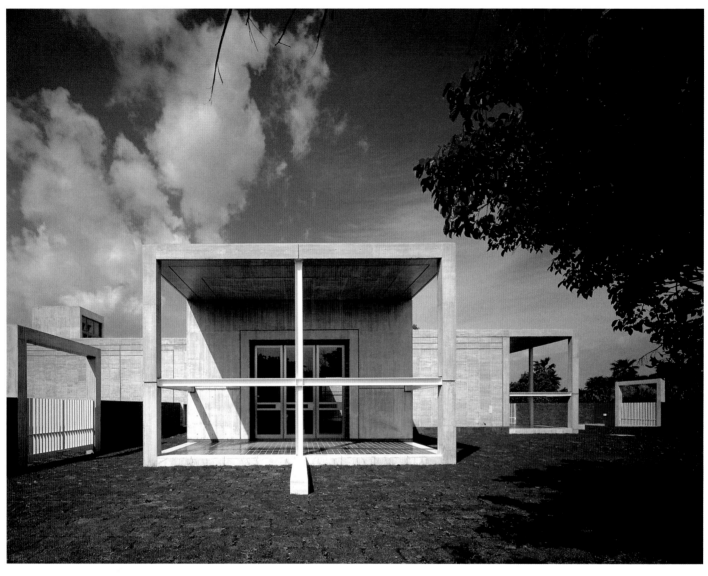

Porches adjoining the exhibition rooms are marked with a ( + ) motif, symbolizing the containment of a cubical void (the steel crosses also reinforce the concrete frame).

The Iwasaki Art Museum and its annex, the Craft Museum, are set in a lush green, semitropical landscape at the southern end of Kyushu Island overlooking the ocean. The rugged character of the terrain seems far removed from the world of urban types and patterns of use that characterize most of our other projects during the same years. Instead, the museum buildings developed, each in its own way, around very basic ideas of shelter, expressed in a simple but rich architectural vocabulary based on house types.

We designed the original museum in the spirit of an informal villa, sheltered from and yet inextricably tied to the surrounding landscape. The building as a whole has a very simple vocabulary and is meant to evoke the rough simplicity of early modern architecture. The external finish is exposed concrete with sealer and sprayed-on emulsion paint, which preserves the texture of exposed concrete while providing protection against the high humidity and rainfall of this region.

The interior houses a large exhibition space and three small alcovelike spaces laid out on a gently stepping ground plane that follows the exterior topography. The large exhibition space is lit by two "light-rooms"—large cubical skylights framed in steel—that filter the strong southern light through louvers and secondary screens at the ceiling level, controlling light levels for the comfortable viewing of the museum's modern paintings. Additional light-rooms are located over the stair and in one of the smaller exhibition alcoves. The entrance lobby and the two other upper alcoves have deep porches, which might be termed "lateral light-rooms" since they also allow indirect natural light. The masses of the exhibition spaces and the more delicate frames of these light-rooms together compose a distinctive silhouette.

Two symbolic elements aim at giving the ensemble a cohesive formal expression. One is the figure ( ⌐¬ ), that is repeatedly used in the parts and the whole of the building. ( ⌐¬ ) is a variant of a commonly held image of shelter, ( ∧ ), a form that suggests security, familiarity, and an earthbound quality. The second element is the figure ( + ) that appears in the expression of the porches. As we can gather from children's drawings of houses, ( + ) is a symbol of openings. But at the same time the cross symbolizes the cagelike, closed-off quality of the porch, which is not intended to be accessible like normal terraces. For this reason the horizontal bar of the cross is located at eye level, cutting off the view to the horizon.

While the main building exhibits primarily modern Japanese and Western fauvist paintings, the Craft Museum, built eight years later, is intended to exhibit Japanese-style paintings, calligraphy, ceramics, and folk art. It is designed as a separate entity, linked to the main building only by an underground passage. If the original Iwasaki Art Museum is modeled on a villa typology, the Craft Museum gives the impression of a more self-enclosed storehouse (Japanese *kura*).

From the Craft Museum's transparent glass entry vestibule, one proceeds to the darker, vaulted space of the main gallery. Here, several elements—the *shoji*-inspired screens, stepped floor surfaces, freestanding columns and beams, and small openings admitting natural light—are reminiscent of traditional Japanese folk house construction. Natural light filters down into the main gallery from the clerestory window above. To the rear of the raised stage in this gallery is a room for the display of Japanese paintings. A stair to the second floor is housed in a towerlike void space. On the second floor, a ceramics gallery leads to a lounge with a view out over the ocean—the view originally denied to the first museum.

Together, the two buildings explore contrasting themes: lightness versus darkness, horizontality versus verticality, Mediterranean versus Japanese typology. Rather than merely extending and repeating ideas from the earlier building, the annex introduces new elements and themes, attempting to give new identity to the museum complex as a whole composed of two unequal but complementary parts.

Iwasaki Art Museum seen from the south. Two "light-rooms" over the main exhibition gallery provide diffused natural light.

Axonometric of Art Museum

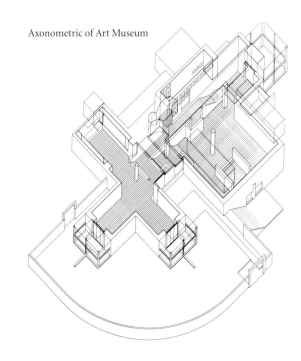

View to courtyard

Main gallery space

Main exhibition hall of the Craft Museum. The exposed structural beams and columns and the limited natural light introduced at the top of the tall space recall the interior of a traditional Japanese folk house.

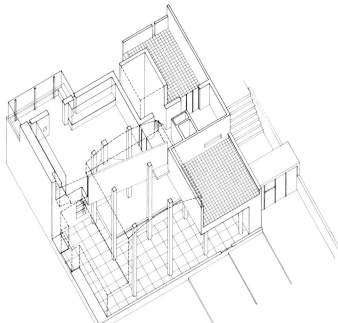

*Above:* Axonometric of Craft Museum

*Top right:* Stair seen from calligraphy gallery

*Bottom right:* A porch admits side light to the main gallery through a steel grille.

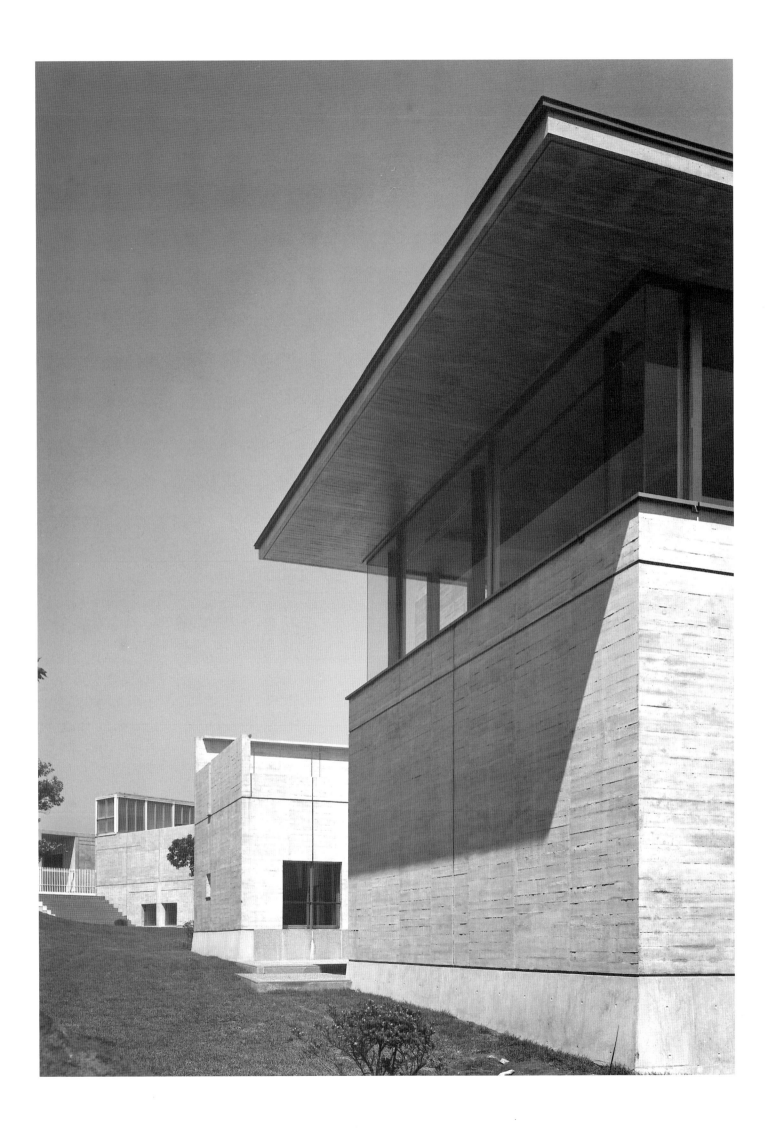

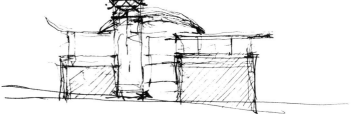

*Top right:* Detail of exterior wall

*Facing page:* Iwasaki Craft Museum (*foreground*) and
Art Museum (*beyond*)

# YKK GUEST HOUSE

Kurobe, Toyama 1982

In the early 1980s the YKK company, a leading manufacturer of zippers, asked us to design a guest house to provide lodging and conference spaces for their distinguished visitors. The spacious site is located in the wooded countryside of the foothills of the Japanese Alps, about one hour's drive from the city of Toyama. Given the remoteness of the site and the desire to create an atmosphere of warm hospitality, the building is designed in the image of a large manor house, with a pitched roof and bay windows playing a prominent role in expressing this primary symbolic reading.

At the core of the house is a multistory living room space that faces the south garden and serves to link all elements of the building visually. The space features exposed beams and columns—reminiscent of Japanese farmhouse interiors—and a freestanding staircase to the upper levels encased in a translucent glass cage. The interior has a luxurious yet informal atmosphere, articulated not only in modern materials such as concrete, aluminum, steel, and glass block, but also through the abundant use of wood.

Wishing to provide an intimate atmosphere within the house as a whole and considering that some guests may have extended stays, the individual rooms are a bit more accommodating than ordinary dormitory rooms, while avoiding the formality of hotel rooms. In addition to spaces for sleeping, working, dressing, and bathing, each room is provided with a glazed alcove looking out on the scenic landscape of wooded hills. On the facade these alcoves serve another function, which is to reduce the apparent mass of the house by linking second- and third-floor rooms into the expression of a single window element; these bay windows thus form the *piano nobile* of a tripartite villa facade.

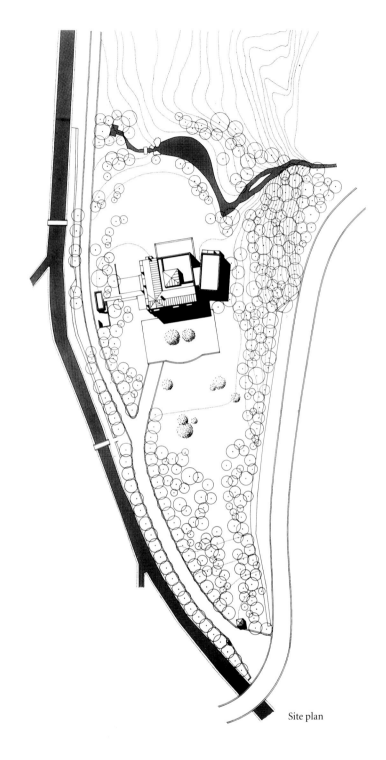

Site plan

View from the driveway entrance—the Guest House recalls an English country manor house.

The high ceiling and exposed columns and beams in the living room evoke the image of the traditional Japanese folk house. The central staircase leading to guest rooms on the second and third floors is encased in translucent fiberglass panels recalling a *shoji* screen.

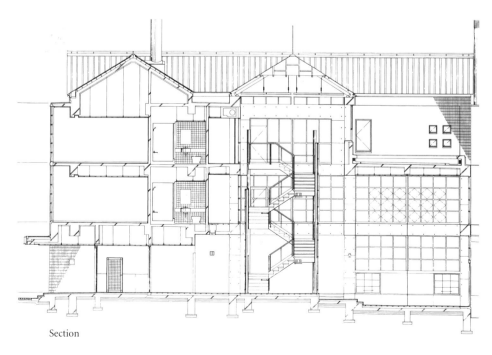

Section

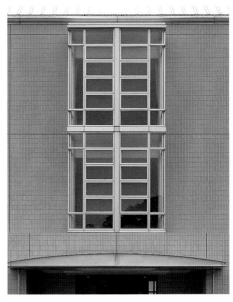

Typical guest room. Each room has a floor-to-ceiling glazed alcove, which provides a feeling of spaciousness not commonly found in hotel accommodations. On the facade, second- and third-floor alcoves are unified into a single bay window element.

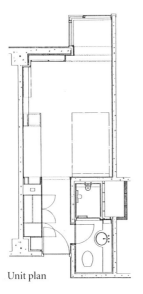

Unit plan

*Above:* Seminar room in library wing

*Facing page:* View from the south lawn, with the two-story living room seen between the gabled guest wing (*right*) and library wing (*left*)

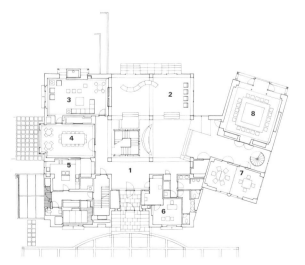

First-floor plan

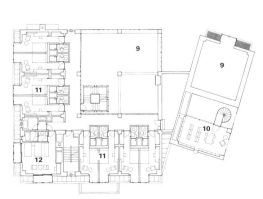

Second-floor plan

1  entry hall
2  lobby
3  lounge
4  dining room
5  kitchen
6  office
7  meeting rooms
8  seminar room
9  void
10  library
11  single guest room
12  double guest room

# TOKYO CHURCH OF CHRIST

Shibuya, Tokyo  1995

For forty years this site in the Tomigaya neighborhood of west central Tokyo housed a modest wooden church, tucked away behind layers of greenery facing Yamate Boulevard. As part of a comprehensive plan to improve traffic flow in the city, the government decided some years ago to widen the street, and for this purpose it acquired the front portion of the church's property—roughly one-third of the land. Upon ceding the land where part of the old church rested, the project to build a larger facility to meet the present congregation's needs and aspirations began.

The church's most urgent need was a significant increase in seating capacity. Over the years the congregation had clearly outgrown the old building, and, hoping to accommodate further growth, the church requested a main hall space that would seat 700 people. At the same time, the now smaller site imposed some restrictions. Since the plot borders a small-scale residential neighborhood to the rear, the building was subject to strict regulations concerning sunlight access. The building's volume and its disposition of parts were largely determined by balancing the conflicting demands of casting minimum shadows on neighboring sites while providing maximum floor area for a large congregation. Given the limited volume in which to build, we allocated most spaces related to the daily functioning of the church—offices, a lounge, children's rooms, and a fellowship hall—to the ground floor. The main hall required a tall volume, so it was raised up to the second-floor level where its ceiling space could expand freely to create a symbolic roof line for the whole building. A simple, shallow arch shape appeared in the early sketches as a way of expressing a metaphor for the celestial vault.

The main hall was to be filled with natural light. However, the visual chaos of the surrounding city—similar in certain ways to the urban chaos we celebrated in the Spiral's facade—provided unsuitable scenery for a space of spiritual reflection. In order to catch abundant light that would enhance rather than distract from the quiet mood of the hall interior, a translucent wall of light across the front of the main hall was created. Recalling the image of a large *shoji* screen on the interior, the "light-wall" is revealed as a double-layered modern curtain wall on the exterior.

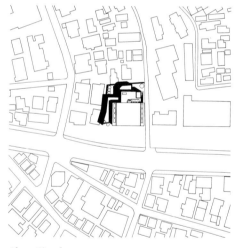

*Above:* Site plan

*Facing page:* Facade detail at entrance

70

View from stair landing to entrance. Finish materials such as wood and stone were selected to create a warm interior. The interior material palette also includes an exposed concrete wall, which takes on the texture and color of the cedar boards used for its formwork.

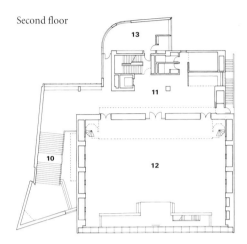
Second floor

First floor

1 entrance lobby
2 lounge
3 children's room
4 nursery
5 meeting hall
6 reception
7 office
8 parking
9 garden
10 main stair
11 foyer
12 main hall
13 conference room
14 balcony
15 projection
16 machine room

Ceremonial stair leading from the entrance lobby to the main hall on the second floor. Beyond are children's rooms and a lounge looking out on a small garden.

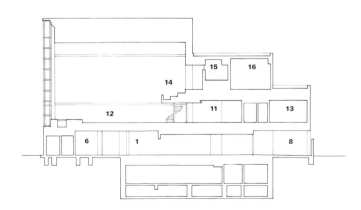
Section

Interior of main hall in morning light

The filtered light entering through the curtain wall is balanced on the interior by natural light highlighting the canted side walls from above.

The curtain wall is made up of two composite layers of glass on a 1.3 meter square grid, separated by 80 centimeters of air space. The construction is supported on a jungle-gym-like Vierendeel truss wall structure of steel. The exterior membrane is made up of paired glass, the outer pane of which is treated with a silk-screened ceramic dot pattern, subtly veiling the truss structure and the second layer of glass behind. The interior layer is composed of two panes of glass sandwiching thin layers of fiberglass tissue, thus producing a translucent *shoji* effect. The double curtain wall has the additional advantages of offering substantial acoustic insulation from Yamate Boulevard's traffic noise and of creating a natural convection current in the air space so that rising solar-heated air assists the hall's ventilation system.

Major exterior materials are glass and cedar board-formed concrete, with discrete use of hammer-finished granite along the most public pedestrian areas. On the interior natural wood is used extensively—for flooring, handrails, doors, and screens—to give a more intimate, almost residential atmosphere (we originally thought of the church in the image of a large house). From the entrance lobby and lounge through the grand staircase to the hall's foyer, we created a series of interrelated spaces, with benches and seating areas where members of the congregation could feel free to relax, to linger after the sermon, to get together for a variety of social activities. At the same time, the sequence through these spaces approaching the main hall is designed progressively to filter out visual and acoustic distractions from the city outside. By the time congregation members enter the hall, turning back toward the front facade to see the glass wall from the interior this time, the commotion of the cityscape lying just beyond has been transformed into pure light filling a quiet space.

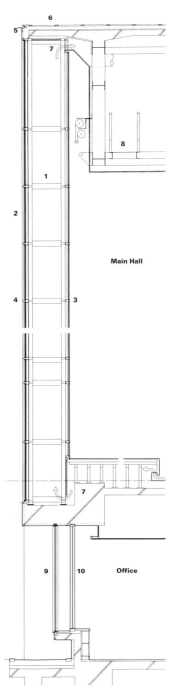

Curtain wall section

1 Vierendeel truss wall
2 paired glass with ceramic frit pattern
3 paired glass with fiberglass tissue between
4 extruded aluminum sash
5 aluminum spandrel panel
6 stainless steel roofing, 0.8 millimeter
7 return air grille
8 catwalk
9 steel sash
10 sliding wooden screen

*Above:* On evenings when the hall is being used for worship services or congregational meetings, the translucent curtain wall glows like a giant lantern, signaling to passersby that some communal gathering is taking place inside.

*Facing page:* The translucent glass wall of the main hall changes with the light of the day.

# CHILDREN'S HOUSE

Oswiecim, Poland 1990–

This house is designed as part of a Children's Village for orphans in Oswiecim, Poland. The village is dedicated to the memory of Dr. Janusz Korczak, a philanthropist who organized homes for orphans in prewar Poland. Architects from several countries, including Poland, are working together to create an environment that will embody Dr. Korczak's ideas about a child belonging both to a family and to a larger community. Professor Tomasz Mankowski of Krakow Technical University developed the master plan, which consists of twelve individual houses grouped around a common recreation space, a community center, and administration buildings. The program for each of the houses is quite modest: living quarters for eight children, three months to eighteen years old, and a single foster mother. Our site in the southeast corner of the village is 25 meters by 25 meters, with a total building floor area of 200 square meters. In keeping with vernacular materials, we chose to work primarily in brick and wood.

The Children's House presents the unmistakable figurative image of a house. Yet its central tower expresses something extraordinary about the structure of the family within—the slight imbalance between upper and lower volumes introduces some doubt about conventional definitions of "family." This tower, containing two loft floors (one for girls, one for boys), rises above the lower mass of the communal spaces, giving the older children smaller residential zones within the larger house. Rooms for the mother and two infants are on the ground floor, more convenient to the house's central functions. Spatially the house interior is structured as a series of interlocking L-shaped zones: cooking-eating-gathering spaces, mother's and infants' rooms, and boys' and girls' loft quarters. The inherent flexibility of the "L" (left open or subdivided) allows the house to change and accommodate unforeseen developments in the family. On the ground floor places of communal importance—dining table, reading alcove, fireplace, entryway facing the common green—provide space for family interaction.

Site near Oswiecim

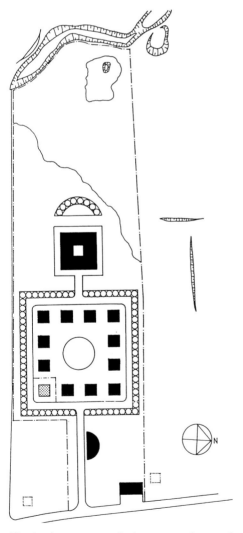

The site plan arranges twelve houses around a central playground; our designated lot is on the bottom left.

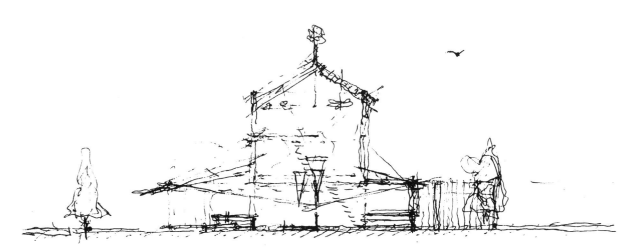

Tokyo - Singapore
Oct. 28 90

7 pm 29°c

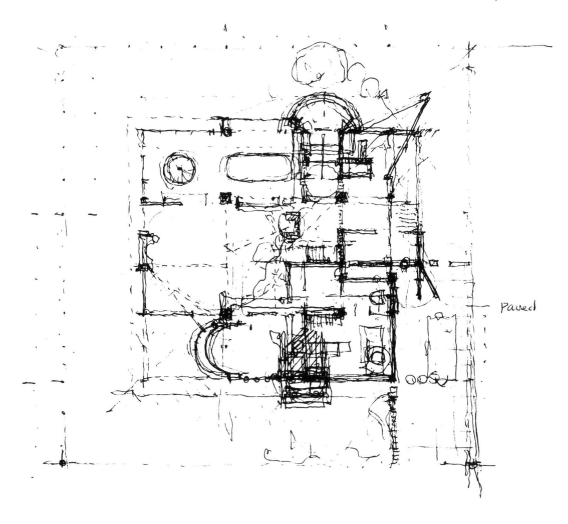

Paved

· own plate
· collections of the house
· Fireplace. Pit.

庄叶尺. roof   skylight

East elevation

North elevation

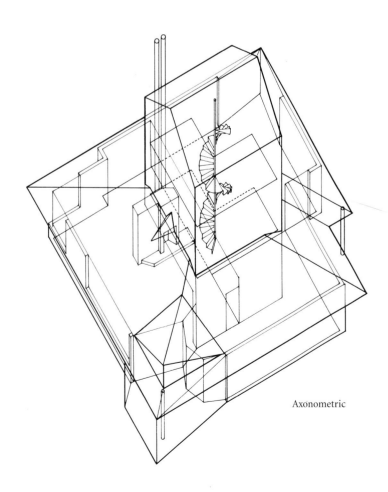

Axonometric

South elevation

West elevation

First floor

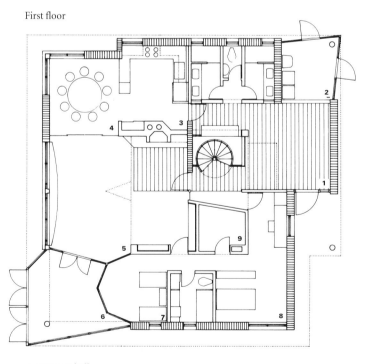

Second/third floor

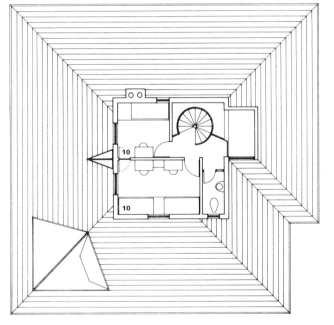

1 entrance hall
2 work room
3 kitchen
4 dining room
5 living room
6 screened porch
7 infants' room
8 mother's room
9 storage
10 bedroom

# ZEEBRUGGE SEA FERRY TERMINAL

Zeebrugge, Belgium 1989

Through its efforts to provide for the rapid handling of ships and their cargo in Europe's expanding economy, the port city of Zeebrugge in northern Belgium has developed a reputation for introducing innovative technologies. In 1989 the city sponsored a competition for a new international Sea Ferry Terminal aimed at developing new concepts for accommodating travelers and vacationers. Our competition proposal not only recognizes a ferry terminal's need to convey a symbolic image as a gateway for passengers traveling between Belgium and England, but also looks at the potential for a new transportation center to act as a regional attraction in its own right. The proposal was thus conceived as a popular destination for both the international traveler as well as the visitor who comes to the Belgian coast for leisure and recreation.

The site is on an exposed strip of land jutting out into the North Sea and is, by any definition, a site without context; the terminal would have to become a world unto itself. A vast circular base was designed to serve as an organizing element from which all other elements would be generated. We thought of this form as a kind of metaphor for the universe, a celestial vault on whose surfaces the various structures of the center would be mapped out. The circular base is 141 meters in diameter and rises 14.5 meters above ground level; inside we have allocated spaces for parking, loading, and cargo storage for the ferry terminal.

The roof plane of this volume in turn provides a plateau on which four quasi-sculptural elements—the terminal office tower, a fitness center, a Ferris wheel café, and a restaurant—are placed, each differing in form and function. If the base represents the celestial vault, these four elements as a group metaphorically suggest the constellations used for sea navigation, or alternately elements associated with the ocean (a compass arrow, an iceberg, the wings of a seabird in flight). The ground surrounding the Sea Ferry Terminal is planted with dense *allées* of trees, so that from several viewpoints only the sculptural passenger- and recreation-related elements are visible, floating above the treetops, set apart from both land and water. Viewed from an approaching ship, the changing silhouettes of these diverse crystalline elements appear as a mirage on the horizon—a fascinating, unearthly image.

The inclusion of diverse activities such as weight-training rooms and a swimming pool, a cinema complex, and a Ferris wheel café serving light snacks (a slight reversal of the conveyor belt cafeteria), together with more conventional facilities for travelers, recognizes that a terminal building need not be a building simply to be passed through as quickly as possible. Instead of languishing in departure lounges while waiting for a delayed vessel, travelers could catch a film or swim a few laps. In the summer months the recreational facilities of the terminal allow it to become a fun center, a destination rather than a transit point for the local population and tourists alike.

Site in Zeebrugge, Belgium

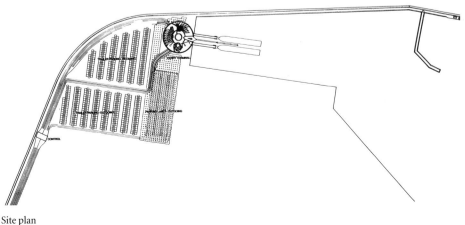

Site plan

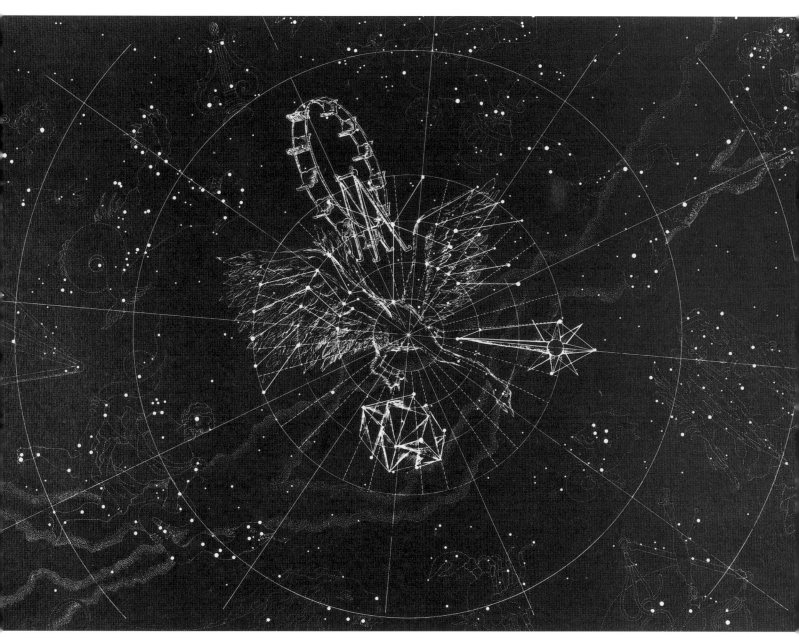

A constellation of elements provides an image for the complex.

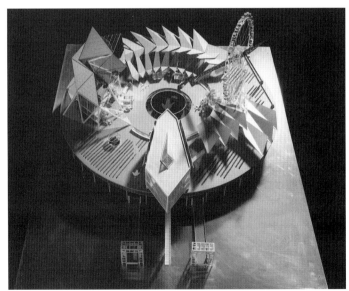

A group of sculptural objects set on a circular terminal base offers ever-changing silhouettes as seen from approaching ships. The skyline elements are, clockwise from the bottom, the passenger lobby, terminal office tower, fitness club, café, Ferris wheel, and restaurant.

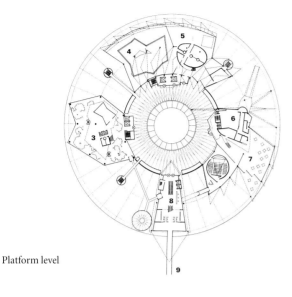

Platform level

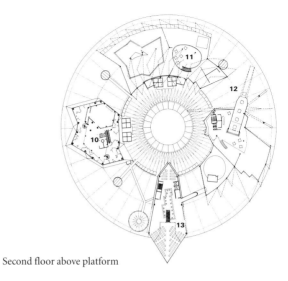

Second floor above platform

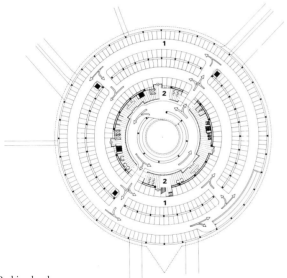

Parking level

1 parking
2 lobby
3 garden atrium
4 pool
5 gym
6 kitchen
7 restaurant
8 reception
9 ship access
10 foyer
11 café
12 café wheel
13 waiting room

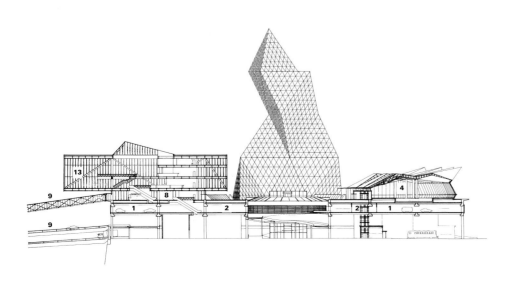

The terminal would appear as a miragelike silhouette across the waves.

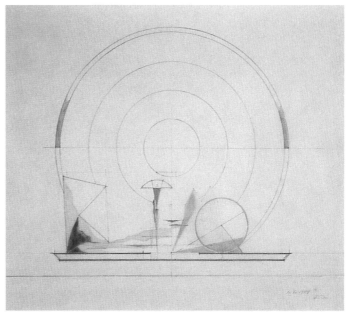

Section/elevation

The roofs of the fitness club and restaurant hover like the wings of a seagull.

# PALAZZO DEL CINEMA

Lido, Italy 1990

Our competition proposal for the reconstruction of the Palazzo del Cinema on the Lido—home of the Venice Film Festival—attempts to express the spirit of the city, both eternal and temporal, in one striking entity: a glass palace on the water. Changing from day to night, its clearly defined mass is gradually transformed, dissolving into a glowing, festive illusion. In twilight an alluring image of glass appears—a reflection of the ephemeral state of Venice seen through a screen of fog. It is a vision of a world that exists only through the magic of light, the medium of cinema itself.

The Palazzo del Cinema acts as a meeting place of two worlds: the decaying, yet timeless, city of old hotels and summer villas along the Lido's narrow canals on one side; on the other the expansive beaches of the Adriatic Sea teeming with tourists and entertainment seekers—and, during festival times, with film producers, rising starlets, and hordes of reporters as well. When approaching the Palazzo del Cinema on foot or by car, visitors arrive at a hard-paved festival plaza fronting the beach. Under the hovering canopy facing the beach are an open-air foyer, a 1,500-seat outdoor cinema, and a café terrace, all intended to generate new activity on this part of the beach. When the festival plaza hosts pageants, parades, and outdoor exhibitions, the canopy provides shade for the spectators. In the evenings when the open-air cinema is utilized for film showings or other events, screens can be draped along the front of the building to protect the space from inclement weather and from the light of passing traffic. Approaching the Palazzo del Cinema's canalside by boat, visitors see a more illusionary aspect of the complex: wrapped in a voluminously curved membrane of glass, the Palazzo resembles a crystalline boat floating silently on the surface of the water.

Inside the Palazzo proper seven cinema rooms of different sizes and shapes are arranged on several levels. The larger cinemas—seating 1,200, 600, and 100 viewers respectively—are located on the lowest level. There the foyer for the Sala Grande is near the waters of the canal. From here a series of ascending and descending public paths connect a variety of lounges, terraces, and gardens, and lead to the smaller cinemas on the upper levels. The cascading layout of these public spaces gives the building the appearance of an Italian hill town captured in an envelope of glass.

Rooftop terraces are located on two levels: the lower, a garden terrace facing the canal and surrounded by greenery; the upper, a reception terrace offering a panoramic view of the Adriatic and Venice. In the distance the domes, turrets, and towers of the city recall its rich historical heritage as a place where Eastern and Western cultures have met. Echoing the distant towers the Palazzo's own

eight masts soar into the sky and serve to secure canvas tents to provide additional protection from the weather. As a gesture to the popular culture of the beach town, a symbolic observation deck in the shape of a film reel has been placed atop the roof.

Oceanside view of the site on Lido beach

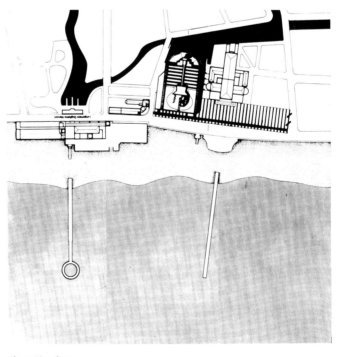

*Above:* Site plan

*Facing page:* Image model: a glass palace

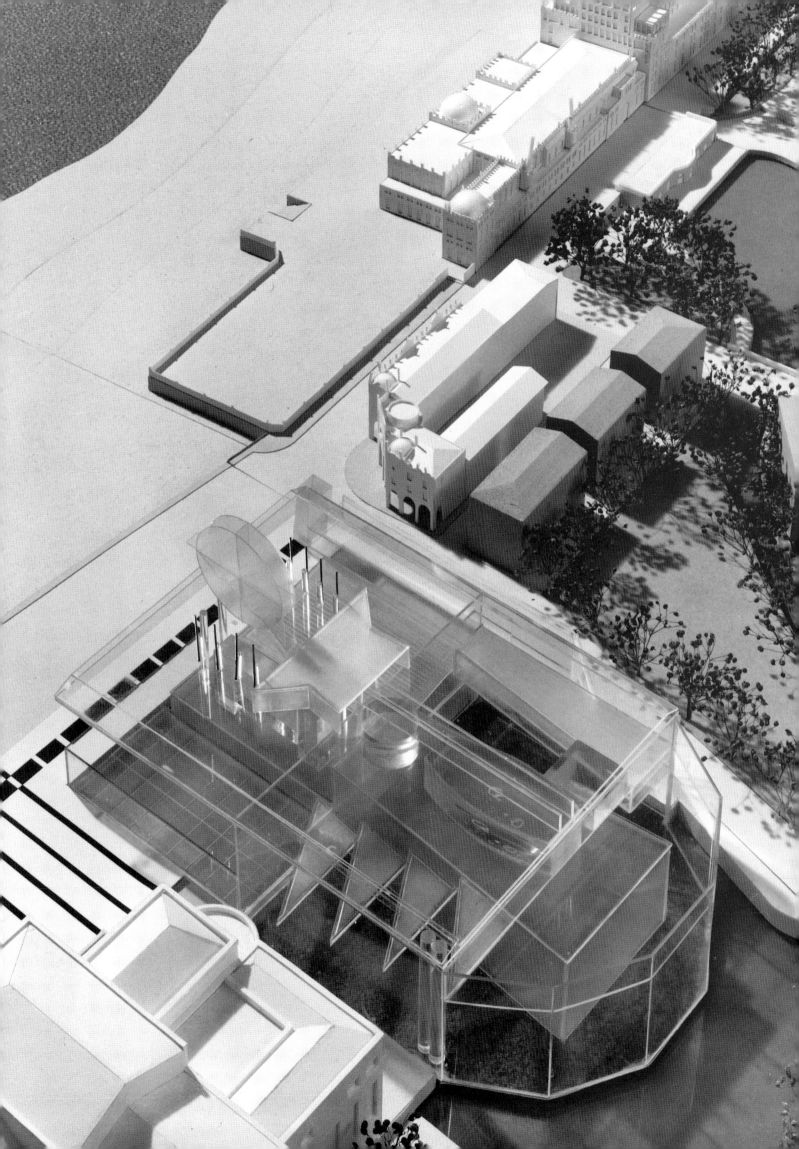

*Above:* View from third-floor café with Lido beach to the right. Below is an exterior covered plaza that can be used to show films in the evening.

*Facing page*: Canalside entrance

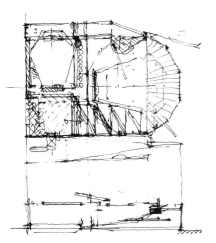

Beachside approach

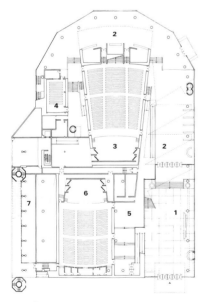

First floor

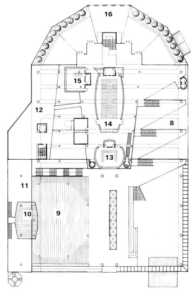

Third floor

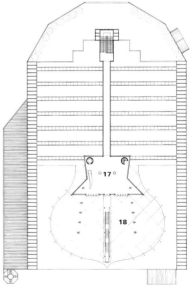

Roof level

1 entrance plaza
2 exhibition space
3 Sala Grande
4 100-seat cinema
5 foyer
6 600-seat cinema
7 shops
8 lounge
9 1,500-seat cinema

10 café
11 restaurant (below)
12 offices
13 60-seat cinema
14 Sala Volpi
15 40-seat cinema
16 garden terrace
17 reception room/bar
18 reception terrace

View from the Adriatic Sea. A statue of a griffin, historical symbol of Venice, stands at the center of the entrance facade.

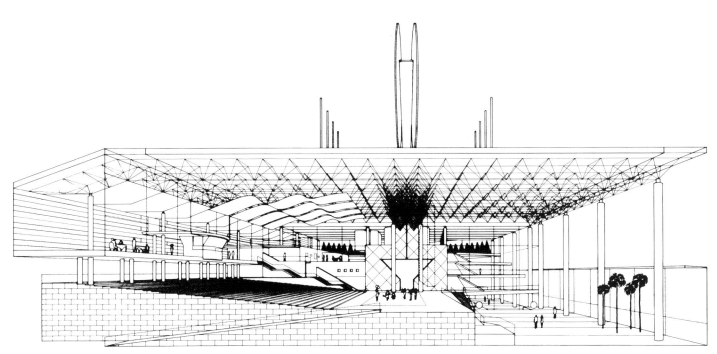

Sectional perspective of the exterior covered plaza

# FLOATING PAVILION

Groningen, Netherlands  1996

The Floating Pavilion seen in silhouette traveling through the countryside

The city of Groningen, Netherlands, has been active in securing architects from a variety of countries to design many of its public facilities. In 1994 we were invited to design a permanent multiuse structure, the Floating Pavilion, which would be used seasonally for many of the city's creative ventures. The pavilion was first used for Groningen's summer festival, "A Star is Born," which was held in August 1996 in conjunction with the opening of the town's new art museum. Traveling along the system of canals, towed by a tugboat from various places in the city to the countryside, it hosted a wide range of activities from festive musical/theatrical performances to tranquil poetry readings, thus capitalizing on the pavilion's ability to be in harmony with different settings and landscapes.

The spirit of the pavilion, developed in collaboration with Dora van der Groen, an avant-garde director/producer based in Antwerp, was inspired by keywords mapping the design: movement, memory, silence, dream, freedom, and surprise. These themes were translated into the architectural form of an open stage 6 by 25 meters sheltered by a steel network and white semitransparent polyester canvas configured into a double-helical structure. This non-site-specific architecture possesses a commanding presence because of its dynamic and unique form. Transfiguring itself in relation to one's vantage point, it may appear as a snail, a heron, or a cluster of clouds. By capturing the colors and light of its immediate landscape—buildings, trees, lawn, water, sun, and sky—it transforms itself into something new, unfolding an unexpected drama. The reciprocal synthesis of changing object and changing background brings to Groningen a new environment and ephemeral landscape.

The Floating Pavilion and Groningen townscape

Plan of central Groningen, with the pavilion's canal route marked in red

"Super and Popular"

red dots = route of Floating Pavilion    F. Maki

1  Kleine der Aa                R. Koolhaas
2  Noorderplantsoen      J. Nouvel
3  Grote Markt                F. O. Gehry
4  Top of the Damsterkade  H. Hollein
5  Brinkflats                  R. Koolhaas
6  Glass video gallery      B. Tschumi
7  Groningen Museum     A. Mendini
8  Music video bus stop    R. Koolhaas

The pavilion consists of a set of abstract stage elements, covered by an ephemeral, cloudlike canopy made of polyester canvas. Side benches made of perforated metal can be folded down during performances for better visibility from canalside. Storage space and dressing rooms are provided below deck.

Thinking of the city and what it needs, there are five elements:

| silence | space | movement | play | dream |
|---|---|---|---|---|
| comes from | water | given by | joy | desire |
| water | air | water | surprise | fantasy |
| balance | movement | change | wonder | recognition |
| trust | freedom | moment | remembrance | future, moment, memory |

Freedom has six directions:    upwards, to the air
downwards, to the water (as a reflection)
to the right, to the left
forwards, backwards. Turning, it should be like a globe,
which is wholeness, fullness, and emptiness all in one.

The pavilion shall be a pavilion of silence, the well
The motto is:    serene love
The most important items are:    transparency—light—colors
silence—the sounds will not be loud
arriving—departing

For this city, there will be a dream place on the water.    (Dora van der Groen)

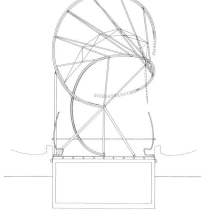

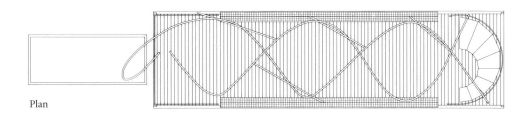

Plan

# KIRISHIMA INTERNATIONAL CONCERT HALL

Kirishima, Kagoshima 1994

Hidden in a range of volcanic mountains on southern Kyushu Island, the Kirishima region each year hosts an internationally acclaimed music festival with distinguished musical performers and educators from around the globe. For several weeks in the summer professional and student musicians come to this mountain retreat for intensive training, and during this time local residents and visitors to the region are treated to a variety of outstanding classical music performances. In response to the growing reputation of the Kirishima International Music Festival as well as to the heightened activity of local music organizations, the government of Kagoshima Prefecture decided to establish a permanent home for the festival in a beautiful rural setting.

The concert hall incorporates three separate components: a main concert hall, with seating for 770 listeners; a group of practice and rehearsal rooms, to be used primarily for music education; and an outdoor amphitheater for larger, more informal musical events, with space for 4,000 spectators. Given a relatively large and sprawling hillside site for this music campus, one of the biggest challenges was to discover and enhance the particular character of several different places within the site, which were addressed by relating views and degrees of enclosure to particular programmatic functions. On a large scale the gesture of two major architectural entities—the concert hall and the outdoor amphitheater—embedded in the sloping ground of the hill provides the basis of an overall spatial unity. Though facing different directions, the hall and amphitheater both seem to emerge from the hilltop, and between them they cradle a broad, flat picnic ground facing the Kirishima Range. Within the context of this simple site gesture, the individual qualities of various spaces for performing, gathering, learning, and relaxing are subsumed into a larger sense of place, a musical genius loci.

Of the three components the main concert hall is the most prominent visually. The hall itself is devoted to performances of classical music, with particular emphasis on chamber music. Its arching volume is enclosed in a metallic roof shell with a unique polyhedral silhouette. This irregular, angular form not only reflects the aesthetics of the acoustical shell contained within, but also responds to the rugged angularity of the surrounding volcanic landscape.

A sweeping glazed lobby enwraps the hall and provides a continuous visual link to this landscape from the interior as well. Its shape recalls the figure of a light, streamlined vessel, somehow epitomizing the festive spirit and the sense of collective experience associated with musical gatherings. This unusual boat-object is the first thing concert-goers see in an unfolding sequence as they proceed up to the hall along a sloping wooded path. Once having entered the building, they double back—still stepping up—toward the foyer windows which reveal a panoramic view of the Kirishima Range. Continuing on around the foyer, they can climb a stair leading to a second-floor terrace from which Kagoshima's famous active volcano, Sakura-jima, is visible to the south.

Practice and rehearsal rooms are located to the rear of the concert hall on the second-floor level. Together they surround an inner courtyard, creating a calm visual center for the music education wing. Open on one side, the courtyard looks out over the wooded site to a network of footpaths and to the outdoor amphitheater, thus providing a sense of visual connection among the disparate parts of the program.

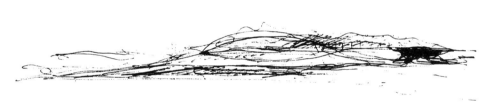

Kirishima Concert Hall. In the background the active volcano Sakura-jima can be seen.

*Above:* View at twilight. The prismatic shell of the concert hall floats above the curving glazed volume of the foyer.

*Left:* View down the hillside, with small hall in foreground.

*Facing page:* View from southeast

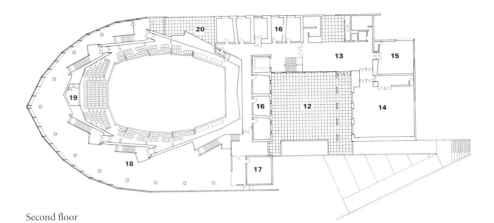

Second floor

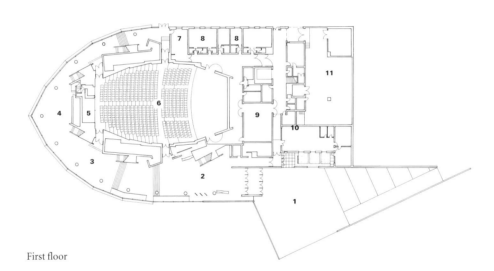

First floor

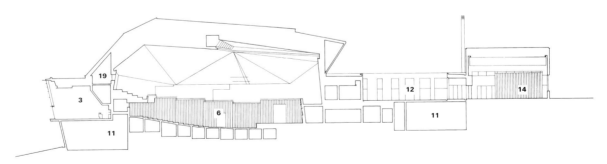

Longitudinal section

| | |
|---|---|
| 1 entry plaza | 12 concert courtyard |
| 2 entry | 13 lobby |
| 3 foyer | 14 small hall |
| 4 bar | 15 rehearsal room |
| 5 control room | 16 practice room |
| 6 concert hall | 17 sound simulation |
| 7 artists' lounge | chamber |
| 8 dressing room | 18 void |
| 9 instrument storage | 19 projection room |
| 10 office | 20 terrace |
| 11 machine room | |

The foyer steps up from the entrance level and its
sweeping glass wall looks out to the Kirishima Range.

*Above:* Balcony seats are arranged in terraced groups wrapping the first-floor seats.

*Facing page:* Concert hall interior: the lower walls are finished in maple; the ceiling, in large triangular surfaces of plasterboard. The polyhedral shape of the ceiling presents an image of a dynamic acoustic space.

## Acoustic Design

The design of Kirishima International Concert Hall posed many interesting challenges, not the least of which was the precise acoustic design of the hall itself. In architectural design concert halls are unique in that they are born from the collaboration of both architects and acousticians—both parties equally concerned with qualities of space, surfaces, and materials. Within this collaboration the acoustical engineer establishes concepts important to concert hall acoustics, usually derived from a combination of past research and new theories or discoveries; the architect then attempts to synthesize the acoustician's theories into the balance of the overall design, crystallizing ideas into form and space.

At Kirishima we began with the premise of an 800-seat hall devoted to classical chamber music. From the beginning we established two design priorities that would affect the acoustics of the hall. Our first concept was to create a space in which the stage is surrounded by audience seats, so as to dissolve the separation of performers and listeners, creating a rather informal concert environment. The second, from an entirely architectural point of view, was to create a visually animated space using only abstract planes and volumes—without resorting to decorative devices—to offer a festive atmosphere suitable for appreciating classical music. Overlaying architectural ideas on acoustical concepts put forth by our acoustician, Dr. Yoichi Ando, we eventually developed a hall with a leaf-shaped plan and a hull-shaped ceiling composed of triangular planes. Breaking the ceiling up into triangles of different sizes and orientations allowed us to shape a continuous nonabsorptive envelope of surfaces, scattering reflected sound to listeners throughout the hall.

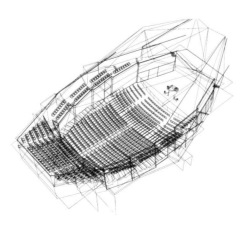

## Using the Computer

During the schematic design phase we began to use a three-dimensional modeling program to study the complex space of this design. Computer-generated perspective drawings aided our presentations, showing in a very literal way how the first-floor audience seats, together with the performers on stage, would be wrapped by the continuous balcony. Although at this point our main objective was merely to represent spatial ideas, it soon became apparent that the computer would be a powerful tool in the preparation of construction documents as well.

The ceiling design at first was a simple folded polyhedron which appeared quite heavy. With the computer, however, we could easily separate out planes and shift them up or down, overlapping them to give a spatial hierarchy and to create zones in which we could locate diffusers and stage lighting. The design was further enhanced by indirect ambient lighting at the base of the ceiling, which makes the ceiling appear to hover above the seating area.

The forms of both the interior ceiling and exterior roof are irregular polyhedrons; similar as they appear, however, the inner and outer forms are actually different in shape and their surfaces all had to be separately plotted. A cavity between the two layers was required to house theatrical lighting equipment, mechanical ducts, and maintenance catwalks, which could only be accomplished by shifting points and ridges as needed, constantly testing the resultant form on a trial-and-error basis. Fortunately, the computer allowed us to study the shapes of the ceiling and roof three-dimensionally, both independently and simultaneously. We were also able to represent the roof as a transparent surface and to obtain cross sections through the forms at any desired location.

Up to a certain stage in the design development, the basic guidelines we had determined still did not include construction information such as the thickness of materials and their joinery; the activities leading to the actual construction of the building thus required increasingly detailed investigations. The roof structure employs a system of folded planes in reinforced concrete—a system selected for reasons of sound isolation and spatial efficiency (i. e., it eliminates the need for girders and beams in the cavity space). Technically, folded planes behave like dome structures in that thickness varies depending on expected loads and stresses. Once the basic guidelines for the outer surface of the roof slab were established, the inner surface of the roof needed to be determined in order to build the formwork. The design of formwork became possible by utilizing the computer's computational abilities. For the first time in the

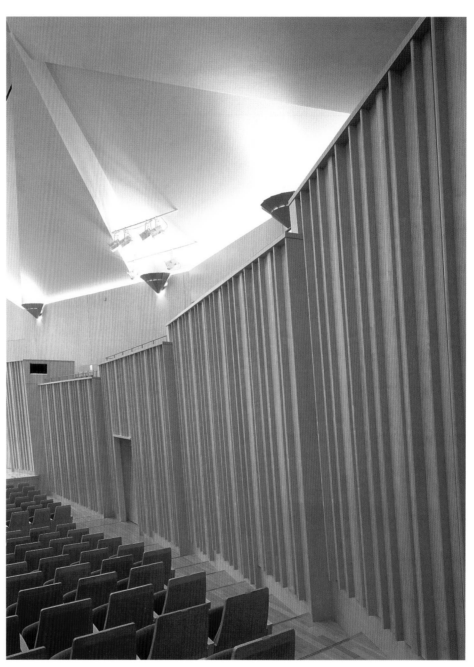

The lower walls are articulated with wood ribs arranged in a random pattern to scatter reflections of high frequency sounds.

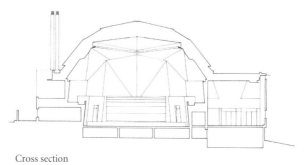

Cross section

design process we were able to derive a three-dimensional matrix locating the points of these complex shapes and forms.

For acoustical purposes the staggered right and left walls of the interior of the hall were to be canted toward the audience at a slope ratio of one to ten. Not only the finish surface but the structural wall was to have this slope, so that the formwork here became complex, and various adjustments with the contractors were again necessary.

Since the early stages of schematic design, we were exchanging data with structural engineers and the general contractor. Our data were delivered in the form of a floppy disk to the contractor who then generated construction shop drawings on site also using computer-aided design (CAD). Shop drawings of projected elevations (giving true dimensions of all polyhedron surfaces) were generated by CAD, and these were consequently used as templates to construct triangular panels on site. These panels were positioned in place at the actual points based on the previously established three-dimensional matrix using a laser surveyor. With the cooperation of the contractor's technical research laboratory, our data were also used to analyze structural settlement and deformation, thus identifying problems that could occur during construction.

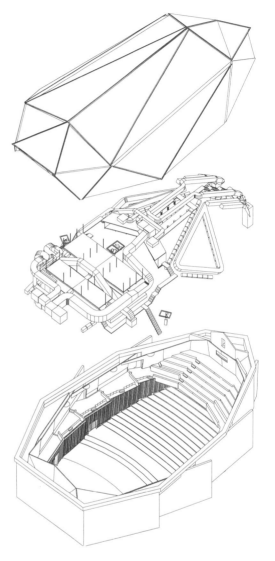

*Top:* Three-dimensional computer modeling was used not only for the inner and outer shells of the concert hall ceiling, but also for verifying the path of service catwalks and air ducts that would have to pass between them.

*Above:* Rehearsal room

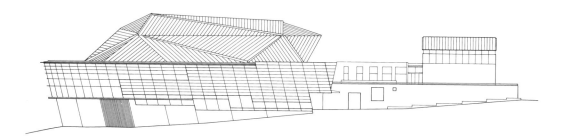

*Top:* North elevation

*Center:* The second-floor court is surrounded by rehearsal and practice rooms on three sides, with its open side facing the Kirishima Range.

*Bottom:* Aerial view

*Facing page:* Detail of foyer curtain wall

# GRADUATE SCHOOL RESEARCH CENTER
# KEIO UNIVERSITY SHONAN FUJISAWA CAMPUS

Fujisawa, Kanagawa 1994

Located outside the loop road of Keio University's Shonan Fujisawa Campus, the curving, semitransparent volume of the Graduate School Research Center stands in contrast to the orthogonally ordered central campus. Perched on a small hill, the building provides a visual terminus to one of the campus' east-west axes, while the stairs ascending up through its transparent entrance hall visibly extend the rising gesture of the axis. The mass of the building can be divided into two major parts in plan: a large curving portion, containing classrooms and open loft space; and the public portion of the building devoted to a cubical, three-story entrance hall.

The increased transparency of the entrance hall makes a gesture of visual communication not only to the existing campus to the east, but also to the site of a future annex to be built on the southern half of the site. The entrance hall provides stairs to the upper floors, lounges on different levels for informal conversation, and a display area for research-related exhibits. Its 12-meter-high curtain wall is layered with a clear hierarchy consisting of round structural columns supporting the roof slab, a steel frame on a 4.2-meter grid supporting the curtain wall, and a 1.4-meter grid of zipper gaskets affixing the glass.

The curved portion of the building has a classically inspired three-tiered section. The ground floor forms a base whose interior is partitioned for an administrative office and seminar and lecture rooms. The second and third floors each provide 600 square meters of open work space for group research and together constitute the *piano nobile*. Counseling and conference rooms occupy the fourth floor which forms the crown of the building.

The second- and third-floor lofts are the most important feature of the program, embodying the experimental and research ideals of the university. Here researchers divide into teams to work on several projects simultaneously, commissioned from both within the university and the outside. Since the composition of these teams is likely to change frequently, the work space needed to be highly flexible with a minimum of permanent interior partitions. The neutrality of these spaces, however, is given architectural interest by wrapping the curvilinear exterior edge with a double-height *brise-soleil* of perforated aluminum panels. This transparent screen not only unifies the interior space but also gives the building a soft glow at night when seen from the exterior. As a major hub of the university's international electronic communications with other important academic institutions around the world, the building is frequently in use around the clock by research students and we were eager to symbolize its 24-hour activity with this veiled luminescence.

Aerial view

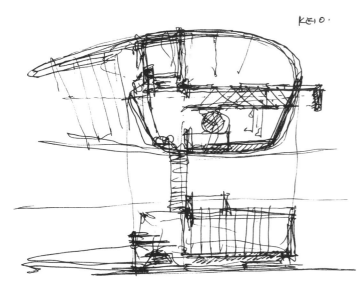

KEIO.

# THE TRANSPARENT GESTURE

Kenichi Echigoshima
translated by Hiroshi Watanabe

Like other facilities on the Shonan Fujisawa Campus of Keio University, the Graduate School Research Center is characterized by transparency. The only anomaly is the shape of the building envelope. The reason for it is not immediately apparent. There seems to be a deliberate avoidance of symmetry and geometry. The outline cannot be called organic or freehand. It seems to suggest a swelling from within. Yet even the *brise-soleil* transmits light. The pursuit of transparency is so thorough as to sacrifice even the sun-shading function of that device. Any qualitative difference between inside and outside is denied; the sharing of spatial extension is emphasized. The projected architectural image thus does not suggest an interior that, having attained fullness, expands outward. The building at first glance is in a transparent, modern style, but it reveals subtle discrepancies. Yet it is not a characterless, abstract space based on some ideal geometrical figure.

The architect explains that the two protrusions on the south side are intended to endow the building simultaneously with a transparency and a multilayered quality, and that the overall outline of the building is not meant to suggest a deficiency such as an oval from which a section has been cut, but "to reinforce the impression of an independent form." One now understands the reason for the outline of the building. It is to emphasize the effect of transparency and to make the building contour itself appear autonomous. The architect does not have faith in geometry, but the situation called for some type of complete form. What he saw was the possibility that an incomplete geometrical figure might in fact produce the effect of autonomy. If one were called upon to characterize the result, it might be described as a distinctive outline that is symmetrical and suggestive, like an airship, of forward movement. Yet inside, the multistory entry hall is located asymmetrically and sets in motion a rotational movement in which the entire building becomes engaged. The shape of the building envelope is thus not a direct reflection of what takes place inside. The experienced space and spatial image suggested by the outline exhibit different characteristics but coexist in the same form. Ordinarily extreme transparency assures the domination of a single principle inside and out and is apt to produce a consistent architectural image. Here, however, different spatial images overlap despite a thoroughgoing transparency. A polysemous quality is indicated, not on a superficial, decorative level, but on

*Above:* Entrance vestibule

*Facing page:* The two-story perforated aluminum *brise-soleil* softly filters natural light entering the research lofts on second and third floors.

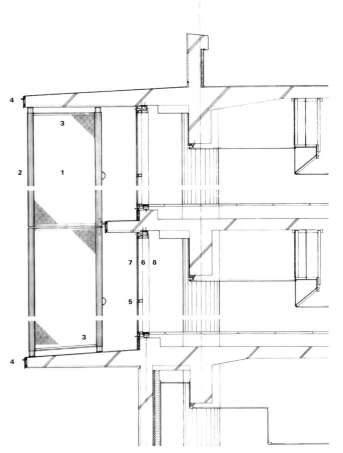

Wall section detail

1 louver screen
2 tubular post supporting screen
3 aluminum frame
4 fascia panel
5 zipper gasket
6 extruded aluminum sash
7 glass
8 mullion support

the deepest level of architectural form, extending even to the inner depths of space because of the transparency of the building.

What concerns us here is the impulse to make a transparent space autonomous, the basis for the quite modern yet nongeometrical act of imagination. A space that is homogeneous and abstract and an outline that is figuratively closed—such an architectural image is basic to the modernist style. What was revolutionary about modernism was the forcible joining of transparency and geometry. The "ground" that substantiated form and the outline that produced the effect of completion shared the spatial image. The impulse to expand and the impulse to achieve completion were both aimed at establishing a homogeneous and characterless geometrical world. There is the beginning in the Graduate School Research Center of a departure from such stylistic consistency and of a transformation of the overall image. The building shuns the kind of transparency that substantiates geometry; while the building contour suggests an autonomous spatial image, a richer transparency is developed. Moreover, the building engages the surrounding landscape and indicates

that it is part of a much larger world of forms. Unlike a geometrical figure, it does not stand isolated. It can relate to movement in the lay of the land because it itself is fraught with movement. The building envelope, while autonomous, is in a dynamic relationship to its environment. It is an earthly gesture that is given transparent form, an act of completion modeled on movement originating in the earth.

Let us look at the Carpenter Center, which was completed while Maki was still teaching at Harvard University. Though the context is different, the form, which constitutes the actual means of response, is similar. The building envelope is such that it closes itself off even as it exerts an influence on its surroundings. There is a gesture, rooted in space, that emphasizes the presence of the inside and is fraught with a shifting tension. However, the *brise-soleil* is deep and heavy, and the effect is to close off the interior. As if to acquaint itself with its surroundings, the building extends a tentaclelike ramp. In Maki's work the space is thoroughly open despite the closed contour of the building, and a feeling of openness with the surroundings is assured. There is no need for a tentacle. That is where the

*Above:* Looking down from third floor to entrance hall and campus beyond

*Right:* The curtain wall is based on a tripartite hierarchy.

*Facing page:* The lobby atrium combines sculptural stairs and lounge terraces to create an active three-dimensional communication space.

*Top:* Loft space

*Left:* Evening view

*Above:* Loft space looking out to greenery

polysemous and integrative significance of the transparent gesture lies. It relates to its surroundings, yet it rotates and suggests moreover a completion of form. Vincent Scully has used images of action to characterize the plastic designs of Le Corbusier's later period, drawing for example an analogy between the columns of the Unité and the muscles supporting an enormous weight. If there is a gestural characteristic distinctive to architectural form, it is probably the assertion of space. Such an assertion is not limited to outward expansion generated by repletion. The assertion of diverse spatial images is possible even with a transparent, homogeneous spatial extension.

In his early works Le Corbusier produced a rich transparency in which simple contours were layered. To that were added, by way of contrast, elements such as ramps that constituted the actualization of human movement. By the time of the Swiss Pavilion the architectural image was torn between a transparent geometry isolated in the air and a curved wall of rubble stone. In altering an approach based on pure solids that had reached a dead end, Le Corbusier himself began by having the wall itself make an earthly gesture to situate itself relative to the surroundings. The

architecture itself took on movement. In Maki's work, that breach in the architectural image is closed by the transparent gesture. It is as if the formal world of the later Corbu were viewed through the eyes of the Swiss architect in his earlier period. Arata Isozaki calls Maki a relativist thinker who "takes note of each condition of a place . . . and then searches for the logic behind the relationships." He describes Maki's maturity somewhat metaphorically as "a flow characterized by lightness and freedom." The form of the Graduate School Research Center can be said to be the direct translation of that notion into an architectural image. A gestural image related to the surroundings and conceived relativistically provides the impetus in an attempt to realize an architectural image characterized by flow. In this formal world the response of transparent spatial acts to diverse conditions reveals the significance of an autonomous contour. This form, which never isolates itself, never forms a space around itself, yet does not readily commit itself to its surroundings—this form which situates itself in its context yet remains independent reveals Maki's essential quality as a relativist thinker.

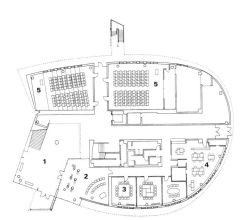

First floor

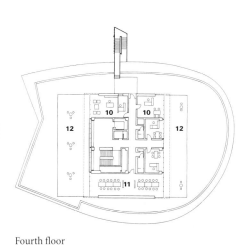

Second floor

Fourth floor

1  entrance hall
2  gallery
3  seminar room
4  office
5  lecture room
6  loft
7  group research laboratory
8  lounge
9  void
10  laboratory
11  conference
12  roof terrace

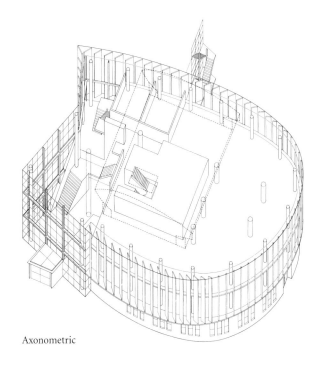

Axonometric

*Above:* View from southeast

*Facing page:* Detail of penthouse corner

# FROM GROUP FORM TO LIGHTNESS

Maki's Architecture "Up" to the Next Millennium

Botond Bognar

"What then shall we choose? Weight or lightness?... The only certainty is: the lightness/weight opposition is the most mysterious, most ambiguous of all."                 —Milan Kundera, *The Unbearable Lightness of Being*[1]

"Unlike most of his contemporaries, Maki unites within his practice two rather contradictory positions; on the one hand an ethical commitment to the provision of an architecture that is both rational and appropriate, on the other, an ironic disposition capable of acknowledging the aporias of the modern world and of confronting the ever-escalating implosion of information and development. Maki regards the inescapably disjunctive character of this last with a dispassionate, Olympian eye. Generous to a fault, he will acknowledge that the programmatic indifference of Deconstructivist Architecture is an understandable reaction to the schismatic character of our time. At the same time he remains detached and judicious, resisting, without becoming reactionary, the temptation to indulge in the plastic and iconographic excesses of the younger generation. Instead his work is informed by a disconcerting and contradictory combination of anxiety and optimism. On the one hand he remains extremely skeptical, while, on the other, he projects the... idea of hope."
—Kenneth Frampton, *The Pritzker Architecture Prize 1993: Fumihiko Maki*[2]

## Introduction/Context

Since the late 1950s the evolution and flourishing of Fumihiko Maki's architecture, one of the longest, most distinguished, and multifaceted design practices of today, have paralleled waves of rapid developments and dramatic changes in Japanese society and the worlds of architecture and design, which have been both problematic as well as exciting and challenging. Some of these turbulent but by all means germinating events have been experienced in common with other countries, while others have been unique to Japan; many of them have had an undeniable influence on Maki's maturation as a designer and thinker. In turn, his work has contributed in an increasingly significant way to shaping the course of late-twentieth-century architecture and urbanism in Japan and, more recently, beyond; today he enjoys a genuine and well-deserved international reputation that is rare among his contemporaries.

The postwar reconstruction in Japan was followed in the 1960s by the so-called "Japanese miracle," an unparalleled boom in industrial progress and unchecked urbanization, that was both manifested in, and fostered by, the still-prevailing, albeit not unchallenged, hegemony of modernism

and modern architecture. In the 1970s the worldwide energy crisis, the slowdown in the economy, the general disillusionment in the redeeming capacity of modern industrial technology and society, and the breaking down of long-established value systems and their replacements with new and, as of yet, unsettled ones questioned the authority of a single "international style" and hastened the entry of postmodernism in just about every segment of cultural life, led by art and architecture. Promoted by the rapid spread of radically new information technologies and the overall penetration of the media, the 1980s were marked by the rebounding of both production and consumption, as well as by the onset of commodity culture and the beginning of a new type of urbanism. The euphoria that accompanied the apparently unlimited promise of this so-called "bubble economy" in Japan came to an abrupt halt in the early 1990s, leaving in its wake a sober awakening and a less-than-somber mood. And, while this has not changed the basic parameters by which the Japanese economy operates, it has certainly put a brake to its runaway and overheated "machine," and has demonstrated an urgent need to check and reevaluate the course Japanese society and its architectural and urban culture may, or should, take in the somewhat uncertain future.

In this regard, though, it is important to remember that Japan's economy, its recent difficulties notwithstanding, still remains the second largest in the world. The country continues to be an undisputed economic superpower in which the government plays, as it always has, an unusually active role.[3] Such conditions, along with many other factors, have been setting the stage for quite some time for the unique developments of the cultural, architectural, and urban landscape in the country. Even today, in a time of reduced private investment, there are plenty of large-scale, tax-funded construction projects, that can maintain the tradition of state-promoted and sponsored building in Japan. As a result, in the past few decades—the new "golden age" of Japanese architecture—the country has played an increasingly important role in the international design scene. The sheer volume, not to mention quality, of outstanding projects and completed works produced in Japan, particularly since the early 1980s, has surpassed the output of most other countries; these achievements have elicited in the West a steadily growing interest in and admiration of, if not always understanding of, the Japanese architectural progress.

The success, while attributable to many forces—social and economic conditions, availability of advanced technologies, exceptionally high standards of construction[4] coupled with a penchant for innovation, and features of the physical and cultural environment of Japan—has also been stimulated by waves of talented Japanese architects. Many individuals have taken turns as the most influential leading designers in Japan. In addition to Kenzo Tange, who has long enjoyed national and international reputation, Arata Isozaki, Fumihiko Maki, Kisho Kurokawa, Tadao Ando, Kazuo Shinohara, Kiyonori Kikutake, Toyo Ito, Itsuko Hasegawa, Shin Takamatsu, and others have become well known both at home and abroad. In their own particular and often singular ways, which together form an unusually broad spectrum of design intentions, they have substantially contributed to the evolution of a new architectural and urban culture in Japan.

The Japanese ability to foster a high-quality architectural culture on a broad scale, beyond the accomplishments of individual architects, is remarkable indeed, because it is something that only a few countries have been able to achieve in our age of globalization, multinational economy, and universal civilization. Kenneth Frampton, in his book *Modern Architecture: A Critical History* (1992), has identified only Japan, Finland, France, and Spain as representatives of a rich, *modern* architectural culture today.[5] In Japan, this has been reached despite the vagaries of prevailing chaotic urban conditions, although one might argue that the innovation of contemporary Japanese architecture is actually and paradoxically derivative of these conditions. Indeed, Japanese architectural works, especially the most outstanding ones, cannot be properly understood, appreciated, and evaluated without grasping their profound, although often ambiguous, relations with the city, whose overwhelming presence Chris Fawcett properly referred to some time ago as "Japan *the* City."[6]

Japanese architects have increasingly shown their capacity to deal with the excessively complex and contradictory context advanced by the society in which they operate, while combining innovative departures with critical gestures and poetic poignancy. If such an observation holds true in general, it does even more so for Maki and other architects of exceptional caliber. Perhaps more significant are those provisions, commitments, features, and qualities that are unique to Maki's work. Benefiting from various sources and approaches, yet remaining aloof from the excesses of any "isms," Maki has defined and follows his own direction in architecture. And, it is safe to say, his achievements, particularly in the last ten years, are really nothing short of the astonishing, even when compared with the most accomplished designers around the world.

After more than three and a half decades of teaching and practice, Fumihiko Maki seems to be at the peak of his career; today he is more active and creative than ever. This is amply proven by the growing number of his outstanding projects: cultural, commercial, education, convention, and sports facilities. In recent years his office has completed several major projects in foreign countries as well, including the Center for the Arts Yerba Buena Gardens in San Francisco (1993) and the Isar Büropark near Munich (1995), and is now busy with several others in Germany, the Netherlands, and Poland. For his consistently excellent work, Maki was honored with the Pritzker Prize (the most prestigious international award in architecture), the fourth UIA Gold Medal, and the third Prince of Wales Prize in Urban Design, to mention but a few of his more recent awards.[7]

**Origin/Background**

Educated in both Tokyo and the United States, Maki has been able to fuse the influences of the evolution-oriented Japanese and the object-oriented Western cultures in his designs, while never yielding to trivial or formalistic historicism. Moreover, being both a distinguished academician and an active designer, he has tied his practice to extensive scholarship. As much as his research into the theories of architecture and urbanism—conducted while teaching in various foreign and Japanese universities—has consistently informed his practice, so much have the results of his completed projects directly guided his theoretical investigations. His works are characterized by a programmatic rationality of design, modular dimensioning, and the extensive yet selective application of new industrialized materials, components, structural systems, and technologies, as well as by a growing interest in and sensibility to details, craftsmanship, spatial articulation, and, most importantly, the experiential qualities of place (*basho-sei*)[8]; while satisfying society's needs, they are both aesthetically vibrant and profoundly in tune with their times.

As Maki's architecture has progressed through several stages, both its scope and complexity have steadily broadened. There are therefore numerous interrelated aspects and intentions that have shaped his work, and through which it has to be discussed. Nevertheless none seems to be as important and consistent as his long-standing commitment to promoting a meaningful, modern, public architecture in the progressively heterogeneous, contradictory, and even "anarchical" conditions of the contemporary Japanese city.

In the above statement there are two points that need to be equally underscored and elaborated upon; the first is "modern," the other, "public." Maki, has always been considered a modernist at heart, though the label "modern" can only be used with limitations when describing his architecture. While building upon much of what modern architecture has achieved—especially with regard to a discernible rationality in conception and an abstract vocabulary—and while adhering to its ethos of socially responsible design, Maki has been critical of many of its premises, especially its inability to produce a meaningful urban model and generate well-functioning, active public spaces in the city. Therefore the two basic provisions of his architecture—the dimensions of "modern" and "public"—are interrelated, yet, to some extent, in a paradoxical way.

Such predisposition of Maki's design enterprise can be traced back as far as the very beginning of his career, and perhaps to an even earlier time in his life. Among his contemporaries in Japanese architecture, Maki is one of the few, who, upon graduating from Tokyo University in 1952, went abroad to continue his architectural education in the United States, where he earned two Master of Architecture degrees, one in 1953 at the Cranbrook Academy of Art and another in 1954 at Harvard's Graduate School of Design.[9] His experiences abroad introduced him early and directly to the latest developments in Western architecture at a time when modernism was still reigning with full power. At Harvard in particular, a stronghold of the modern movement where he subsequently taught between 1962 and 1965, Maki was nourished in the long-standing traditions and legacy of many leading figures of modern architecture, such as Walter Gropius, Marcel Breuer, Jerzy Soltan, and Shadrach Woods, who had taught or were still teaching in the school. Most important was the influence of Josep Lluís Sert, the dean of the school while Maki was at Harvard, for whom Maki worked from 1954–56. From Sert, Maki learned not only the basic vocabulary and principles of urbanism, but also the appreciation and articulation of a reticent yet plastic and spatially enriched architecture. This characterized much of his designs in the 1960s and 1970s, including his first major work, the Hillside Terrace Apartment Complex in Tokyo, which commenced in 1967 and was completed in several stages.

Maki's education, work, and teaching abroad were not the only episodes that provided him with a special perspective on architecture, implanted the seeds of his predisposition and adherence to the cause of modernism, and sharpened his growing interest in urban design. His childhood experiences in Tokyo first drew Maki into the spheres of the emerging modern world and a thriving urban environment. Contrary to his well-known contemporaries, Maki was born and has always lived, when not abroad, in Tokyo. The experience of the capital's special urban milieu had, as it still has, a profound impact on him, directing the trajectory of his career throughout the years. Hiroshi Watanabe has remarked, that Maki was already "An urbanite before he ever became an urbanist."[10] Maki himself has reminisced, "In my childhood in Tokyo (in the

1930s)...the white houses by the Japanese pioneers of modernism...that I chanced to visit in those days were in marked (and refreshing) contrast to other residences in the *yamanote* ("High City") area whose dominant colors were greens and browns and where many trees still grew. Their white spaces suggested visions of the future, and the glass blocks inserted in the white walls and the narrow steel railings were my first introduction to these materials. Eventually, images of automobiles and airplanes were superimposed on my impressions of these houses."[11]

Along the eventful course of becoming an accomplished urbanist, Maki has developed a penchant for public architecture and a profound concern for the city. While he has designed some excellent pieces of residential architecture, the vast majority of his works, and indeed the ones that have made his name well known, are public structures and complexes. Yet even his more private buildings display unique qualities that lend them a discernible civic character. This is evidenced most by his own house in Tokyo (1978), the Iwasaki Art Museum (1979) and Craft Museum (1987) in the open landscape of Ibusuki, and the YKK Guest House in Kurobe (1982). The latter in its pastoral setting appears as an urban villa rather than a rustic farmhouse. It both complements and challenges its natural environment; here artifice and landscape mutually enhance each other.

Maki's work seems unfailingly and unmistakably urban regardless of its location because it articulates his understanding of the relationship between architecture and the city. For Maki there is a sensible continuity between the two as they share certain qualities with each other. The building itself appears to be a "small city" within the larger one, or alternatively, it carries the attributes of an urban enclave, while rendered as a "city-in-miniature." Interestingly, the origin of the idea, if not its actual resolution, harkens back to Andrea Palladio, who, in his *The Four Books of Architecture*, wrote, "The city is as it were but a great house, and, the contrary, a country house is a little city."[12]

Yet Maki's insights were more significantly shaped by other, more contemporary sources, including the activities of Team X (the organizers of the Tenth Congrès Internationaux d'Architecture Moderne [CIAM X]), and more importantly, the Dutch architect, Aldo van Eyck, who was the group's charismatic leader, co-editor of its *Forum*, and its most influential spokesperson. Van Eyck, in his efforts to buttress the new type of urbanism Team X was forwarding, voiced the necessity of the above-mentioned continuity by stating, "We must stop splitting the making of a habitat into two disciplines—architecture and urbanism. Why?...As I have already said, a house must be like a small city if it's to be a real house—a city like a large house if it's to be a real city."[13] Contrary to the rigid functional model

1. Shinjuku Redevelopment Project, 1960. (F. Maki with M. Otaka)

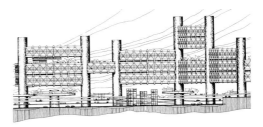

2. "City-in-the-Air," the Joint Core System Project for Shinjuku, 1961. (A. Isozaki)

3. Golgi Structures Project, 1965. (F. Maki)

of modernist urban design, and in a clear revolt against CIAM IV's "mechanical principles of order" laid out in its Athens Charter of 1933, Team X searched for the more complex, structural patterns of urban growth. This opened the way to pluralistic appropriations by the members. The one represented by van Eyck, the most sensitive and critical thinker in the group, was filtered through his anthropological studies in Africa.

Maki, who attended the 1960 Team X meeting in Bagnols-sur-Cèze, near Avignon, France, subsequently worked with several members of the group at Harvard. Thus he became acquainted with their work, and more specifically that of van Eyck, with whom he shared a respect for the genetic elements in urban forms as well as an interest in the architecture of traditional settlements.[14] Van Eyck's and Maki's departure toward a new urbanism was nothing short of a paradox. While they remained strongly committed to the modern cause, they, unlike most of their predecessors in CIAM, as Alex Krieger has pointed out, "managed . . . to harbor high regard for the pre-modern traditions of urbanism. This seemingly contradictory stance of championing modern architecture without dismissing the traditional city was an intellectual breakthrough."[15]

**Collective Form/Group Form**

At almost the same time that van Eyck was investigating the architecture and urban culture of the Dogon, a small African tribe in Mali, Maki, awarded with a Graham Foundation fellowship in 1958, embarked on two extensive research trips the following years: first to Hong Kong, Thailand, Singapore, India, Iran, Egypt, Lebanon, Syria, Turkey, Austria, Italy, France, Spain, the United Kingdom, the Netherlands, and Belgium, then to Israel, Greece, Italy, Spain, France, the United Kingdom, Belgium, the Netherlands, Germany, Denmark, Norway, Sweden, and Finland.[16] During these journeys Maki studied the formal and spatial organizations of various settlements; he pursued a more effective mode of urban integration, or a new "collective form," as he called it—what the alarmingly disintegrating modern cities lacked. Of the many cities and villages he visited, the ones that made the greatest impression on him were communities of houses built with walls of sun-dried brick and tiled roofs, the kind that are scattered along the Mediterranean in large numbers. He recognized that the type of collective form manifested by these communities profoundly reflected the character of their cultures. Together with an architect friend, Masato Otaka, he developed the findings of his studies into his first urban design proposal for the redevelopment of west Shinjuku in Tokyo. The

proposal presented an alternative to the prevailing modernist models (fig. 1). Entitled "Toward Group-Form," it was admittedly "not so much an actual scheme for that area, as [an initial] demonstration of the idea of group-form,"[17] Maki's new organizational type and strategy in design.

As the intentions of this proposal coincided somewhat with those of Maki's contemporaries in Japan, in 1959 he, along with Otaka, joined the so-called Metabolism Group. The primary aim of the Metabolists was the systematization of design and the extensive application of new industrial technology for both architectural and urban renewal. The leaders of the group, Kikutake and Kurokawa, plus the inspirational father of the movement, Tange, and one of his disciples, Isozaki, envisioned the advent of new technopolises; their futuristic and utopian urban schemes were conceived of prefabricated and mass-produced elements, units, and even capsules supported by various megastructures, which were utilized to assure functional and spatial flexibility, change, and growth, plus operational efficiency in, or rather over, the congested existing city (fig. 2).

Although Maki's interest in new modes of urban design were closely associated with those of the Metabolists, he never shared their technological preoccupation with mechanical changeability as the basis for the future city. He was a reluctant warrior in the army of Metabolists, and so his practice at that time could be considered as closer to the margin of Metabolism than its center. He and Otaka were the moderates in the group; their proposal for the redevelopment of Shinjuku (1960) and Maki's equally theoretical urban project with Golgi structures (1965) (fig. 3), while clearly critical departures from the master-planning practices of the modern movement, simultaneously distanced themselves from the rigid (mega)structuralist interpretations of the new city. As such, they were more sophisticated than the urban projects of his fellow Metabolists.[18] In fact, these projects revealed an organic quality, a feature that was further elaborated a few years later in Maki's *Investigations in Collective Form.*[19]

Moreover, even in his early "Metabolist" architecture, Maki was more inclined to approach the issue of urban flexibility from a restrained and practical position, that is to say, from the reality of the existing urban conditions, rather than from the idealistic heights of utopia. Thus his designs implemented the diverse viewpoints of the citizens, but this never resulted in simply populist or trivial pop designs; his works have always maintained a discrete elegance and an aura of dignity.

While Metabolism ruled the architectural scene in Japan for more than a decade, some of its early followers deviated decisively from its original paradigm and practice. Isozaki's shift toward a more art-oriented, highly

4. Rissho University Kumagaya Campus Buildings, 1968. (F. Maki)

6. Senri Chuo Building, Toyonaka, Osaka, 1970. (F. Maki)

5. Osaka Expo–70, Space Frame, 1970. (K. Tange)

7. Collective forms: diagrams of compositional, mega-, and group forms (F. Maki)

conceptual, and ironical-mannerist architecture contrasted Maki's steady move toward a more rational, yet refreshingly "enlightened," design that addressed the public realm of urban architecture as its most important task. Maki's progress in this direction was gradual; indeed, in most respects, Maki, unlike Isozaki, Shinohara, Ito, and most others, can be considered a "gradualist." Therefore, although his early projects, such as the Nagoya University Toyota Memorial Hall (1960) and the Rissho University Kumagaya Campus Buildings (1968) (fig. 4), made initial steps toward mediating between inside private and outside public spaces, and so, toward establishing continuity between architecture and urbanism, they simultaneously displayed some unmistakable features of the prevailing style in Japan, including massive, unfinished reinforced concrete structures and emphasis on enclosed vertical circulation shafts.

The growing disparity between the work of Maki and his fellow members in the Metabolism Group was highlighted by the numerous projects built for the 1970 Osaka Expo under the leadership of Tange. While Tange and Kikutake designed gigantic space frames (fig. 5) and Kurokawa built various pavilions as systems of capsules, Maki, in the nearby new town of Toyonaka, completed the Senri Chuo Building (1970) (fig. 6), which was articulated on an intimate human scale. It featured a double-level public plaza, a lively, a multistory atrium, or "urban room," with bridges and walkways, and a spatial character that both continues the outside urban space and transforms it into an in-between space.

Maki's unfolding new mode of design made him a leading figure of contemporary Japanese contextual architecture in the 1970s. Based on his studies of vernacular architecture and settlements in both the West and East, including Japan, his publication *Investigations in Collective Form* emphasized the part-and-whole relationship as the fundamental issue of new "collective" or public urban forms. Maki promoted, in contrast to the modernist "compositional form" and Metabolist (structuralist) "megaform," a more flexible and sensitive "group form," an organization in which the parts and the whole maintain a reciprocal relationship (fig. 7). In this system, while the whole supports the function and development of the elements, the elements themselves, empowered with a generative capacity, constitute the "collective" whole as an additive and aggregate form. Unlike megaforms, group forms are not simply determined and ruled by an independent system imposed on them *a priori*. For Maki, such reciprocity—an organic or symbiotic relationship of mutual interdependence—also implied that works of architecture necessarily acquire some basic attributes of urban formations through deciphering and responding to the most significant qualities of their given built environment.

Maki's approach systematically, albeit gradually, undermined the primacy of the static whole, resulting in more complex, but "weaker" or "incomplete" overall forms, which were open to a multiplicity of human associations and meanings. This translated into a design strategy of breaking down an architectural program into its functional and/or formal elements while retaining their perceptible references, both functionally and symbolically, to the larger whole (for instance, as a classroom refers to the notion of school). Having articulated the parts in a distinctive way, Maki devised various intermediary realms or spaces, often as extensions of the spatial units themselves, that formed a loosely connecting aggregate system or, more precisely, organized the elements into an ambiguous whole, with a spatial matrix of what van Eyck called "labyrinthine clarity."[20] Several of Maki's projects in the 1970s exemplify this mode of design. They include the Kato Gakuen Elementary School in Numazu (1972), the Osaka Prefectural Sports Center in Takaishi (1972), the Tsukuba University Central Building (1974), and the National Aquarium of the Okinawa Marine Expo (1975). Yet, the one that best represents the idea of group form is his most renowned early work, the Hillside Terrace Apartment Complex in Tokyo (1969, 1973, 1976). Through its porous matrix of formal disposition and spatial fluidity of interstices this mixed-use, low-profile, and "informal" urban project of residences, studios, small offices, shops, and boutiques mediates not only between two adjacent yet sharply divergent urban areas—a quiet park with a Shinto shrine and a busy, major road—but also between the "outside" public and "inside" private realms by filtering their spaces into an attractive system of semi-open and semi-public, in-between courtyard plazas. In this urban complex, the result of careful spatial modulations, "exterior spaces...first serve as the generators of the interior spaces, and become eventually the interior spaces themselves."[21]

It is important to point out that while Maki's definition of the whole, along with his gradual loosening of the relationship among the parts, tended toward an increasingly ambiguous quality that eventually reached the stage of collaged and fragmentary compositions, his early designs yielded, almost invariably, rather stable, although not necessarily univalent, overall configurations. Owing to his experiences with European and Asian vernacular settlements, his interpretation of "collective form" in the 1960s and most of the 1970s resulted in more solidly grounded buildings and complexes. Several of them were admittedly inspired by the "silhouette of medieval towns with the highest building in the center."[22] Often shaped as piles of cubical elements, projects such as the National Aquarium in Okinawa (1975) and the Iwasaki Art Museum in Ibusuki (1979) also alluded to the images of ancient stepped pyramids, and decidedly, as in

8. Row House at Sumiyoshi, Osaka, 1976. (T. Ando)

9. Urban Landscape of Tokyo at Shibuya, 1991.

10. *Tokyo: Form and Spirit* exhibition installation, 1985. (F. Maki)

the case of the Tsukuba University Central Building (1974), to mountains.[23] A similar formal articulation can be detected in Maki's few residential buildings, thus providing yet another suggestion of their having urban dimensions.

On the other hand, one cannot but notice a curious feature of many of Maki's public buildings, including large ones in urban settings; they display some latent but unmistakable attributes of residential architecture, and they often embody the image of the paradigmatic house. The Iwasaki Art Museum (1979) and Craft Museum (1987), the YKK Guest House (1983), and the Tepia (1989) in Tokyo reveal their remote origins in either the Japanese urban residence, or the Western palazzo, or both, while they show an indebtedness to several canonical works of early modern residential architecture.[24] The explanation for this may reside, partially at least, in the unusual traditions of Japanese public architecture, or, rather, the lack of such traditions. Indeed, one of the most striking characteristics of Japanese urban and architectural history is that public buildings in the conventional sense did not develop until the modern era. In the Edo period (1603–1868), theaters, magistrate's offices, and schools were built as auxiliary facilities of samurai residences, temples, or shrines, and as such were architecturally only variations on these buildings. In addition, traditional residential and religious architecture had a common origin in prehistoric storehouse (*kura*) architecture, and therefore did not differ from each other as much as they did in the West. In this light the somewhat dichotomous character of Maki's public architecture becomes more understandable.[25]

Although the evocation of the whole, that is the "collective form," has changed significantly in Maki's subsequent work in order to meet the demands of a vastly accelerated Japanese urbanism, his articulation of an architectural complex as a metaphorical small city has continued, as has his recollection of the urban realm and its public dimension within smaller, "individual" projects. In this respect, his architecture differed considerably from the intentions of most other designers of the 1970s New Wave. In the wake of deteriorating urban conditions in Japan—congestion, pollution, the erosion of privacy, and, most importantly, the onslaught of uncontrolled consumerist urbanism—many architects such as Ando, Shinohara, Ito, Hasegawa, Hiroshi Hara, and Takefumi Aida took an explicitly negative stance toward the city. Their inward oriented and defensive architecture was shaped as "hermetic microcosms" often centered around tiny, isolated courtyards in order to protect the owners from the disturbing outside world (fig. 8). Whereas most others harbored "encapsulated urban utopias" within the closed and private domain of

small individual buildings, Maki designed works to engage the city and to make sense within it. Neither Maki nor his peers proved to be completely successful in providing a meaningful solution to the prevailing social and urban predicament, particularly with regard to the quickly transforming public realm of the city. Therefore, the beginning of the 1980s signaled the necessity for new directions in Japanese architecture.

## Surface/Depth

In the age of proliferating privatized architectural rhetorics, which commenced in earnest sometime in the 1970s in both Japan and the West, Maki has continued to work, albeit with a changed syntax and shifting strategy, toward maintaining a well-differentiated though common language embodied in the public dimension of architecture and the city. His intentions might have paralleled the somewhat similar commitment of European contextualists or neorationalists, notably that of the Italian Aldo Rossi. Yet, Maki's idea of the city has little to do with the classical language of architecture and the classical traditions of Western urbanism; rather it is derivative of the Japanese city, which is substantially different when compared to both its traditional and contemporary Western counterparts.

Tokyo best represents such differences. It is both the epitome of accelerated urban culture in Japan, and one of the foremost examples of new, informational world cities. Tokyo has continued to exert the most significant impact on Maki's changing course of design (fig. 9), nurturing, what he calls his "city sensitivity." Maki summarized his insights in his contribution to a large-scale exhibition entitled *Tokyo: Form and Spirit*, which toured the United States in 1986, after being on display in Japan.[26] Maki's project was comprised of seven pillarlike structures, each symbolizing a particular quality of Tokyo: a city of chaotic heterogeneity, a city of endless or continuous unfolding, a city of constant construction and destruction with both a sense for the future and with a scent of decay, a city of eyes watching through masks, a city of both strong collective memories and a flood of anonymous information, a city both real as well as fictional, and a city of depth with an invisible center (fig. 10).

In addition to their reference to the contemporary city, Maki's designs reveal a sensible affinity with the ambiguous spatial definition of traditional Japanese architecture. A more conscious reliance on this affinity, along with an attempt of a lightness of appearance and a predilection for certain elements of mannerism, introduced a new stage in Maki's work in the early 1980s. Gradually, he has also enriched his architecture by extending his concerns beyond the physical/formal aspects of the built environment to include the cultural, social, and technological landscape as well. More precisely, in addition to the spatial relationships entailed by actual architectural settings, or "primary landscapes," the images and symbols of "imaginary landscapes," which Maki sees as part of the collective memory of the Japanese, have come to play a significant role in his designs. This is best shown in the YKK Guest House in Kurobe (1982), the Fujisawa Municipal Gymnasium (1984), and the Kyoto National Museum of Modern Art (1986). The orthogonal grid on the facades of the museum, for instance, is not used as a negative device to defamiliarize and eliminate meaning (as it is for Isozaki and Fujii); rather, it is used as a positive symbol to reference Kyoto's original gridiron urban structure.

Maki has managed to evoke such imaginary landscapes without reverting to postmodernist, historicist clichés. Around the mid 1970s, he began to respond more noticeably to the layered, collagelike quality of the heterogeneous urban environment in Japan. He articulated his designs with sequentially layered spaces that, similar to traditional architecture and gardens, involve the intricate arrangement of surfaces, various screens, and thin, membranous elements, thus conjuring up of a phenomenological depth (*oku*). Such spatial disposition of traditional Japanese architecture and urbanism—in significant contrast to its Western counterpart, predicated on the laws of perspective conception and perception of space—constituted a manifestly "unperspective" paradigm of space. This difference in spatial paradigms reflected the predominantly center- and individual-oriented Western culture, and the strongly group-oriented Japanese culture.[27] As Maki points out in his seminal essay "Japanese City Spaces and the Concept of *Oku*," the Japanese city has always been characterized by a sense of depth in addition to a kaleidoscopic quality in lieu of a dominant center and an easily perceptible order.[28] Maki also acknowledges that "in Japanese . . . architecture, public character is expressed through the use and design of territory—in the sensitivity to borders, both marked and unmarked; in the multiple layering of space by means of . . . screens; and in spatial arrangements structured not by the idea of a center but by the idea of depth (*oku*)."[29]

Maki insists that by embracing the ethos of *oku* in the careful spatial design of public architecture, "The illusion that there can be secret places must be sustained."[30] Therefore, he has detached building envelopes from the tectonic body and freely manipulated them, often like signs. They are configured so as to bring about and "perform" a continuously "unfolding" architecture, in which everything is not revealed; as much as they fragment the overall composition, they also tend to obscure the "object of

desire," that is to say, they de-objectify architecture. In the "labyrinthine" spatial matrix of such design, where there is always a hint to some imminent yet perpetually receding spaces, meaning is conduced to be withheld rather than clearly expressed, or, alternatively, it is released but only slowly, piecemeal, and never completely. As evidenced well by the Spiral Building (1985) and Tepia Science Pavilion (1989), both in Tokyo, and even more so by his recent projects for the Palazzo del Cinema (1990), the Salzburg Congress Center (1992), and the Graduate School Research Center of Keio University (1994), Maki's increasingly liberated and lightweight membranous enclosures are capable of dissolving, to an amazing degree, architecture's solid mass and substantial materiality.

Unfolding within the "depth" of his uniquely choreographed buildings is a symbolic space, or a system of spaces that, endowed with a manifest elegance and dignity, engender a sensible urban or public character. These "nested" spaces are often reached through or made a part of a relatively long and intricate entrance sequence, such as the gallery and spiral ramp in the Spiral and the multistory hall with the main stairway in the Kyoto Museum of Modern Art. However these spaces differ from the recently popular atriums found in many commercial buildings. Maki's designs foster as well as celebrate gathering and the emergence of *random* human events, rather than simply promote sale as the primary goal of the space; in so doing, they are always dignified and often ceremonial, sometimes overly so.

Maki's progressively "dematerialized" and increasingly ambiguous architecture has revealed additional departures with several new qualities. One of the most important among them is a shift in his understanding of the relationship between the part and the whole, insofar as he is now more inclined to pay attention to the definition of the constituent elements than to their totality. While he brings the parts into sharper focus, he simultaneously renders the overall form "fuzzier" and more elusive, but by no means obliterated or destroyed. In his essay "Modernism at the Crossroads," Maki put it this way, "If a strong totality, with suppressed parts and a hierarchical composition are characteristic of classicist architecture, active and assertive parts are characteristic of Gothic architecture, and the early works of modern architecture. Today, I find myself more strongly attracted to the second organizational type. One reason is that working from the parts permits a freer formal interpretation of how various formal and environmental demands—including those of historical and symbolic nature—are to be met."[31]

Indeed, the surface-depth relationship is a significant aspect of Maki's design intentions particularly when compared to the general develop-

11. Spiral Building in the context of Aoyama Boulevard, 1985. (F. Maki)

ments of contemporary architecture, wherein too often merely the superficial surface of architectural definition is explored at the expense of spatial depth. Anthony Vidler in his *The Architectural Uncanny* has observed, "Such an aesthetic…in a society of spectacle committed to the suppression of all phenomenological depth, would indicate that the long tradition of anthropomorphic embodiment in architecture has been finally broken, with spatially uncanny consequences."[32] Maki, continuing the ethos of Japanese traditions so different from that of Western ones, aims at achieving a sense of depth precisely with the disposition of surfaces while eschewing the dichotomy between the uncanny and the homely in architectural space. This is so, insofar as his procedures of fragmentation, or "dismembering the body" of architecture, are as much derivative of the "disjunctive" and neither anthropomorphic nor anthropocentric conception of Japanese architecture, amply exemplified by the Katsura Imperial Villa (seventeenth century AD) in Kyoto,[33] as they are akin to Bernard Tschumi's "architecture of disjunctions," seen particularly well in his Parc de la Villette in Paris (1984).

### Technology/Fiction

Maki has long questioned the standard notions of an integrated whole or the "synthesis" of form. Along such investigations, now with a heightened interest in more assertive components and active spatial events, his works have attained both an explicitly fragmentary and collaged disposition and an implicitly theatrical quality. This new mode of design—in effect, an *integration without synthesis*—has reached such a high level of sophistication as warrant the term "poetics of fragmentation." As the parts have grown in independence and number, they have opened themselves further to the influence of various sources and precedents. Maki's designs continue to be inspired by both the works of the pioneers of modernism and the futuristic achievements of late-twentieth-century technology, but they have also begun to incorporate elements of various other architects, especially certain mannerist architects, such as Carlo Scarpa. Thus, in his recent projects, as Kenneth Frampton has correctly observed, "notwithstanding Maki's unwavering commitment to programmatic rationality, the final expression is subtly mannered"[34] and, one might add, sometimes distinctly so. The result of Maki's more acutely personal design sensibility—exemplified also by Isozaki's mode of mannerism[35]—is, as a matter of course, "an architecture of quotation *par excellence*."

The Spiral reveals its inspiration as much in the classical architecture of the Athenian Acropolis as that of the Katsura Imperial Villa; parts of Tepia

reflect equally Gerrit Rietveld's Schröder House (1924), Le Corbusier's Villa Shodan (1956), and the 1914 Werkbund Building by Gropius; while certain aspects of the Salzburg Congress Center reference both Rem Koolhaas and Toyo Ito's architectures. It is also interesting to note that on the Keio University Fujisawa Campus, the four units of classroom buildings almost directly quote Le Corbusier's Villa Savoye (1931); in turn, the research buildings behind them allude to the rationalist paradigm of Giuseppe Terragni. Thus the Villa Savoye has been lifted from its "ideal plain" and repeatedly deployed in a "dense urban" setting to find itself contributing in a curious way to Maki's evocation of group form. On the other hand, the group is here patterned along a Cartesian grid, displaying some remote affinity with Tschumi's la Villette project, as David Stewart has pointed out.[36] To continue the list, several of Maki's recent buildings, most notably the Kyoto Museum of Modern Art, are replete with Scarpaesque elements.

Engendered by personal reminiscences, "imaginary landscapes," and even dreams, as well as by his interpretations of "collective memories," the various "disconnected" elements of Maki's designs have gradually lent a festive, if not to say theatrical, character. These details, often articulated with translucent screens, with delicate and reflecting surfaces, and with the orchestration of filtered light effects, are meant to evoke elusive scenes in cinematic sequences, episodes without an all-encompassing story. In them, like in unforgettable movies, reality and fiction seem to overlap. Maki has written about his fascination with the transitory illusions of the cinema screen, "Architects are like movie directors. I don't think movie directors make films out of stories; I think the story is not the most important part of the movie. The most important thing in a movie is what kind of scene or scenery he wants to produce at the critical moment. Then to justify those sceneries he uses a story or, he makes up a story.…I am eclectic enough, probably, not to be afraid of setting up different sceneries within one building, or indeed of making buildings look to some extent like chaotic Tokyo"[37] (fig. 11).

These sceneries unfold along carefully modulated systems of movement: entryways, passages, sequences of folded spaces, and, very importantly, ceremonial stairways; they fade in and out of focus as strolling visitors wind their way through what may be called "esplanades," like the ones in and around the Spiral, the Kyoto Museum of Modern Art, the Fujisawa Municipal Gymnasium, the Tokyo Metropolitan Gymnasium, and other buildings. Frequently, however, the scenes are encountered as sharp snapshots that freeze both time and space and wherein experiences verge on the hallucinatory or the surreal. Such scenes can be glimpsed on

12. Ukiyo-e *View of Nihonbashi* from the series "One Hundred Famous Views of Edo" by Ando Hiroshige, 1858.

the rooftop terraces of the Spiral, Tepia, and the Kirishima International Concert Hall (1994); each, in its own way, recollects equally well the stillness of Giorgio de Chirico's paintings and some haunting scenes from the films of Akira Kurosawa, Sergei Eisenstein, Federico Fellini, Michelangelo Antonioni, or from Alan Resnais's *Last Year at Marienbad*, one of Maki's favorites.[38] Yet, nowhere else has the affinity between Maki's new architecture and the cinema been brought home more poignantly than in his 1992 competition entry for the Palazzo del Cinema in Venice, Italy. Designed with extensive layers of specially treated large glass surfaces and various translucent screens, the transparent and dematerialized volume of the Palazzo reflects the ephemeral state of Venice, a city afloat, as much as a "vision of a world that exists only through the magic of light (as in the cinema itself)."[39]

Nevertheless, experiencing Maki's recent architecture is profoundly akin to experiencing not only the ephemerality of the fragmented contemporary world, but also that of the "floating world" of the traditional Japanese *ukiyo-e*. These wood block prints depicting fleeting moments or scenes, small-scale "spectacles," and everyday human pleasures, thus altogether the transitoriness of life in the decadent urban milieu of Tokugawa Era Japan (1603–1868), unfolded in a discontinuous series, like pictures on a tapestry, or like the still frames and episodes in a movie[40] (fig. 12). Like these two media, recording the city in both the past and present, the designs of Maki are forwarded by the "surfaceness" of thin, membranous elements and screens along with the quality of almost transcendental lightness. Regarding historic continuity in Japan, Maki has commented, "Tokyo has undergone many changes in physical appearance over the last century. The city, so decimated by World War II, has had to rebuild from ashes. In its rebuilding it has become—perhaps it has returned to being— a city without heaviness. It was once a city of wood and paper; it has now become a city of concrete, steel, and glass. The feeling of lightness, however, remains."[41] Elsewhere he has added: "The aesthetic that this cityscape generates is one that favors fluctuations, fluidity, and lightness; it suggests the discovery of a new perceptual order,"[42] as well as the recognition of a new metaphor.

Lightness in Maki's designs is achieved not merely by employing lightweight materials and structures, but also by creating a new perceptual order capable of mediating between, and so integrating the numerous motives and "subtly" disjunctive elements into an architecture that, though tenuously eclectic, appears to be fluctuating between presence and absence. Lightness as a metaphor is the manifestation of a "new" understanding of the world in flux. Such an understanding, however, is similar

to the ethos of traditional Japanese *sukiya*-type residential architecture, which distinguished itself from its more formal predecessor, the *shoin*. The informal and fluid spatial disposition and the eclectic milieu of *sukiya* brought about by various borrowed elements, decorations, and ideas were shaped by the idiosyncratic aesthetic sensibility of the owner and/or designer, always a man of sophisticated taste. Writing about the architecture of Togo Murano (1891–1984), one of Japan's greatest contemporary designers who worked in the spirit and style of *sukiya*, Maki recognized, "The dissonances [in Murano's works] are enjoyable because there is lightness. . . . Lightness is here not just a visual quality. It is a matter of touch, color, and the feeling of space. It is the product of relationships between various elements that have been established according to a [uniquely] defined world view."[43] With this commentary, Maki implicitly acknowledges his indebtedness to the architectures of both the historic *sukiya* and Murano. Despite their tremendous differences, Murano's and Maki's architectures, at close scrutiny, display numerous features in which the two unmistakably intersect. Beyond a common tendency toward eclecticism, refinement, and lightness, they also share a common and strong predilection toward craftsmanship and extensive and meticulous detailing. Of course, their design modes are dissimilar. In strong contrast to Murano, Maki uses the latest high-tech materials, technologies, and, when necessary or possible, the most innovative structural solutions.

Yet, Maki's preoccupation with details goes far beyond the intent merely to resolve technical problems faultlessly; they also serve him well in generating evocative motives and design elements, in providing scale, rhythm, and tactility, and in making up for the "unbearable void" left by modern architecture, which robbed architecture of its details for which its forms could not compensate. Although Maki's extensive detailing is not really decoration per se, it causes some of his designs to be occasionally referred to as decorous (*tansei*). This detailing, being increasingly industrially crafted high-tech solutions, is one of the most significant aspects of his recent unique architectural constructs and, as such, contributes greatly to the evocation of their impalpable lightness and elusive appearance. Seemingly, lightness for Maki, as for Italo Calvino, "goes with precision and determination, not with vagueness and the haphazard."[44]

All this is demonstrated in a particularly astonishing way in Maki's project for the Congress Center in Salzburg, Austria (1992). In this scheme a light, steel-frame structure and layers of extensive glass surfaces, perforated metallic screens, and louvers comprise a "box of light" 48 by 48 meters in plan and 36 meters in height. The various "light" layers here, more than in any of Maki's previous buildings, include not only the vertical, but also the horizontal planes—canopies, ceilings, and floors—that have been rendered and made visible as thin membranes. Here for the first time, Maki shaped even the flat roof with perforated metallic screens. Nestled within this loosely and ambiguously defined boxy matrix of interlocking spaces are two "suspended" spatial units similar to those in Rem Koolhaas's project for the National Library of France (1989). These units, floating inside and partially outside of the space of the rooftop terrace, form a wrapped-core structure that is both spectacularly lucid and mysteriously intriguing; it is as illusive as Maki's Palazzo del Cinema in Venice (1990). Although the Congress Center has not been built, its exquisitely constructed model and computer-generated plans and details, displayed in the MoMA exhibition Light Construction in New York in 1995, left no doubt that, in spite of being a smaller building than Koolhaas's library, it is its equal and, with respect to resolution, perhaps also superior to the library (which, like Maki's project, had to remain only a proposal).

Moreover, the Congress Center's solution for the two-story oval volume inside anticipated the unique lightweight structural system of Toyo Ito's Mediatheque Project in Sendai (1998).[45] Ito was a pioneer of "light construction" in his generation. His 1984 house, the Silver Hut in Tokyo, championed a form of "nomadic architecture." Since then, he has developed an "architecture of the ephemeral" with a vision of space as flows of (electronic) information—a new, "aperspectival" paradigm of space—the model for which he has found in the Japanese city.[46] It has to be mentioned here that Ito is not the only architect in Japan whose architecture of lightness is analogous to Maki's new direction in design; in the 1980s, numerous, generally younger architects turned toward similar explorations. Itsuko Hasegawa combined such sentiments with her special views of nature and artifice. Kazuyo Sejima, Hiroshi Hara, Riken Yamamoto, and others soon followed suit. They share with Maki a preference for using industrially produced, lightweight, high-tech materials and often arrive at similarly fragmentary compositions. Maki's works, however, can be distinguished from these equally outstanding lines of design in that they have never been derived from the prototypical "primitive hut," which often guides these other designers (especially Ito) as a metaphor; instead they continue to be forwarded through an extreme sophistication and refined detailing, though most of them have grown in scale to reach immense proportions.

Although the Salzburg Congress Center was not built, much of the qualities that characterize its architecture—wrapped-core plan, screened transparency, and, above all, a delicate lightness—have been realized in Maki's design of the Keio University Graduate School Research Center in

Fujisawa. Like its predecessors, this work expresses Maki's evolving new architecture, which appears to occupy or, rather, "float" in a metaphorical in-between realm. First, it purposes to mediate—yet by no means synthesize—between various, often opposing or contradictory entities and phenomena: inside and outside, individual and society, part and whole, monumental and organic, past and future, machine age and information age, and East and West. Second, it establishes a feasible link between modernism and postmodernism, spanning, as David Stewart has noticed, "the culture gap between Walter Gropius and Zaha Hadid."[47] It is clear that Maki, always a voice of reason in the upheavals of contemporary architectural discourse, has been able, in most instances, both to benefit from, yet also to *transcend*, each aspect of the above polarities.

### Tectonics/Lightness

"What most strikes the…imagination is not the conditioning of everything and everyone by the inevitability of its own weight, but rather the balance of forces that enables heavenly bodies to float in space."
—Italo Calvino, *Six Memos for the Next Millennium*[48]

Consistently expanding the horizon of modern design in Japan, Maki's architecture has been, from the beginning of his career, evolutionary rather than revolutionary. While this holds true for his work in general, a series of major projects since the mid-1980s has greatly accelerated this evolution. They display numerous features and qualities that are new not only in Maki's oeuvre, but also in contemporary Japanese architecture; they represent the cutting edge in architectural design and production in the world today. The Fujisawa Municipal Gymnasium (1984), Makuhari Messe (1989, 1998), Tokyo Metropolitan Gymnasium (1990), Berlin Olympics Sports Halls (1992), and Kirishima International Concert Hall (1995), and their "counterparts," the Spiral (1985), Kyoto Museum of Modern Art (1986), Tepia (1989), Salzburg Congress Center (1992), and Isar Büropark (1995) are indeed superb representatives of a new and most productive stage in Maki's architecture.

These major works can be put in two groups: the first is characterized by medium-sized buildings, generally flat surfaces, and an orthogonal geometry; the second is comprised of enormous complexes shaped, without exception, with curving forms, huge, undulating roof structures, and metallic surfaces stretched tightly over the structures. Although the two groups share much in common in their exploration of new directions—design sensibilities, materials, technologies, detailing, and craftsman-

13. Olympic Gymnasium, Tokyo, 1964. (K. Tange)

ship—the second group displays a dimension that is unparalleled in scale, architectural articulation, and structural engineering. It is this group that now deserves our attention.

The completion of the Fujisawa Municipal Gymnasium in 1984 introduced Maki's new line of design and set the direction and tone for the buildings that followed. Yet, because of each consecutive design's varying program, size, and location, the original model was readjusted and further developed. The Fujisawa Gymnasium, although one of the smallest among these large projects, seems to manifest the boldest architectural statement. The extent to which Maki has questioned and done away with prevailing notions of "stable" architectural compositions and the predictability of preconceived forms are the most striking, if not the most refined, here. In this respect the project is often and properly compared to Kenzo Tange's Tokyo Olympic Gymnasia (1964) (fig. 13).

Through this comparison one can amply measure the degree to which Maki has deviated from the compositional principles and, one might say, the metaphysics of orthodox modernism. While the two designs take the tradition of high-tectonic culture as their common point of departure, and while they are equally comprised of two interconnected volumes with an overall curvilinear geometry, they articulate the "collective" architectural form in diametrically opposite ways. Tange's design is a masterpiece of compositional unity wherein every element in a strict hierarchy supports a fully integrated, homogeneous, and complete totality. Maki's masterpiece, on the other hand, follows a fundamentally different sensibility; not only are the two arenas different in form and structure, but also their constituent elements and motives, including all the various parts of their roofs, claim a large degree of independence; that is to say, they go a long way to undermine, prevent, and/or suppress the emergence of any one dominant system of form or a coherent, finished, and harmonious composition. Every new vantage point of this fragmentary and collaged assemblage of parts reveals an unexpected face, mask, or facade, and a new silhouette; in other words, each "perspective" suggests another reading of the "whole." As a result, the Fujisawa Gymnasium displays a perpetually shifting or, more precisely, perceptually "unstable"—and therefore excitingly vibrant—image. Moreover, coupled with a sculptural energy and the glistening of the stainless steel covered roofs, Maki's design attains a hallucinatory brilliance.

The other projects in this second group, except the Kirishima International Concert Hall, had substantially larger programs and called for considerably more complex solutions in terms of both design and structural engineering—particularly in the cases of the sports and multipurpose arenas, whose dimensions are manifold of those of the Fujisawa Gymnasium. Nevertheless, these projects retain the curvilinear and some other qualities that best characterize their predecessor, and, while complementing them with new ones, further develop the inherent ideas Maki has explored. The huge main arenas of the Tokyo Metropolitan Gymnasium and the Makuhari Messe are articulated with circular plans and shapes similar to the roof form of Fujisawa, while the Berlin Olympic Sports Halss have, almost literally, the form of a shell. The largest of these structures is by far the Makuhari Messe, an urban-scale convention center; the 540-meter-long exhibition hall of the first stage (1989) is covered with two segments of longitudinally arched roofs, while the 216-meter-long structure of the second stage (1998) is spanned by a combination of transversally arched and softly folded roof segments. Latest among the completed projects, the Kirishima International Concert Hall complex is an exception among its peers, not merely because of its smaller scale, but also because of some new features in the design, such as a roof shaped as a slightly "disfigured," multilateral, prismatic dome, wherein every segment of the sharply folded surface is triangular, almost like in *origami*, the traditional Japanese art of paper-folding.

Additional elements in each of these extensive complexes are perhaps even more numerous and disparate than those at the Fujisawa Gymnasium. The swimming pool and smaller arena of the Tokyo Gymnasium, the conference center of the Makuhari Messe, and the outdoor amphitheater and small recital hall of the Kirishima Concert Hall are such parts; they all broaden the multitude of architectural components to comprise fragmentary, diffused, and thus open-ended architectural, and more so, urban compositions. These works, being dynamic rather than static, are best revealed and appreciated as—and in—motion. The experience—particularly of the Tokyo Gymnasium—is a curious *mise-en-scène*, very much like those in *kaiyushiki-niwa*, the traditional Japanese stroll gardens,[49] where the episodic character of all scenes and vistas never yields a definitive whole, or leads to any final arrival, or produces a singular story. Rather, it forms a continuously shifting collage with a manifest lack of perspective quality, alludes to a fluid and floating world of "no-thingness," and conjures up a profound sense of lightness.

Yet, in these large projects, lightness has another dimension. It is related, both directly and metaphorically, to articulating the enormous roofs that the nature and size of such projects inescapably entail. For Maki, there are three important aspects of these roofs, namely their structural solution, how their silhouettes shape the skyline, and their skin. In the 1970s, most of his structures (or "group forms") were perceptually sta-

14. Congrexpo Center of Eura-Lille, Lille, France, 1995. (R. Koolhaas)

15. Sketch of the Tokyo Metropolitan Gymnasium, Tokyo, 1991. (F. Maki)

ble and, so, "simpler" constructs; their pyramidal formations were firmly grounded in the landscape or the "context" of the urban fabric. As such, they engendered a form of regional architecture. Although this aspect of his design continues in his recent works, including to some extent these large complexes, it is now complemented by, and often even entirely replaced with, more complex, or multivalent systems.

Whereas the event hall of the Makuhari Messe is spanned by a cylindrically vaulted homogeneous space frame, the large arena of the Fujisawa Gymnasium is bridged by a pair of huge, vertically arched lattice work trusses that soar impressively high above the extensively cantilevered concrete structures of the grandstands and arenas. Even bolder, more complex, dynamic, and innovative is the structural design of the much larger, 9,000-seat main arena of the Tokyo Gymnasium. Its multiplicity of tilting, contracting, and dilating arches together with their sensuously curving lines and a system of more streamlined shell surfaces epitomize an architectural achievement that surpasses even the bravura of the two predecessors. From inside, the space seems to be inflated while its "receding" membranous enclosure is held up by the equalization of multidirectional forces. From outside, the swelling form appears to depart from the ground and levitate above the public plaza beneath. Because of the structural/formal design of their large spaces, their applied technologies, their intricately curving shapes, and their delicately textured and reflective surfaces, these projects radiate a phenomenal or ephemeral quality, whereby, despite their tremendous size, they appear light, almost miragelike, and always on the verge of disappearing.

These works of Maki can be properly compared to the best designs of such architects as Norman Foster, Renzo Piano, Richard Rogers, and Nicholas Grimshaw, whose persistent endeavors to explore the benefits of high technology and a durable constructional fabric in architecture often bring about tectonic solutions that are exceptional in most respects, although not always accompanied with a quality of lightness. It is perhaps Grimshaw and Piano who have achieved a more profound sense of levity in some of their designs, such as, respectively, the Waterloo International Terminal in London (1993), and Kansai International Airport near Osaka (1994). On the other hand, Maki's Makuhari Messe can also be likened to Rem Koolhaas's enormous Eura-Lille Congrexpo Center (1995) in France (fig. 14), and "architecture of bigness." Yet, while the two are comparable in terms of scale, architectural program, and thought, the Makuhari Messe certainly surpasses its French counterpart in terms of resolution, tectonic articulation, elaborate detailing, and, above all, evocation of an elegant lightness.

The lightness in these projects is not merely the "simple" outcome of "dematerialized" constructs conceived primarily of thin, membranous, and atectonic materials, although they do participate in the evocation of this quality. More importantly, lightness is achieved by the special handling of the very tectonics, or structural entity; in other words, lightness here is evoked not as opposed to or in spite of the forces of gravity, but precisely *because* of a unique sense of gravity. For Maki weightlessness is not regarded as an absence of gravitational forces, but rather as the sustained and delicate equilibrium of all gravitations in motion or, as Greg Lynn put it, "differential gravities." He wrote, "Unlike . . . normative views based on a resistance to weight, the concept of differential gravities is based on a more flexible notion of the ground and grounding. . . . Where gravity and weight are thought in complex, differential terms, lightness is distinguished as the complication, not the simple loss, of ground."[50] Thus the levitating, floating sensation experienced in Maki's large projects is primarily the result of "lightly grounded" structures, which, although they "depart" from a base of solid ground, do not give up the specificity of the site.

This in-between quality of visually hovering above or of barely touching the ground is further emphasized by the second aspect of Maki's design, the shaping of the skyline in all his works. Maki has long been fascinated with the silhouettes of vernacular settlements, hillside towns, and other urban formations as representatives of a collective form and spirit. Yet now, perhaps more than before, he is concerned not only with the manner in which his buildings land on the ground, but also how they "depart" from it and meet the sky. His recently published (1989) sketchbook, *Fragmentary Figures*, clearly reveals just how important this is to him.[51] This publication documents the design process from the initial conception of images through their transformations to an architectural *parti*, to actual structures. Here the early sketches of these large projects are shown to be derived from first envisioning their roofs or skylines (fig. 15). The softly undulating, collaged lines and surfaces invariably, and admittedly, suggest the silhouettes of rolling fields, hills and "cloudlike" formations, and thus also insinuate a floating quality.[52]

It is important to emphasize that these sketches have been conceived of, and can be interpreted in, two ways: the roof lines in them seem to outline as much the continuity of the land or landscape as the image of the sky. Thus Maki's architectural forms are both earth bound and sky related, or both terrestrial and aerial; they hover between earth and sky. In the introduction to his sketchbook Maki wrote, "A sketch leaves things uncertain even to oneself and incorporates areas of emptiness. A sketch is appealing precisely because it records a dream that will not be fulfilled."[53] Many of Maki's completed works, however, seem to prove him not quite right; they testify to the high degree in which he has achieved the realization of his dreamed skylines. One such project is his Isar Büropark (1995), a low density office complex near the international airport in Munich. Here two large glass roofs tilt toward a central *allée* and float above open terraces. By capturing the light of the sky, they act as an artificial second sky that dips down toward the earth like a crevice. From a distance the two roofs also appear to continue the surface of the ground that they almost reach.

Within this group of new buildings, Maki "gravitates" toward an architecture that fluctuates between presence and absence. In this regard we have to turn now to the skin of the curving roof surfaces, the third aspect of Maki's roof designs. For covering these immense and often formidably shaped structures, he has, in each case, employed thin stainless steel sheets. Since the Fujisawa Gymnasium and Makuhari Messe are located close to the sea, and the Tokyo Gymnasium in one of Tokyo's busiest areas adjacent to a train line and an ever-congested, elevated expressway, the selection of this material is justified because it is resistive to the corrosive effects of salty air and air pollution. However Maki's use of this material exceeds functional requirements. Intricately textured by the extensive seam lines by which they are put together, these highly reflective surfaces both bring alive and dematerialize the forms they define under different light conditions. Maki has written about the Fujisawa Gymnasium, "Seen against a clear sky, the stainless steel skyline possesses an aura like that of the sun during an eclipse, and the roof loses all material presence."[54]

The ambiguity of the overall image in all of these designs invites a wide range of interpretations that encompass both contemporary and traditional experiences. Depending on one's viewpoint to the building proper, one can equally perceive a UFO, spacecraft, zeppelin, car or other high-tech vehicle, turtle, seashell, traditional Noh mask, samurai helmet, and a *mokugyo*, the wooden gong used in Buddhist rituals. Moreover, the Tokyo Gymnasium, with its softly rounded forms, emerges as a vision of a B-52 bomber, while the Concert Hall, due to its sharply angular, prismatic shapes, comes through as an F-117 fighter, both stealth planes that can elude detection.

According to this analogy, Maki's recent architecture may appear and disappear almost by stealth. However paradoxical it may seem, it does suggest that these buildings of "cloudlike forms" cannot effectively be seen according to the rules of perspective or comprehended in ordinary ways; they demand to be viewed in a new "light" in which they tend to turn "invisible." Like formless forms, they are manifestations of a "vanishing

architecture" that is both there and not there. In effect, these complexes can be seen as futuristic versions of the quintessential Japanese rock garden; the more one gazes upon them, the more they seem to disappear, while reappearing in a curious way, internally, "within" the perceiver. In these new projects Maki does not commit himself to the false dichotomy of weight and lightness. Rather he edges toward an entirely "new" design paradigm, which, as a process of liberation, is free from all dichotomies, and what both Zen philosophers and Friedrich Nietzsche would have understood well.

In the final analysis then, this much is evident: these superbly crafted, new projects prove that Maki has been able to coalesce a meaningful contemporary urban architecture and spaces of public appearance. Building upon modernism's respect for materiality, significance of tectonics, and social commitment, this architecture surpasses much of its predecessors and contemporaries not only with its aspirations to phenomenal lightness, but also with its sensitive capability to respond to, and, as a critical agent, engage in a multiplicity of ways its natural, urban, and cultural contexts, as well as to incite a much broader spectrum of human experience without falling victim to shallow scenography or the triviality of simulation. Recognizing moreover the significance of both advanced technology and the diverse nature and dynamism of contemporary "post-ideal" urban society, Maki continues to pursue an architecture that is enduring, yet amply multifaceted and superbly fit for our pluralistic age of information. Kenneth Frampton put it this way, "[With his recent works] Maki has been able to render his concept of a fragmentary urbanism at a higher symbolic level, in which these modern 'cathedrals' stand out against the chaos of the Megalopolis, as civic catalysts.... [They] imply...a new kind of urban enclave with which to engender and sustain a more fluid and shifting conception of public space."[55]

Maki's enlightened practice proves that in the "age of the ephemeral" only the slightest distinction can exist between criticism and conformity. His expressions of an individual sensibility respect the particulars of Japanese urban conditions and are some of the most hopeful, universal messages about the possibilities of architecture today, not only in Japan, but also beyond. As such, Maki's work aspires to a truly world-class architecture. Maki once remarked that with and within his architecture he intended "to offer unforgettable scenes."[56] Owing to their unique designs, sparkling brilliance, impressive civility, and urban sensibility, Maki's new projects, like mnemonic devices, possess the qualities of memorable landmarks; they are among the few with which the course of contemporary Japanese architecture, the Japanese city, and, in general, the global cultural landscape at the turn of the millennium will have to be both measured and remembered in times to come.

## Notes

My subtitle is an obvious reference to Italo Calvino's *Six Memos for the Next Millennium* (New York: Vintage Books, 1993), in which he specifies six values as the most significant ones for literature: lightness, quickness, exactitude, visibility, multiplicity, and consistency.

1. Milan Kundera, *The Unbearable Lightness of Being* (New York: Harper Colophon, 1984): 5–6.

2. Kenneth Frampton, "Thoughts on Fumihiko Maki" in the brochure *The Pritzker Architecture Prize 1993: Fumihiko Maki* (Los Angeles: Jensen & Walker for the Hyatt Foundation, 1993).

3. Ever since the Meiji Restoration in 1868, when Japan's modernization was launched by the government, the country's economic progress has been strongly patronized and controlled by the Japanese government. A good recent example is the *Kumamoto Art Polis*; within this project, since the mid-1980s, many outstanding Japanese and foreign architects have been invited to design significant public facilities all across Kumamoto Prefecture.

4. Most Japanese construction companies have evolved from medieval family-run carpenter guilds, many of which, with the help of the government after 1868, developed into gigantic general contractors. The five largest, the so-called "Big Five," are the Shimizu, Kajima, Taisei, Takenaka, and Obayashi corporations.

5. Kenneth Frampton, *Modern Architecture: A Critical History* (London: Thames and Hudson, 1992): 331–343.

6. Chris Fawcett, *The New Japanese House* (New York: Harper and Row, 1980): 24.

7. In 1993 Maki became the second Japanese architect to receive the Pritzker Prize in Architecture, since it was first awarded in 1979. Kenzo Tange was the 1987 recipient, while Tadao Ando received the prize in 1995.

8. Maki actually uses the term "place character" (*basho-sei*), which is a more direct expression of his aims than the more sublime, and by now also more nostalgic, *genius loci*. See Fumihiko Maki with Kiyo Matsuba, "My Approach to Modernism: Freedom and Originality in Architectural Design" (in Japanese), *Space Design* (January 1986): 137.

9. Maki's few contemporaries who continued their education and/or worked abroad are Yoshinobu Ashihara (b. 1918), who received his Master's Degree from the Harvard GSD in 1953, then worked for Marcel Breuer in New York for a few years; Minoru Takeyama (b. 1934), who received his Master's Degree from the Harvard GSD in 1960, then worked for Josep Lluís Sert and Harrison Abramovitz in the United States and for Jorn Utzon, Arne Jacobsen, and Henning Larsen in Denmark; and Takamasa Yoshizaka (1917–1980), who worked for Le Corbusier from 1952–1954 in his Paris office. Other noted architects, such as Tange, Isozaki, Kikutake, Kurokawa, Shinohara, Hasegawa, and Ito received their education in Japan and had no extended work experience abroad.

10. Hiroshi Watanabe, "Spiral, Sports Arenas, and Spirit of Place: Recent Works by Fumihiko Maki," *Japan Architect* (March 1987): 57.

11. Fumihiko Maki, "New Directions in Modernism," *Space Design* (January 1986): 7.

12. Andrea Palladio, *The Four Books of Architecture*, Book 2 (1570; reprint, New York: Dover Publications, 1965): 44.

13. Aldo van Eyck, quoted in Alison Smithson, ed., *Team 10 Primer* (Cambridge, Mass.: MIT Press, 1974): 27.

14. Following their first meeting in Bagnols-sur-Cèze, Maki met van Eyck on several occasions, including one in 1960 when van Eyck was a visiting professor at Washington University in St. Louis, and in 1965 when van Eyck was a visiting professor at the Harvard GSD.

15. Alex Krieger, "(Ongoing) Investigations in Collective Form: Maki's Quarter-of-a-Century at Hillside Terrace," *Japan Architect* 16 no. 4 (1994): 240.

16. Maki's first trip took place during May–August in 1959, and the second during April–September in 1960. Such extended study trips abroad by a Japanese architect of that time were rare, and Maki was again alone among his peers to have this opportunity.

17. Fumihiko Maki, "Notes on Collective Form," *Japan Architect* 16 no. 4 (1994): 248.

18. Camillo Golgi (1844–1926) was an Italian physiologist who conducted neurological studies and who first observed a network of fibers (Golgi structures) in 1909, which eventually led to the discovery of the neuron.

19. Fumihiko Maki, *Investigations in Collective Form* (St. Louis: Washington University School of Architecture, 1964).

20. Aldo van Eyck, in Smithson, *Team 10*, 41.

21. Fumihiko Maki, quoted in Michael Franklin Ross, *Beyond Metabolism: The New Japanese Architecture* (New York: McGraw Hill, 1978), 32.

22. Fumihiko Maki, in *A New Wave of Japanese Architecture*, Kenneth Frampton, ed. (New York: IAUS, 1978): 75.

23. Maki has called the building a "glassy mountain," in reference to the nearby Tsukuba Mountain. Quoted in Ross, *Beyond Metabolism*, 120.

24. Among such canonical works are Gerrit Rietveld's Schröder House (1924), Le Corbusier's Villa Shodan (1956), and Walter Gropius's Werkbund Building (1914).

25. In traditional Japanese architecture the elevated and simple wooden structure of ancient storehouses (*kura*) was a prototype from which both Shinto shrines and residential architecture evolved. Throughout the centuries the two retained a manifest similarity in general shapes; this is even more striking, when compared with the strong disparity between religious and domestic architectures in most other cultures, particularly the Western.

26. See the exhibition catalog, Mildred Friedman, ed., *Tokyo: Form and Spirit* (Minneapolis: Walker Art Center and New York: Harry N. Abrams, 1986).

27. Since the Renaissance in Western art and culture, the development and domination of the perspective mode of spatiality have represented the evolution of the person as an individual with an awareness of the self that is an indivisible and independent entity, a singular point of view. As such, Westerners have come to understand themselves apart from the world, according to the rules of perspective. In the world of perspective then things always appear in front and "at a distance." Western perspective also reinforces the idea of a world dominated by a strong center. This world view, absent from Japanese history, remained largely unchallenged in the West until the dawn of recent developments in modern—particularly avant-garde—art, architecture, and philosophy that include chaos theory, concepts of fractals, etc. Our rapidly progressing age of (electronic) information probes even further into the hegemony of the idea of space constituted solely according to the laws of perspective. For further details see Botond Bognar, *Contemporary Japanese Architecture* (New York: Van Nostrand Reinhold, 1985): 28–61. Furthermore, an excellent elucidation of the concepts: "unperspective," perspective, and "aperspective," especially in regard to Japanese architecture, is found in Günter Nitschke, "From Ambiguity to Transparency: Unperspective, Perspective, and Aperspective Paradigm of Space," *Japan Today* in the *Louisiana Revy* 35 no. 3 (June 1995), Copenhagen (English supplement).

28. Fumihiko Maki, "Japanese City Spaces and the Concept of *Oku*," *Japan Architect* (May 1979): 51–62.

29. Fumihiko Maki, "The Public Dimension in Contemporary Architecture," *New Public Architecture: Recent Projects by Fumihiko Maki and Arata Isozaki* (New York: Japan Society, 1985): 16.

30. Fumihiko Maki, "City Image, Materiality," in Serge Salat and Françoise Labbe, *Fumihiko Maki: An Aesthetic of Fragmentation* (New York: Rizzoli, 1988): 10.

31. Fumihiko Maki, "Modernism at the Crossroads," *Japan Architect* (March 1983): 22.

32. Anthony Vidler, *The Architectural Uncanny: Essays in the Modern Unhomely* (Cambridge, Mass.: MIT Press, 1992): xiv.

33. The Katsura Imperial Villa in Kyoto was, as many other examples of residential architecture in Japan were, designed and built piecemeal over almost one hundred years, by its several aristocratic owners, who consecutively added new sections to the previously built ones, thus changing the "original" architecture according to their own intentions and taste. The same can be observed in the architecture of the Katsura garden, whose "disjunctive quality" Walter Gropius noted with rather much dissatisfaction when he visited the compound in 1954. He summarized his views on Katsura in Walter Gropius, "Architecture in Japan," *Perspecta: Yale Architectural Journal* 3 (1955): 9.

34. Frampton, "Thoughts on Maki," 2.

35. It has to be mentioned that while Isozaki's "architecture of quotation" has shown in recent years a discernible tendency toward "heaviness" with explicit signs of classicism, Maki's on the other hand has moved steadily toward "lightness."

36. David B. Stewart, "Apollo in the Age of Deconstruction," *Japan Architect* 16 no. 4 (1994): 73.

37. Maki, "City, Image, Materiality," 29.

38. "Last Year at Marienbad" (*L'année dernière à Marienbad*), France, 1961.

39. Fumihiko Maki, "Palazzo del Cinema," *Space Design* (January 1993): 172.

40. Many wood block-prints (*ukiyo-e*) by such famous artists as Katsushika Hokusai (1760–1849) and Ando Hiroshige (1797–1858), for example, were made in extensive series, wherein they unfolded in a "discontinuous continuity" or were laid out like in a mosaic or tapestry; *Fifty-Three Stages of Tokaido* (1833) and *One Hundred Famous Views of Edo* (1858) by Hiroshige are good examples of this.

41. Fumihiko Maki, "The Roof at Fujisawa," *Perspecta* 24 (1988): 120.

42. Maki, "City, Image, Materiality," 8.

43. Fumihiko Maki, "Introduction," in Botond Bognar, *Togo Murano: Master Architect of Japan* (New York: Rizzoli International, 1996): 24.

44. Calvino, *Six Memos*, 16.

45. Toyo Ito designed his project, the Mediatheque in Sendai, to be completed by 1998, with an entirely new structural system, wherein the vertical support of the lacy and transparent seven-story building is formed by twelve meshlike tubular steel hyper-shell shafts wrapped in translucent glass. This solution lends the building a sense of extreme lightness.

46. Nitschke, "Ambiguity to Transparency," n. p.

47. Stewart, "Apollo in Deconstruction," 68.

48. Calvino, *Six Memos*, 23.

49. Japanese stroll gardens (*kaiyushiki-niwa*) are not laid out geometrically; they are designed with episodes of various sceneries that unfold with alternating turns (*oremagari*), while repeatedly changing from hidden to revealed (*miegakure*) by the spatial layers.

50. Greg Lynn, "Differential Gravities" *ANY, Architecture New York* 5 (special issue on lightness) (March/April 1994): 21–22.

51. Fumihiko Maki, *Fragmentary Figures: The Collected Architectural Drawings* (Tokyo: Kyuryudo Art Publishing, 1989).

52. About "cloudlike" totalities Maki has written, "An order in which the relationship of the parts to the whole is systematic might be labeled a 'clock,' and a condition in which the parts and the whole are in an unstable equilibrium might be labeled a 'cloud.'... [In other words, here] the whole remains indeterminate and cloudlike." Maki, "City Image, Materiality," 10–11. In regard to Maki's interest in the boundaries between architecture and the sky, one should notice the often numerous and conspicuously arranged lightning rods on the roofs of his buildings.

53. Maki, *Fragmentary Figures*, 6.

54. Fumihiko Maki, "Fujisawa Municipal Gymnasium," *Japan Architect* (March 1987): 18.

55. Frampton, "Thoughts on Maki," n. p.

56. Fumihiko Maki and Roger Connah, "To Offer Unforgettable Scenes—A Discussion with Fumihiko Maki," *Japan Architect* (March 1987): 68.

BOTOND BOGNAR is Professor of Architecture at the University of Illinois and author of numerous books on Japanese architecture, including his latest ones, *The Japan Guide* (New York: Princeton Architectural Press, 1995), *Togo Murano: Master Architect of Japan* (New York: Rizzoli, 1996), and *World Cities: Tokyo* (London: Academy Editions, 1997).

# TSUKUBA UNIVERSITY CENTRAL BUILDING

Tsukuba, Ibaraki 1974

The Central Building at Tsukuba University houses classrooms, offices, and other facilities for the art and physical education departments, and was planned as a symbolic gateway to the future university campus. The main axis of the campus passes directly through its central atrium, which, located between two flanking wings housing classrooms and seminar rooms, acts as a meeting place for students of the two different departments.

Severe time constraints on the construction period led to a design using preassembled or "dry" construction techniques, which had much to do with determining its expressive nature. Floor plates are made of skeleton steel deck plates; interior partitions, of cast aluminum panels and lightweight steel studs; and the building cladding system, of large panels set with glass block. At this time in Japan glass block had never been used in construction to the extent that it was used at Tsukuba University. We became very attracted to their unique qualities—providing abundant natural light without giving complete transparency, and maintaining excellent heat and sound insulation. We were interested in devising a new way to treat them, improving on the traditional system of hand laying them like units of masonry; in this way we felt we might contribute to the development of a new vocabulary for curtain wall design. Under the constructional system we devised, glass blocks are fitted into heat-pressed steel frames laid out on the ground for ease of construction; the panels are then lifted by crane and attached to the building in rapid succession to create the outer envelope. Each panel is fitted with a small, clear, operable window at eye level to provide views out from the classrooms and for ventilation. Within the fabric created by the glass block panels, large clear window units are substituted at appropriate points in the composition—indicating the presence of the lobby or a special-use classroom behind the facade.

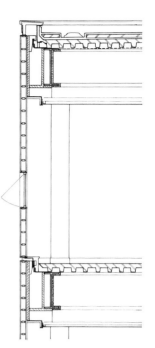

*Above:* Assembly of glass block curtain wall during construction

*Right:* Curtain wall section detail

*Facing page:* Detail of glass block curtain wall panel at the Library, with the Central Building seen beyond

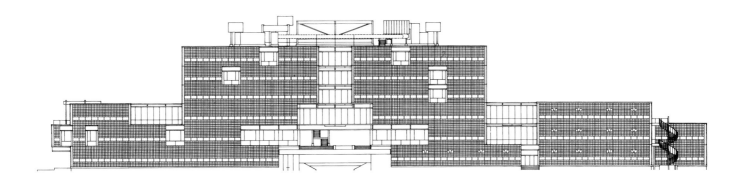

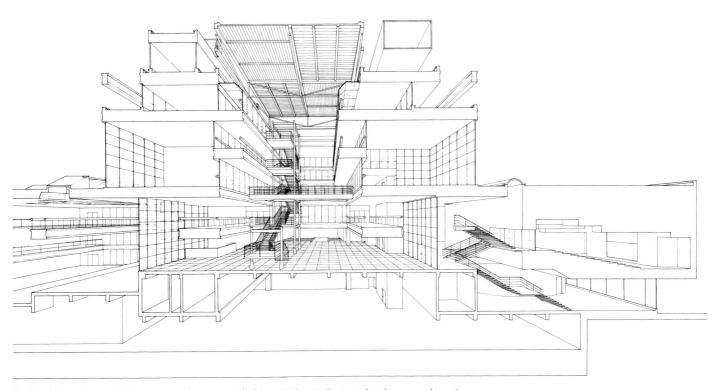

*Top:* South elevation, symbolic gateway to the campus. The large windows indicate student lounges and meeting areas.

*Above:* Sectional perspective through central atrium

*Facing page:* Steel staircase of the central atrium

# OSAKA PREFECTURAL SPORTS CENTER

Takaishi, Osaka 1972

The Osaka Prefectural Sports Center was designed to provide a broad range of athletic amenities for an industrial district on the outskirts of the city on Osaka Bay, newly developed in the early 1960s. The center's facilities include a main gym and a sub-gym for indoor sports, a swimming pool, meeting rooms, offices, lounges, and restaurants. Set alongside a canal that divides the industrial belt of Rinkai from a sprawling residential neighborhood, the Sports Center also acts as a threshold element between the factory and housing districts.

The center's architectural expression is largely conveyed through its innovative roof structure, which presents an undulating skyline composed of prefabricated beam and truss units of Cor-Ten (weathering steel)—chosen for its resistance to industrial pollution. The individual structural units—huge tubular roof beams connecting bow-shaped truss sections spanning 21.6 meters—suggest the industrial imagery of the factories across the river, although we consciously used these structural units to create an irregular, sloping skyline which might also recall the aggregational form and scale of the nearby residential neighborhood.

Seen from below the undulating roof structure encased in a light metallic ceiling mesh emphasizes the spatial qualities of individual gymnasium and pool interiors as well. The tubular roof beams are used not only structurally, but are also linked to the air-handling system for use as exhaust ducts. Due to the amount of prefabrication made possible by this structural system, the entire above-grade structure, including the ducting system and ceiling of wire mesh, was erected in only twelve days.

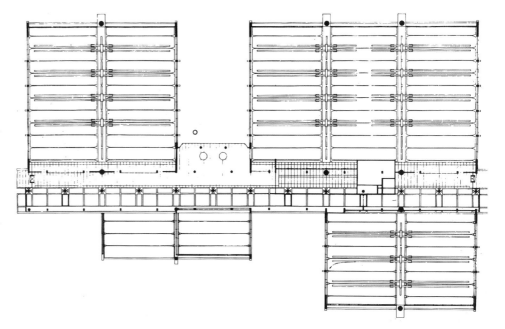

Reflected ceiling plan, showing aggregation of structural units and air ducting

The roof structure was designed to be constructed of intermediate-scale prefabricated elements, consisting of spindle section transverse beams connected by bow-shaped truss units. Each truss was factory produced, prefitted with ductwork and ceiling panels while still on the ground, and later hoisted into position within the main skeleton.

Entrance plaza

The Sports Center acts as a transition between a residential neighborhood and an industrial zone located across the canal.

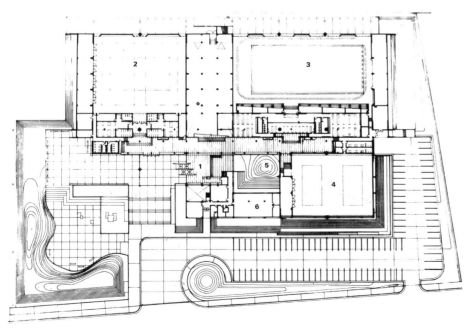

1 entry hall
2 main gymnasium
3 swimming pool
4 subgymnasium
5 courtyard
6 office

First floor

Interior of swimming pool. A translucent glass curtain wall provides suffused natural light.

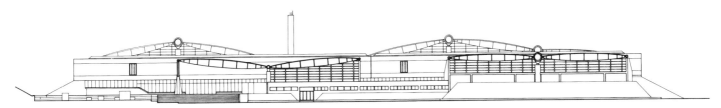

East elevation

# NATIONAL AQUARIUM, OKINAWA

Bise, Okinawa 1975

Territorially an independent island of Japan, the subtropical prefecture of Okinawa is in many ways culturally closer to southern China and Micronesia. It enjoys strong sunlight, a blue sea, and wildlife quite distinct from anything found on the main Japanese islands. When we received the commission to design a large aquarium on Okinawa as part of the International Ocean Exposition of 1975, we realized that the particularities of this locale would place a different set of demands on the architecture—related both to the subtropical climate and the limitations of skilled construction labor on the island at that time.

To offer relief from the brutal summer sun, the aquarium building proper is shielded with a series of exterior arcades. The arcades provide shade not only for large number of spectators lining up to see the exposition events and exhibitions but also for pedestrians walking along the ocean shore. It is articulated as a series of alternating precast concrete arches that provides a frame for watching the ocean and sets up a lyrical rhythm for procession. To express the regional character of Okinawa, the precast arches are painted brown to match the color of local infill bricks, and a sculpture of Okinawa's protector—a god of peace—stands at the entrance.

Although the configuration of arches results in a fairly sophisticated, complex form, the technique of precasting greatly shortened the construction time and eliminated the demand for highly skilled labor for the erection of the arcade structure. Involving only wall elements (two of which make up a three-hinged arch) and floor/roof slabs, the system designed achieved maximum flexibility with minimum means. Nearly 300 arched elements and 150 floor slabs were used to create a stepping, pyramidal building mass.

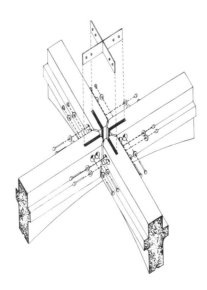

*Top:* Aerial view of the aquarium complex

*Middle:* Axonometric drawing of the arcade

*Bottom left:* Individual concrete arch sections were precast off site, transported individually, and hoisted in place for bolting.

*Bottom right:* Bolting, the simplest and most primitive method of connection, was employed to minimize the need for skilled labor. Once the system was perfected, workers were able to erect one cubical module a day.

View to the sea from the arcade at sunset

Fish tanks

The aquarium interior also included some innovative design features. We were eager to avoid making the display a typical collection of small tanks resembling the windows of a train. We proposed instead to show the natural environment of many varieties of fish in two large tanks—one for a coral reef and one for the open ocean. The ocean tank, containing 10,000 fish (including a large shark), was the largest in Japan at the time of its completion. In order to provide an unobstructed panoramic view of the cruising fish, we decided to eliminate bulky vertical and horizontal mullions from the tank wall. Instead the wall is composed of five layers of 5-centimeter-thick acrylic sheet chemically bonded together. Effectively a cantilever structure supported only at its floor connection, the 25-centimeter-thick, completely transparent tank wall sustains the immense lateral pressure of 1,500 tons of water contained inside.

In contrast to the strictly "functional" design approach prevalent in many aquarium exhibit rooms, we surrounded the deep-sea tank with a carpeted lounge area so that visitors could recline in alcove seats and listen to soft electronic music while observing the flowing three-dimensional patterns that 10,000 fish quietly and ceaselessly create.

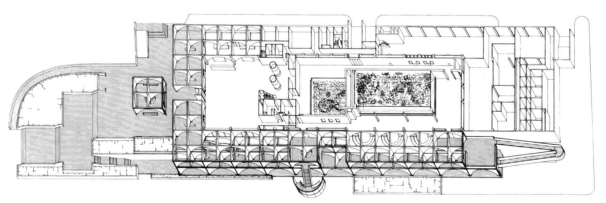

Axonometric drawing showing the relationship between the precast concrete arches and the hybrid structure of the exhibition rooms

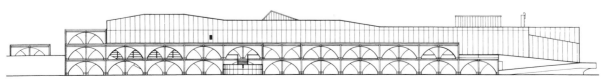

*Above:* Oceanside elevation

*Facing page:* The simple arch elements are configured to produce a rhythmical arcade along the seaside.

# FUJISAWA MUNICIPAL GYMNASIUM

Fujisawa, Kanagawa  1984

North elevation of main arena

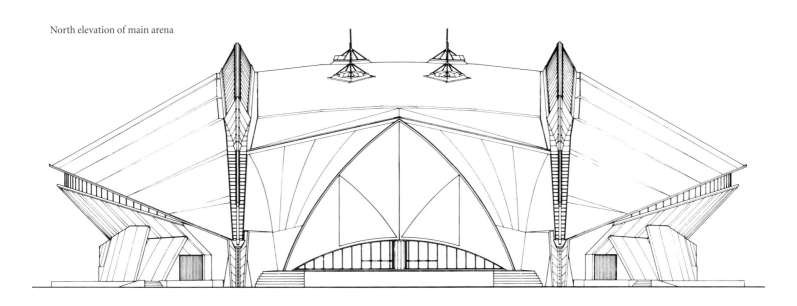

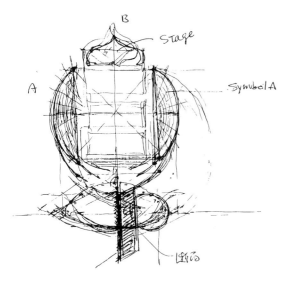

# THE ROOF AT FUJISAWA

Fumihiko Maki

It is a well-known fact that Japan began to modernize rapidly after the Meiji Restoration. In the more than one hundred and twenty years that have passed since that restoration, Japan has developed into what is arguably one of the most industrialized nations in the world. In metropolises such as Tokyo and Osaka, traditional buildings that have survived natural disasters, fires, the war, and the effects of rapid modernization are very limited in number and scale. Old, preindustrial streetscapes that remain fully intact are virtually nonexistent. This trend toward industrialization will undoubtedly accelerate in the future as the densities of these cities increase and, concomitantly, new construction continues to occur at a more rapid rate. Moreover, such rapid growth will be combined with increasingly stringent building codes intended to mitigate the destructive effects of natural disasters by way of particularly lightweight and sophisticated systems of construction. This is the situation in which the contemporary practitioner of architecture in Japan finds himself.

In this sense the evolution of the industrialized city and the emergence of modern architecture—from which contemporary architecture developed—must be seen as interrelated phenomena. The theoretical foundations of modernism—including references to mass production, trabeate construction, investigations in new and lightweight materials, free planning and functionalism—all suggest obvious comparisons to the world of industrialization.

We have witnessed this expanding industrialization with some concern. The most extreme position insists that such industrialization will undermine our culture, fracture our relationship to history, and bring about the formation of a forbidding urban landscape without reference to place. The Western world has given voice to similar concerns as well. For an architect in such a predicament a pressing question reveals itself: What is the role of history and place in this industrial city and how does one contribute works of authenticity and resonance to such a landscape?

Going south in Manhattan along the East River, one encounters a series of huge concrete and steel bridges. Their stone foundations have been exposed to the elements over many years and are coated with moss. They remind one of the ruins of Roman aqueducts and the world of Piranesi.

The factories and the tall expressionless apartment buildings standing nearby are also weathering products of an early industrialized society, and appear before us as strangely reticent monuments of modern history. Cityscapes of this nature greet one in London and Manchester as well. In contrast to these examples of Western industrial vernacular that testify to the glories of a weighty past, the industrial vernacular of Japan has an entirely different aspect. The factories, high-rise apartment buildings, and gas tanks that stand crowded together in the vast area reclaimed from Tokyo Bay visible from the expressway describe a world of abstract form. One can discern here a kind of lightness, a frail optimism that approaches lyricism. The past does not weigh down this cityscape as it does the cityscapes of the West, because here it is not allowed to accumulate. The human traces in this transitional landscape can be dated back only a few decades at the most. Features distinctive to Japan, everything from signs, vending machines, and plastic products to entire urban infrastructure, participate on an equal basis with cheaply constructed buildings in the formation of the surface of the city. If one looks closely enough, one can see in this surface composed of concrete, metal, glass, and plastic, the layered tactile quality that is distinctive to Japan. The aesthetic that this cityscape speaks of is one of fluctuation and fluidity. It is possible to recognize the existence of a unique perceptual order here.

The phenomenon of the modern city cannot be understood as a manifestation of the industrial imperative alone. Notwithstanding the expectations of early twentieth-century theoreticians—who foretold the development of our cities along models provided by this industrial revolution—it remains possible to identify significant distinctions between one modern city and another. The proportion of new construction to old, the persistence of local preferences, and the particular characteristics of a regional culture all contribute to this diversity. While it is true that modern frame construction must conform to laws of tectonics independent of the specifics of place, that particular quality of place still finds expression in our buildings.

The Japanese variation derives primarily out of a historical phenomenon. Japan has many strong traditions of craft, custom, dress, and family structure. We do not, however, possess an accumulated stock of

traditional architecture around which our cities could be formed. In this sense our traditions persist in the form of intangible as opposed to tangible structures. The imprint of Japanese culture on the industrialized city is felt not in the juxtaposition of old and new artifacts as is seen in Europe, but in the overlay of an entirely new architectural landscape on a very old culture. The integration of the two results in a very distinctive experience of the Japanese city.

It is this experience—this persistent expression of culture—that must form the basis of a true modern vernacular. The design and construction of individual buildings capable of speaking to both the traditional past and industrial future of Japan depends on a sensitivity to this historical fact. The challenge facing the architect today is to understand and contribute to this integration of intangible traditions with tangible artifacts; to link together the historical character of our culture with the development of a built urban landscape that cannot literally recreate its own history. Such a challenge involves the investigation of industrial artifacts with an eye for their more evocative natures, searching among them for a specific character related to regional tradition.

This search for a meaningful integration of the past with the future has dominated my thinking in recent years. Much of my work has been undertaken in pursuit of this integration. For an architect committed to building, this investigation is deeply involved in formal and technical matters of construction, such that the entire issue becomes manifest in their resolution. As can be seen in the battered and monolithic stone constructions of England's industrial past or the lightweight and luminous assemblies scattered along the edge of Tokyo Bay, these issues related to place and character may be deciphered in essentially physical terms. For this reason I believe it to be critical to the design process that one constantly reference the material nature of one's proposals to both their historical and geographic context. The study of primary architectonic elements—the foundations, walls, columns, and, perhaps of most importance here, roofs—related to any particular construction must be undertaken with a sensitivity to the material history of that element to ensure that this architecture speak to more than its own occurrence.

The capacity of a single architectural element to possess this dialectic was made clear to me in the conception of the roof for the Fujisawa

*Left:* Interior detail at base of arch

*Below, left:* Section of main arena

*Facing page:* Detail of roof cladding along main structural keel arch

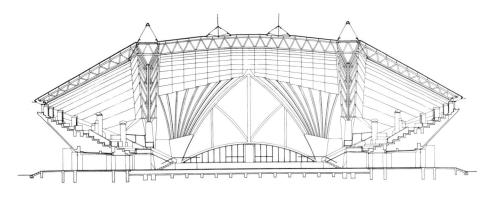

153

Municipal Gymnasium. In fact, the stainless steel roof to be seen here has a complex history of its own, intimately tied up with the specifics of its coming to be—its technical and formal inception along with its actual production in the field. It is necessary to speak at some length about this technical history in order to communicate the intention of the roof as a cultural artifact, as a *constructed* artifact that stands in a complex relationship to history. In this way I believe it is possible to see the roof itself as a metaphor for the coming together of two traditions.

Fujisawa is a city located very close to the seashore, about thirty kilometers from Tokyo. The landscape of this area is, in fact, quite bleak. The particular site chosen for the new sports complex lacked any distinguishing characteristics of its own and remains surrounded, for the most part, by smaller structures arranged in a loosely defined configuration. The introduction of a very large structure of the scale required by the program assured that the new building would assume a strong presence in the city. We recognized early on that the successful accommodation of this program would necessitate the construction of two very large rooms, each of which would have a definition and a nature of its own. Given our experi-

ence with this particular building type, we understood the critical issues of scale that such constructions inevitably present. We also knew that the roof itself would most profoundly influence this eventual reading of scale. The manner in which this roof was conceived and developed would be crucial to the final character of the building.

Several considerations led us to choose stainless steel as the primary material for this roof. Many of these considerations had to do with specific physical characteristics of the steel itself: its great resistance to the degenerative effects of salt air, its considerable luminosity, its capacity to be shaped and bent into fairly complex segments, and certain inherent qualities of scale suggested by its extreme thinness and fragility. We regarded each of these characteristics as advantageous to the formal and technical ordering of the roof. Their cumulative effect was to provide a point of departure of considerable rigor, a set of limitations demanding precise calculation and significant investigation of relevant construction procedures.

We determined through our investigation that each steel sheet would be limited to 40 centimeters in width and only 0.4 millimeter in thickness,

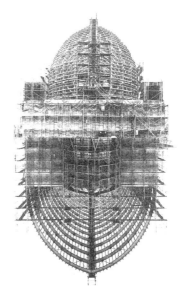

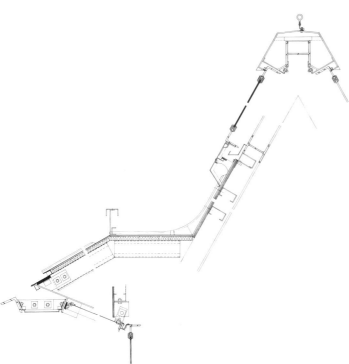

*Left, top:* View of roof under construction

*Left, bottom:* Roof detail at the skylight

*Above:* Collage image of the subarena under construction

*Facing page:* Steel frame of the roof under construction

155

a thickness of such fragility and susceptibility to creasing and wrinkling that extraordinary measures would be required in its manipulation. Such thin sheet steel would not be capable of maintaining an even surface in the life of the building, nor, for that matter, during construction when particularly extreme concentrated stresses would be exerted on each sheet in its transportation and manipulation. When seen against the sunlight, these inevitable imperfections would become particularly apparent. Working with the manufacturer, we were able to devise a method for producing systematic wrinkles in each sheet in such a way that these deformations would appear uniform and intentional, providing a certain texture to the roof and allowing another scale reading to be manifest in the surface itself. This texture might then speak of the nature of steel in the same way that grain speaks of wood or the visible composition of minerals speaks of stone.

The manner in which these steel sheets might be fabricated and joined was studied carefully so as to avoid a repetitive or mechanistic assembly, or conversely, a homogenous, membranelike appearance that might belie the building's truly assembled nature. To this extent we wanted very much

to avoid the "inflated" quality that such large structures commonly suffer. Through many attempts in model, we were able to determine a configuration of individually fabricated segments which collectively achieved the desired whole, while maintaining the integrity of the part. Each of these steel sheets was in itself quite unique. Rather than accept a repetitive subdivision of the roof by way of highly complex curved segmentation which we learned would be quite difficult to manufacture, we made liberal use of trapezoidal segments, requiring certain adjustments to be made at critical points in each sheet. Many of these adjustments had to be modified, even conceived, at the construction site itself.

Several members of the design team were present at the site throughout construction to supervise this on-going process of study and correction. In fact it was necessary to set up a small office at the site where the design team could work, maintaining day-to-day contact with the builders—even assisting in the construction itself—to ensure that each connection and each detail were executed correctly.

In an effort to make apparent the hovering quality of the roof—to disassociate it from the more massive base of its support—we developed a

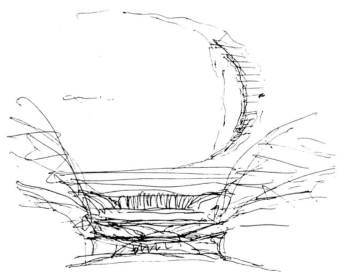

*Left:* Skylights introduce light into the main arena along the main structural arches.

*Facing page:* Practice gymnasium on the third floor of the subarena

South facade of the subarena. The stainless steel roof and mirror-finish ceramic tiles produce a glimmering surface.

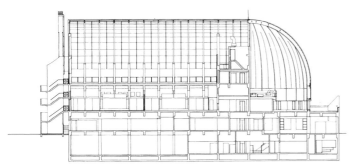

Longitudinal section through subarena

Third floor

1 entrance hall
2 lobby
3 main arena
4 stage
5 training gym
6 office
7 kendo arena
8 gallery
9 void
10 café
11 judo arena
12 subarena

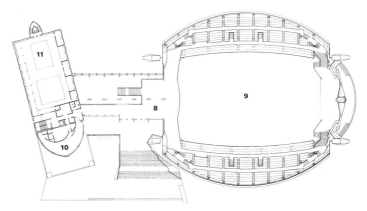

Second floor

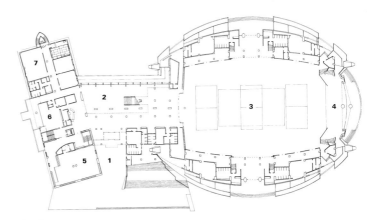

First floor

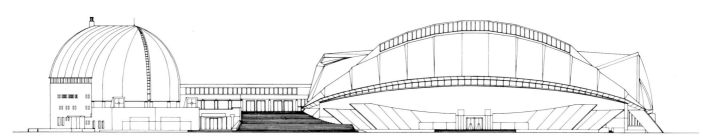

East elevation

View from main arena to subarena. The two opposing curves of the roof edges interact, constantly changing as the visitor walks around the gymnasium periphery. A perforated metal roof edge for the main arena emphasizes the thinness of the roof's stainless sheets.

series of pin connections where the meeting of these two elements could be poignantly accomplished. Such a meeting further reinforced the apparent lightness of the roof, allowing it to maintain an identity of its own that speaks of an almost ethereal presence. Through the development of these pin connections we were able, as well, to underline the assembled nature of the steel-clad roof structure, reinforcing once again our ambition not to fall victim to that "inflated" appearance so contrary to the proper definition of scale.

The reality, or the spirit of the steel itself, seemed to be very much related to its sharpness, its precision, its capacity to define an unequivocal edge. This was always on our minds as we studied each corner and intersection, and particularly as we explored the termination of the roof near its base. But such luminous metal has another evocation as well. I have observed that at certain times of day in very particular light, this luminous steel virtually disappears into the sky, suggesting an aura not unlike that of the sun during an eclipse. Its reflection of such bright light is so complete as to absorb wholly the material itself in the act of reflection. This is its paradox and mystery.

These facts are important insofar as they document the coming together of a traditional procedure of construction with the development of a new and highly sophisticated building material. In a strict sense the manner in which the Fujisawa Municipal Gymnasium was built cannot be considered innovative. Many of the procedures we evolved here might even be considered medieval. The building was constructed with the active participation of an attendant workforce; a supervisory team responsible for both the conception and execution of detail was present at the site at all times; and the work being performed was of a singular and unique nature. This was not a building composed of repetitive elements, mechanically produced in great quantities for use in buildings other than Fujisawa itself. Accordingly, the complex speaks of a fundamentally traditional reality. Its character is determined by the piecing together of carefully crafted individual components in a complex assembly not unlike its Japanese predecessors. It is here that the intangible traditions of craft and method referred to earlier exert themselves on the production of otherwise entirely modern artifacts.

Such a reading, however, is inevitably challenged by our sense of its definitively unique character as well as by its relationship to modern industrial construction. We see in the formal language of the building—in its scale and in the precise fabrication of elements that make it up—a type of construction that is not familiar to us through the traditional world of

hand-crafted production. Despite its connection to that past, it cannot be wholly explained by or absorbed in it.

A similar and intended ambiguity exists in the associative qualities of the sheathing itself. What does this metal roof mean? Of course, we cannot speak of this with any precision. Metal has many associations with both an industrial and a traditional reality. It is a material of hardness, precision, strength, and great reflectivity, thereby making reference to a future populated by the artifacts of an advanced science. But it also recalls the tools and equipment of an earlier time, a world of medieval helmets and weaponry, of artifacts from an iron age marked by a great fascination with such metals. This luminous steel thereby shares a past with a future—a complex relationship to time and place alongside an insistent industrial character intended to assure it a vital history.

Tokyo has undergone may changes in physical appearance over the last century. The city, so decimated by World War II, has had to rebuild from ashes. In its rebuilding it has become, perhaps it has returned to being, a city without heaviness. It was once a city of wood and paper; it has now become a city of concrete, steel, and glass. The feeling of lightness, however, remains.

We now return to the notion of specificity of place that introduced this essay. The sports complex at Fujisawa represents an attempt to address this problem by way of a set of material and constructive considerations guided in turn by an image of place and a sense of history, such that the eventual building demonstrates an unequivocal geographic inevitability. Paradoxically it has been necessary to allow the building an ambiguous relationship to history—to both the past and the future—in an effort to define this specific connection to place. The temporal associations possible in any interpretation of this building, therefore, are manifold and complex, while it remains our intention that its geographic relationship be without ambiguity. In this way the Fujisawa Municipal Gymnasium might speak to a specific regional history, to the lightness and architectonic precision of its constructive legacy—as it is intrinsically tied to that region. In short, we wish the building to be free in time so as to be fixed in place.

The suggestion of a modern or industrial vernacular of rigorous architectural character might be found in this process. This has certainly been our struggle. If the metal roof at Fujisawa finds an evocative place among the industrial artifacts of its milieu, making explicit the ambitions of a culture in search of a more resonant architecture, we will have successfully catalyzed an investigation critical to the Japanese future.

FROM:
Fumihiko Maki, "The Roof at Fujisawa," *Perspecta: Yale Architectural Journal* 24 (1988): 106–121.

The exterior stair of the subarena became an independent, sculptural element in the composition.

# TOKYO METROPOLITAN GYMNASIUM

Shibuya, Tokyo 1990

The Tokyo Metropolitan Gymnasium replaces an older sports facility that had been built in the early 1960s and that had become quite inadequate to the growing demands on it. The new gymnasium was constructed on the same site of four hectares, with a total program floor area of 45,000 square meters. The new complex consists of a much larger main arena with a seating capacity of 10,000; a subarena primarily used as a practice gym; a swimming pavilion with 50-meter and 25-meter pools and spectator seating for 900; and support spaces, including training and meeting rooms, a sports exhibition space, expanded administration spaces, and a restaurant. This sports complex is open to all residents of Tokyo and serves as a stage for both national and international indoor sporting events.

The site of the Tokyo Metropolitan Gymnasium is part of the larger Meiji Jingu Park and is bounded by Sendagaya Station to the north, residential and commercial complexes to the south and west, and the National Stadium to the east. Finding such a large parcel of open land in densely built Tokyo is quite rare, and the design takes advantage of its generous situation by treating the entire site as an urban park. Sendagaya Station, the gateway for most visitors to the sports park, becomes a pivotal point for access to the main arena, the swimming pavilion, and the public passage between the buildings. Paths to each of these points are dispersed radially from the station and form diagonal vistas through the site from the point of arrival. The urban park is open at all hours and serves as a pleasant route for pedestrians between two major streets; the grounds of the Tokyo Metropolitan Gymnasium have thus become a very active place both day and night.

A height restriction of 30 meters imposed on the site required the main arena floor to be lowered 6 meters below ground level and the swimming pavilion, 2 meters below. By conforming to the height restrictions the design does not fully reveal on the exterior the voluminous spaces required of its hall interiors, and the scale of the buildings harmonizes well with the nearby residential and commercial buildings. While the volumes of the respective buildings in the complex are kept quite low, the roof shape of each building is given a significant architectonic role—thus continuing our investigation of the symbolic role of the roof that began with the Fujisawa Municipal Gymnasium some years earlier. The roof of the main arena curves gently like a shell; the roof of the subarena is stepped like a ziggurat; and the roof of the swimming pavilion undulates and hovers above the outward-curving side walls. Together with the transparent entrance pyramid, outdoor sculptures, and red lighting fixtures, these roofs constitute a new cityscape. Continually changing views of the park and city beyond open up as one moves between the dynamic building masses and sculptural elements. This experience of changing scenery is not unrelated to the compositional principles of traditional Japanese strolling gardens known as *kaiyushiki*.

*Above:* Transparent model collaged against Tokyo's skyline

*Facing page:* Aerial view of the sports complex with Shinjuku's skyscrapers seen in the background

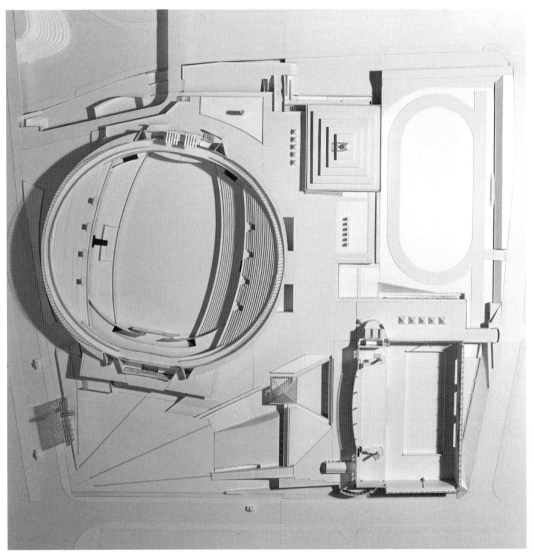

Model

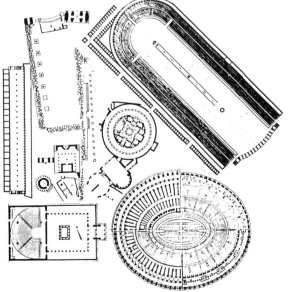

Collage in the style of Hadrian's Villa

The shell-like roof of the main arena, the ziggurat of the subarena, the floating translucent membrane covering the swimming pavilion, and the glass pyramid of the visitors' entrance together make up a campus with a varied skyline.

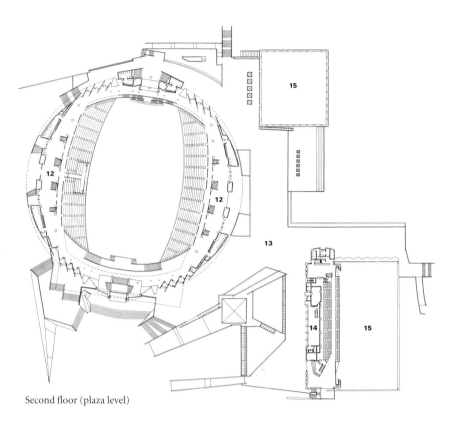

Second floor (plaza level)

1  main arena entrance
2  main arena (below)
3  entrance
4  garden
5  administration
6  training
7  seminar
8  subarena (below)
9  pool entrance
10  50-meter pool
11  25-meter pool (below)
12  spectator lobby
13  pedestrian plaza
14  café
15  void

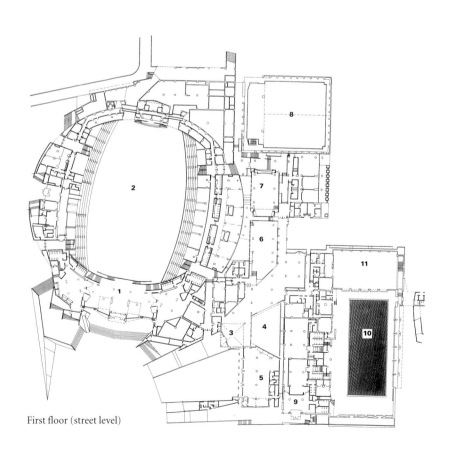

First floor (street level)

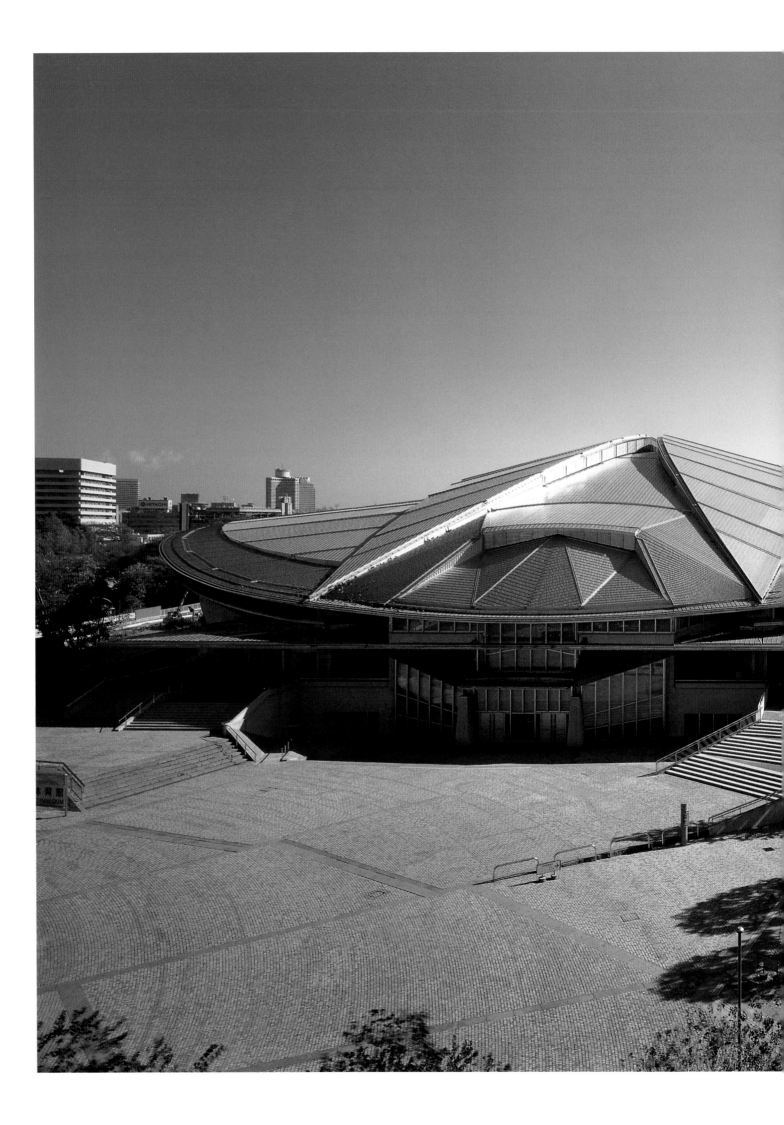

*Above:* A kinetic sculpture by Yoshikuni Iida acts as a focal point for a pedestrian plaza passing between the three arenas. Offices, training rooms, locker rooms, and passages connecting the arenas are located underneath this raised plaza level. The curved roof of nearby Tsuda Hall (also the design of our firm) is seen in the distance.

*Left:* Main arena seen from the exit gates of Sendagaya Station

*Facing page:* Corner detail of the swimming pavilion, with the main arena seen in the background

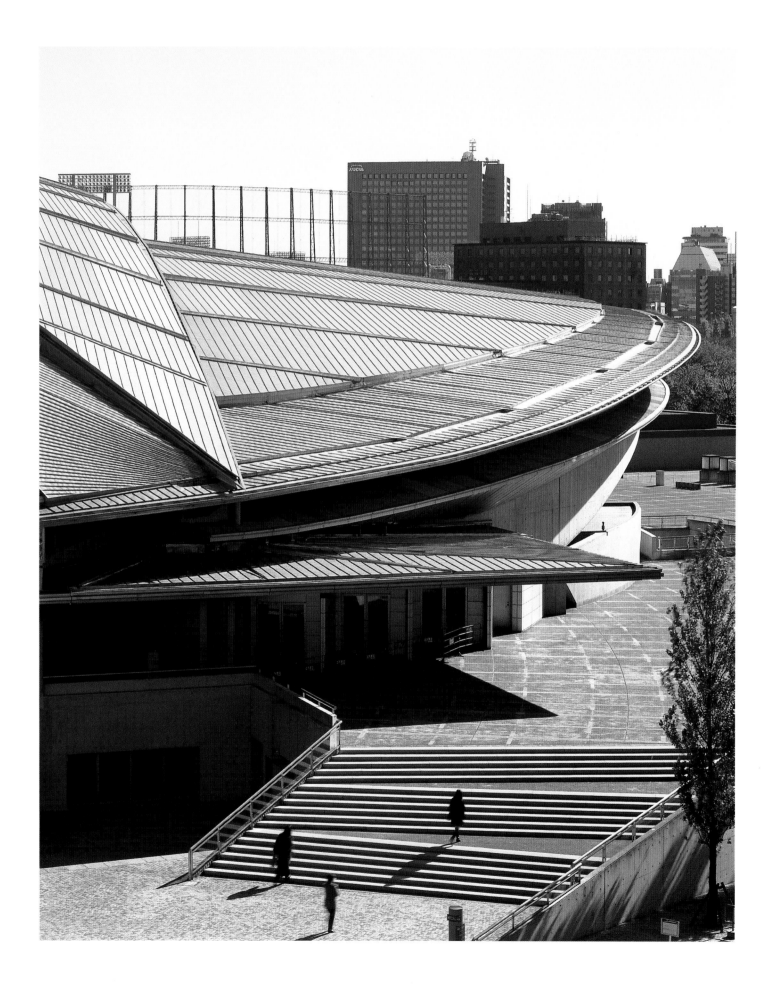

View from main arena to the swimming pavilion. A café-restaurant opening out on the pedestrian plaza is located within the pavilion below its spectator stands.

Competition sketch of skyline

Spectator deck

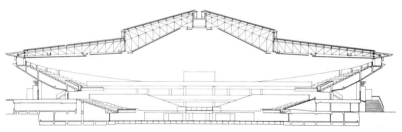

Cross section through main arena

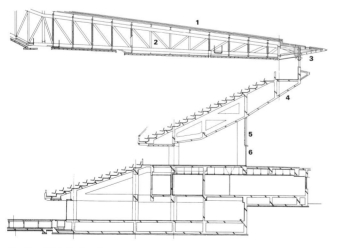

Sectional detail of main arena

1 roof:  seam-welded stainless steel, 0.4 millimeters
         on cement board backing, 25 millimeters + 7.5 millimeter
         urethane/fiberglass insulation sheet
2 steel truss
3 eaves: punched stainless steel sheet
4 exposed concrete with acrylic sealant
5 aluminum sash
6 aluminum flush door

## The Main Arena

The main arena is circular in plan and based on similar spatial intentions as the Fujisawa Municipal Gymnasium—using the dynamics of a long-spanning roof structure to create an animated, voluminous curved space. In order to enclose a space 2.5 times that of Fujisawa (the main arena of the Tokyo facility has a diameter of 120 meters, compared to 75 meters of Fujisawa), a pair of leaflike girders, each comprised of two opposing curved planes made of truss elements, rest against each other, supported on massive piers at four points along the perimeter. This main structure accounts for all of the roof's resistance to seismic forces and carries more than two-thirds of its vertical loads. Twenty-eight columnar supports spaced along the periphery of the arena seating resolve the remaining vertical loads at pin-joint connections. The horizontal forces exerted by the roof structure's pair of outward-leaning leaf-girders are taken by a tension ring along the edge of the circular roof line.

Natural light is essential to appreciating qualities of large spaces; without it, our sense of scale is inhibited and structure and space appear uniform and flattened. In the main arena daylight is admitted through windows along the top of the arena seats. As in the Fujisawa Municipal Gymnasium the roof surface is sheathed in stainless steel; however, in the Tokyo gymnasium, a composite double-packing roof surface with a sandwiched polyethylene sheet between two 0.2 millimeter stainless sheets was developed to provide for higher quality sound insulation. Thus, although it is used primarily as a gymnasium, the main arena is sufficiently insulated acoustically to accommodate a variety of nonsporting events such as concerts, using its state-of-the-art audio/visual system. Electronically operated venetian blinds are installed in double-pane windows located along the perimeter to control the quantity of light or even black out the space for certain events.

Natural light admitted through continuous windows along the edge of the spectator stands gives the roof the appearance of floating.

**The Swimming Pavilion**

The swimming pavilion is characterized by overall lightness and transparency. The four outer walls and the ceiling plane are visually detached from one another by clerestory and vertical slit windows at the corners that allow a generous amount of sunlight directly into the interior space. The spatial tension between the hovering roof and the end walls is further heightened by curving the top of the wall outward. Soft natural light filtering through a translucent Teflon roof and fiber grating ceiling produces an ethereal, floating spatial quality in the bright pool interior.

As in the main arena, the main floor level of the swimming pavilion is submerged a few meters below street level. Here, however, we were eager to take advantage of the building's southern orientation to provide a sunbathing deck along the poolside opposite the spectator stands; so we manipulated the section of land between the pavilion and existing sidewalk to create a gentle slope down to the poolside. The slope is planted with trees and ground cover in order to provide restful views for swimmers and passersby alike, and thus it acts as a buffer zone between the interior and the street.

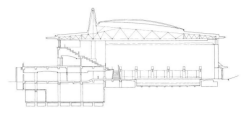

Cross section through swimming pavilion

The swimming pavilion's 50-meter pool. Natural light is admitted not only through clerestory windows but also through the roof membrane itself, which is made of translucent Teflon.

Corner window detail, showing maintenance stainless steel catwalk, fiber grating ceiling, and aerated aluminum panels. Interior finishes were chosen not only for their durability and resistance to chemical corrosion, but also with an eye to matching colors and enhancing the light, watery character of the space.

The low-slung stainless steel roof of the main arena catches the sky's reflections.

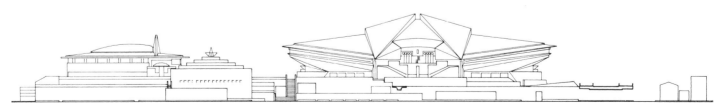

East elevation

Contrasting forms of the curvilinear main arena roof and the glazed pyramid over the visitors' entrance

Roof profile in sketch

# SWIMMING/DIVING HALL + VELODROME FOR OLYMPICS 2000

Berlin, Germany  1994

Velodrome interior

Swimming/Diving Hall interior, showing wavelike undulating roof structure

The city of Berlin, as part of its bid for the Olympic Games in the year 2000, invited us to submit a competition design for two new sports facilities: a Swimming/Diving Hall and a Velodrome. The prospect of Berlin, a city reunited by the end of the cold war, playing host to the Olympics to initiate the new century immediately struck us with its symbolic appeal. But as we began to analyze the site and its context in the eastern part of Berlin, we realized that beyond this symbolic role, the sponsors wished to use the Olympics as a catalyst for furthering the city's reunification process by developing and improving the quality of urban life in the neighborhoods of the former East Berlin. We therefore attempted not simply to provide a pair of sports halls on an isolated site but suggested ways in which the energy and resources devoted to the Olympics might best be harnessed to provide a lasting benefit to the city itself.

The site is conceived as a new Olympic Park where the two main sports halls, a smaller community gymnasium (set at a skewed angle), and a mixed-use commercial structure facing the main street are set within a continuous green landscape of trees and lawns. The two large volumes of the sports halls are positioned in a diagonal relationship to each other, thereby defining two large outdoor spaces: an open space between the Swimming/Diving Hall and the railroad tracks to the north, to be used for outdoor sports, and a raised esplanade serving as a forecourt to both halls. The esplanade rises 5 meters above street level (partially submerging the large volume of the halls) and is connected to the residential neighborhood to the north by a pedestrian bridge spanning the railroad tracks.

The particular forms and structural configurations of both halls respond to the dynamic characteristic of each sport—centrifugal motion in the Velodrome and linear wavelike motion in the Swimming/Diving Hall. The one-way spanning trusses of the Swimming/Diving Hall have gently sagging curves, and their heights are staggered from one another. The resulting slits are filled with clerestory windows in order to dramatize the hovering quality of each section of roof. The shell-like form of the Velodrome roof and the uneven distribution of its seating reflect the importance given to maintaining a strong visual relationship between its interior and the esplanade seen through its glazed entrance facade. This relationship between a vast interior space and an open exterior one would be maintained throughout the year. During seasons when the facility is not used for cycling events, the Velodrome could be converted to a large covered plaza for a variety of festive events, with activity spilling out onto the esplanade.

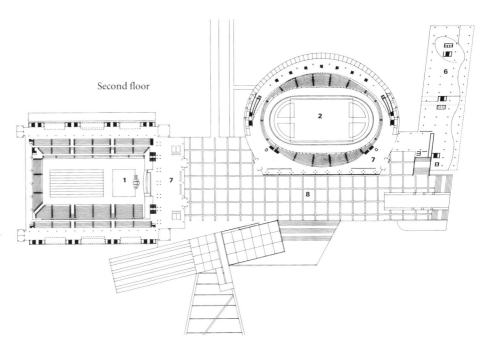

Second floor

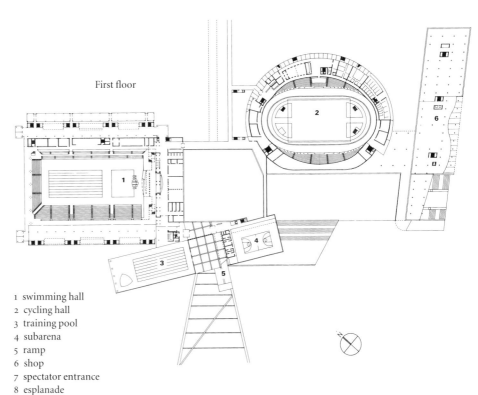

First floor

1 swimming hall
2 cycling hall
3 training pool
4 subarena
5 ramp
6 shop
7 spectator entrance
8 esplanade

183

Early sketch showing roofscape

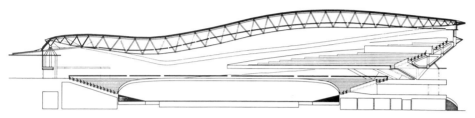

Section through Velodrome

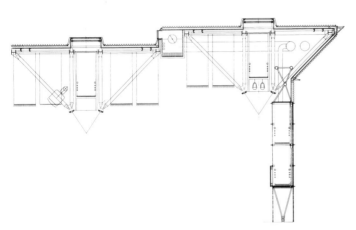

*Above:* Detail section of Swimming/Diving Hall roof structure

*Right:* Overview of sports complex

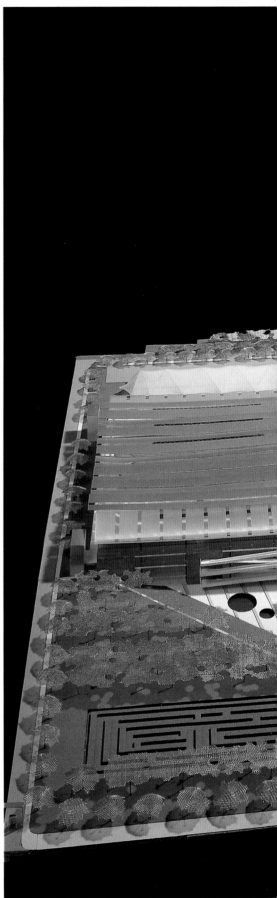

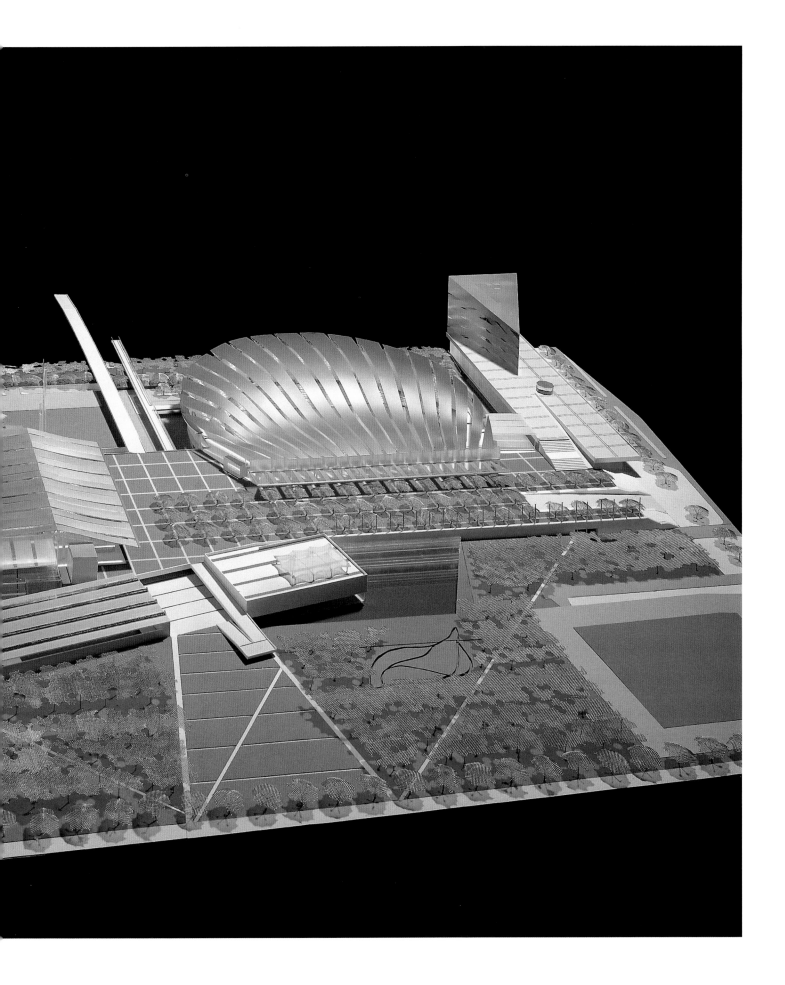

# MAKUHARI MESSE

Makuhari, Chiba 1989

The Nippon Convention Center—more commonly known as Makuhari Messe—is built on a flat parcel of reclaimed land facing Tokyo Bay, located halfway between downtown Tokyo and the international airport at Narita. The convention center was planned as a focus for the newly emerging business/residential center of Makuhari New Town. We received the commission to design Makuhari Messe after winning a national invited competition in the summer of 1986. As a comprehensive convention complex comprising an exhibition hall, event hall, and international conference center, the Messe was unprecedented in Japan at that time. Representing perhaps our office's most ambitious effort, this complex of buildings totaling more than 130,000 square meters was designed in one year and constructed in two.

The planning began with the allocation of separate parts of the program into independent buildings of various geometric and architectonic forms. Responding to the fact that most visitors would approach the convention complex from the train station to the north, the design locates the two relatively smaller buildings—the event hall and the international conference center—on the north side of the site, forming an informal entrance plaza between them. These buildings, with their pedestrian arcades, exterior stairs, and sculptural elements, provide a sense of human scale for visitors approaching the massive complex. Rising beyond them, the arching silhouette of the immense exhibition hall roof is visible.

The generating image for the competition entry shows a village of buildings sheltered by mountains rising gently in the background.

Image model

Competition perspective

Aerial view of the 540-meter arching roof of the exhibition hall, with the event hall and international conference center on the left. Tokyo Bay is to the right.

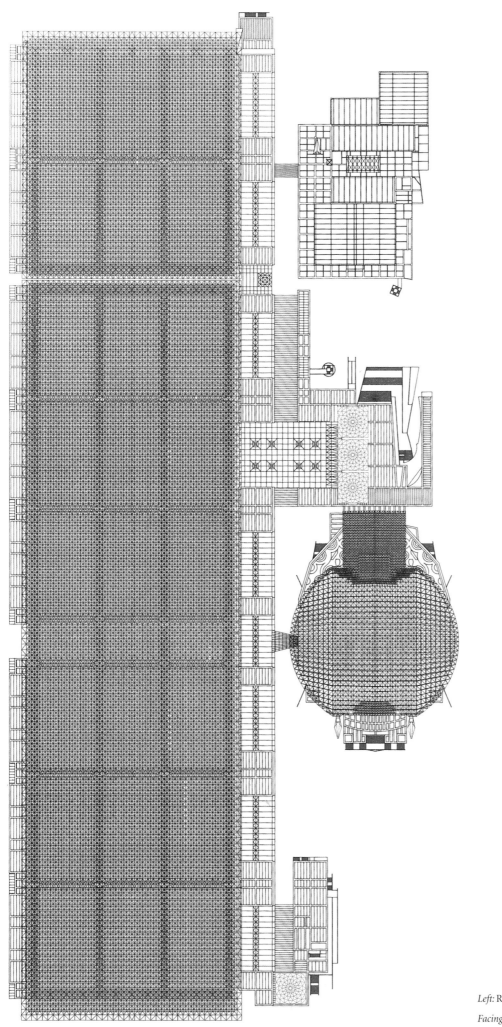

*Left:* Roof structure plan

*Facing page:* Roofscape

189

North elevation

View of exhibition hall from southwest. The open-ended, incomplete gesture of the arching roof silhouette seeks to avoid the static image of a single, closed form at this massive scale.

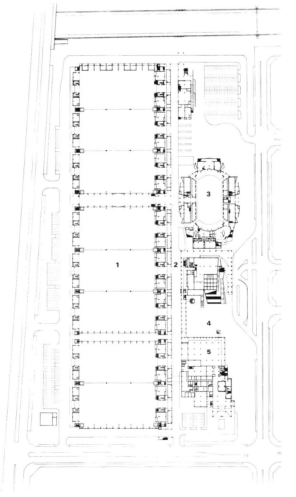

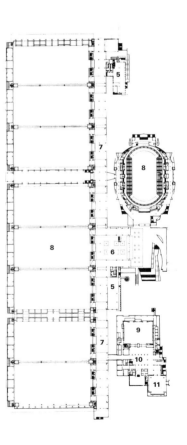

1  exhibition hall
2  service road
3  event hall
4  plaza
5  restaurant
6  main entrance
7  central mall
8  open to below
9  hall
10  lobby
11  international conference center

First floor

Second floor

*Overleaf:* Stairs and escalators leading to
main entrance

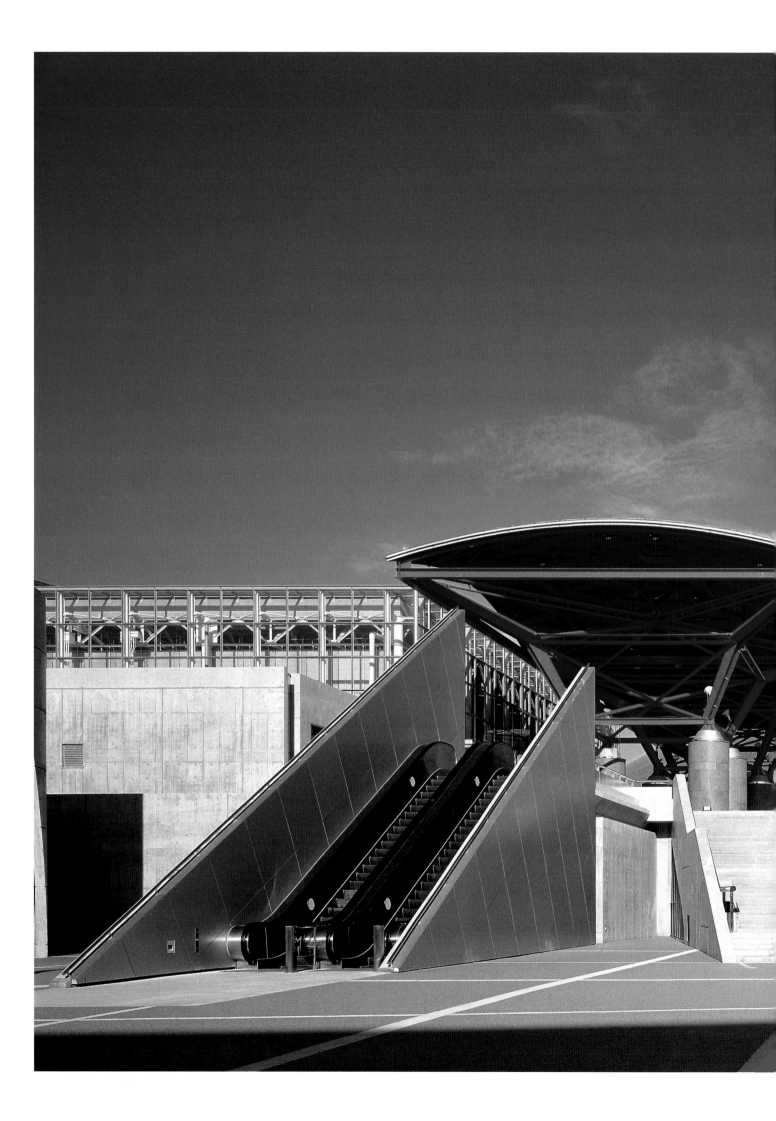

## Exhibition Hall

The largest of all the Messe's facilities, the exhibition hall is comprised of eight identical bays, 120 by 60 meters in plan, covered by a single, arching roof sheathed in 0.5-millimeter-thick, continuously formed stainless steel sheets. The roof rises from a height of 15 meters at its lowest point to 31 meters at its apex. The roof's asymmetrical, open-ended arch form was chosen in order to give the complex a dynamic silhouette—particularly when viewed from a speeding automobile along the highway to the south of the site (here, one's sense of scale should be quite different from the pedestrian entrance to the north). The extensive south facade is articulated as a double curtain wall, provided with a substantial air space between the inner and outer layers for insulation. The exterior layer is clear glass through which the second skin of white glass-wool board is visible, giving the whole construction a liquid texture that reflects the color of the sky.

The eight exhibition hall interiors can be combined into one continuous space, or alternatively each can be used independently, separated by 10-meter-high sliding partitions. In order to preserve the perception of the sweeping, continuous roof structure even when the halls are independently partitioned, the upper portion of these partitions were designed in fixed transparent glass. Entrance to the eight exhibition halls is from an interior mall running parallel to the halls at the second-floor level. Visitors entering at this level are treated to an overview of the exhibits before descending by escalators to the main floor.

The central mall connecting entrances to all eight exhibition halls. The glass of the lower portion of the curtain wall can be rolled down during fine weather to allow natural ventilation in the 540-meter corridor. For reasons of construction staging, the central mall was actually the last part of the Messe to be built; for expedience, all of its components—including the precast columns—were designed to be prefabricated and quickly assembled when the site finally became available.

Exhibition hall in use for a trade fair

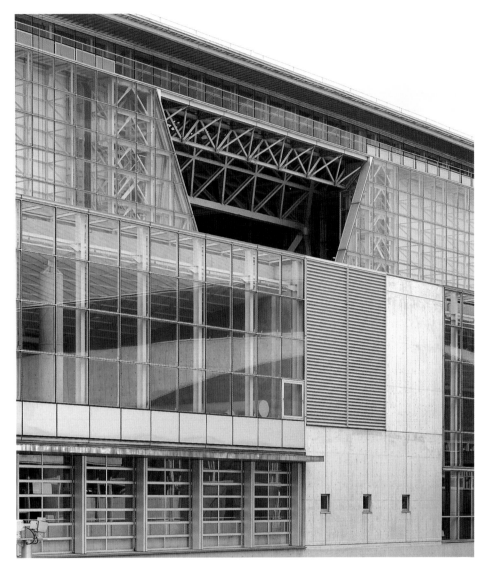

As a building type convention centers tend to be quite massive with nondescript interior spaces due to the users' desire not to receive much natural light. In Makuhari Messe, however, we allowed for strategic openings along the edges of the ceiling in order to lighten the interior mood and for continuous skylights to permit natural light to filter through the intricate tracery of the roof's "space beams."

Makuhari Messe's extremely short construction schedule posed a great challenge—time was in fact one of the most important parameters for determining appropriate structural and constructional strategies. Industrial processes for systematizing and prefabricating materials were used extensively in order to minimize on-site labor and thus conserve time. The massive "space beams" (vast trusses made continuous with the fabric of the space-frame roof) for the exhibition hall, for example, were all preassembled in a factory in order to simplify on-site joinery. Furthermore, all floors of the buildings are composed of a precast concrete system, which had the greatest effect and efficiency in the stepped seating areas in the event hall. Not everything, however, was industrially produced. All of the joinery details for assembling prefabricated products were designed specifically for this project. Thus, it is the combination of industrial products with some site-intensive work and hand-crafted details that gives this rather large building a distinctive quality of its own.

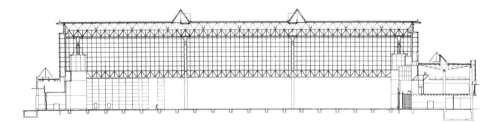

*Above:* Erection of prefabricated "space beams"

*Top Left:* Detail of double curtain wall on north facade

*Left:* Cross section of exhibition hall and central mall

*Facing page:* Detail of support of a "space beam" in the exhibition hall

## Event Hall

The event hall has a capacity of a total of 9,000 seats (6,000 fixed and 3,000 removable) and is designed to accommodate a wide range of sporting and theatrical events. When Makuhari Messe hosts unusually large conventions, such as the biannual Tokyo Motor Show, the event hall is used to provide additional exhibit space. The curvilinear roof of the hall is finished in 0.4-millimeter stainless steel sheets electrically welded together.

The event hall in use during an international table tennis tournament

Though the event hall is outwardly similar in form to the Fujisawa Municipal Gymnasium, a space-frame structure was chosen for its roof due to the scheduling advantages offered by its prefabrication.

## International Conference Center

The international conference center has its own independent entrance and porte cochère, but it is also directly accessible from the mall of the exhibition hall on the second floor. The center includes a banquet hall for 2,000 people, an international conference hall, a variety of smaller meeting rooms, and the administrative offices for the Nippon Convention Center. The banquet hall and meeting rooms have all been organized around a more intimately scaled sequence of lobbies and circulation spaces which provide a spatial contrast to the voluminous interiors of the exhibition and event halls. To harmonize with the other buildings the exterior is clad in metallic 2.5-millimeter-thick aluminum panels with open-gasket joints.

Conference center lobby

Stair leading to conference and banquet halls

# MAKUHARI MESSE, PHASE II

Makuhari, Chiba 1989

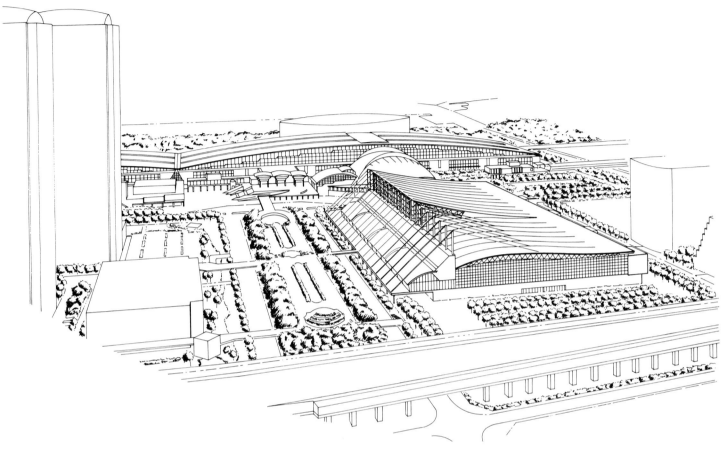

Perspective drawing showing the cable-suspended roof of the new exhibition hall in the foreground, with the existing Messe complex seen beyond

A few years after the construction of the initial Makuhari Messe, it became evident from the increasing scale of its use that additional exhibition halls would be necessary, and we were appointed to design a 33,000-square-meter annex to the earlier complex. The new program required one large exhibition hall of 9,000 square meters (the typical bay of the first phase of Makuhari Messe was 6,700 square meters) and additional smaller bays that could be subdivided in the manner of the first phase.

A site to the west of the earlier complex was available for the annex, and it had been suggested that the addition should merely extend the length of the existing structure with another span of arching roof across the street. After preliminary studies, however, we discovered that the distance one would walk from one end to the other of the exhibition spaces made this option inadvisable. At the same time, reflecting the passage of years, we became interested in using the proposed building to create a new urban complex made up of complementing parts, rather than merely enlarging in a predictable way the already gigantic form of the exhibition hall. This idea follows from our experience in designing projects such as the Hillside

Terrace complex and the Iwasaki Art Museum in distinct phases. In the end an alternative site was chosen to the north of the existing event hall, allowing the new exhibition halls to be planned perpendicular to the length of the original exhibition hall.

As in the original Messe the structural feat of spanning long distances for the exhibition hall interiors meant that the form of the roof would have enormous expressive potential. The original Messe's arched roof had suggested the image of mountains; for Makuhari Messe, Phase II, the silhouette was inverted to create a curve as a metaphor for a wave. The new roof uses a hybrid suspension structure consisting of a series of curved steel trusses suspended from vertical steel poles at 12-meter intervals. The horizontal forces incurred at the point of suspension are stabilized by backstay cables anchored at the edge of the raised pedestrian deck. In addition to their structural function, the tall poles and tension cables are intended to introduce a festive atmosphere to the Messe grounds, particularly as seen in perspective from the approach road.

The roof of the large exhibition hall takes the form of a catenary curve—structurally the most

efficient shape for a roof load in tension—and rises to a maximum height of 32 meters. Clerestory windows around the periphery of the roof are designed to dramatize the lightness of its structure. The roof of the two adjacent halls has a more complex wavelike curve that turns downward at the east end in contrast to the catenary curve. Its 96-meter span is alleviated at midpoint by attaching a suspension cable. From the interior the effect is one of unexpected lightness. Ceilings are clad in aluminum panels (with truss bottom cords and diagonals protruding), creating a more luminous and refined quality than we were able to achieve in the original exhibition hall ceilings.

The sequential and sectional organization of exhibition halls and public spaces remains similar to that of the original Makuhari Messe—entrances to the exhibitions are located on a raised pedestrian deck so that visitors can see the whole exhibition space at a glance before descending to the main floor. An entrance plaza featuring an elliptical conference room pavilion is located at the south end of the site, diagonally across from the larger plaza of the first phase.

South elevation: the glazed elliptical volume contains a special conference room.

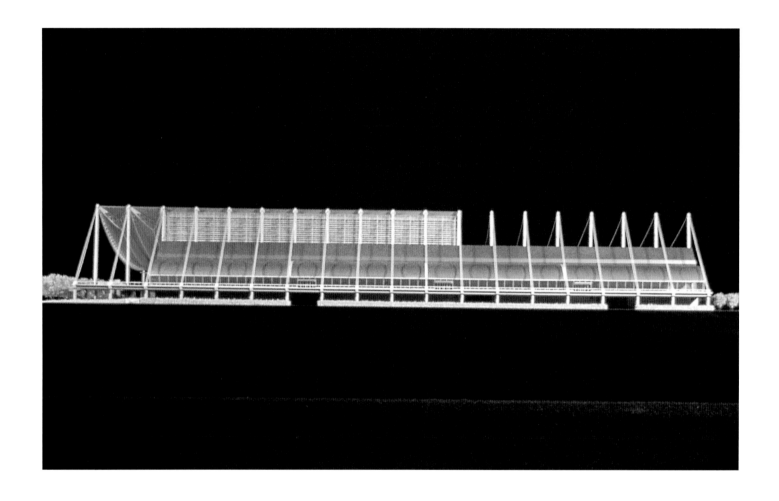

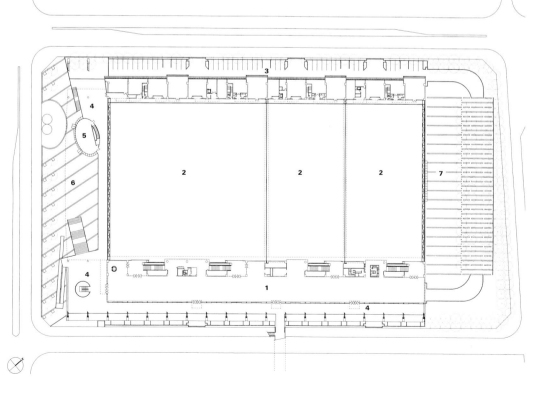

*Above:* East elevation

*Left:* Second floor

1 esplanade
2 open to exhibition space below
3 service zone
4 pedestrian deck
5 conference room
6 south plaza (below)
7 north plaza (below)

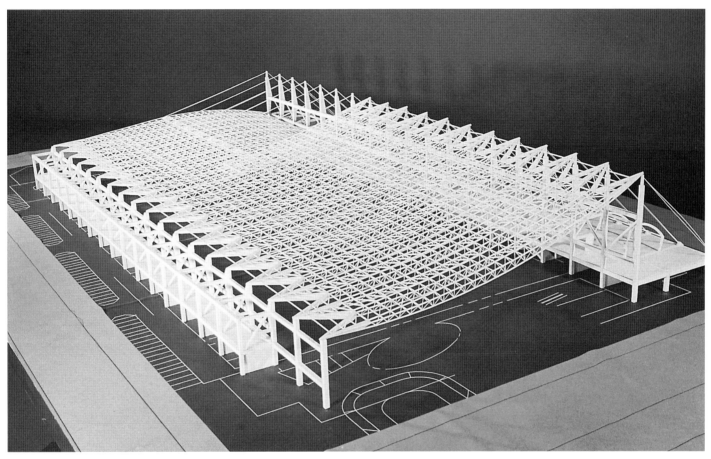

Structural model

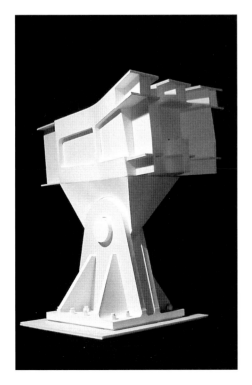

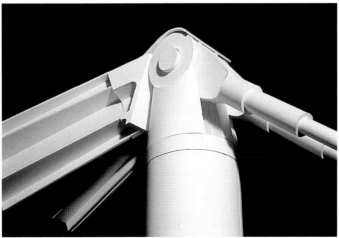

*Above:* Detail model of upper truss connection joint

*Left:* Detail model of lower truss connection joint

# NOTES ON COLLECTIVE FORM

Fumihiko Maki

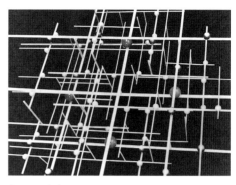

Open-ended system

The summer of 1958 was to prove the most memorable period of my life as an architect. I was teaching in the School of Architecture at Washington University when I received word that I had been selected as a fellow by the Graham Foundation. Established principally to support young artists, including architects, in pursuing research of their own choosing, the Graham Foundation fellowship was perhaps the most generous grant in the world at the time. Among the ten fellows chosen that year, the oldest was Frederick Kiesler, well-known for the Endless House. Others included B. V. Doshi, an architect of my own generation, from Ahmadabad, India, and the sculptor Eduardo Chillida, who lived in San Sebastián, Spain.

I decided to spend most of the following two years traveling in Southeast Asia and the Middle East, regions I had not visited before, as well as northern and southern Europe. It was for me a Journey to the West. Of the many cities and villages I visited on two extended trips in those two years, the ones that made the greatest impression on me were communities of houses built with walls of sun-dried brick and tiled roofs, of the kind that are scattered along the Mediterranean coast in countless numbers. The sight of those houses—their features thrown into sharp relief by deep shadows—linked and piled on top of one another on the hillside under the strong sun and against the background of a deep blue sky, was by itself remarkable. But what was even more striking was the fact that the community, that is, the collective form, was composed of quite simple spatial elements such as rooms arranged around a small courtyard. At that time architects and historians in Japan had not yet begun to undertake surveys of villages. I saw in those collective forms from the Mediterranean an expression of regional culture, that is, a body of wisdom accumulated over many years.

The impressions gathered on that journey are behind the proposal entitled "Group Form" which I presented in 1960 with my friend, the architect Masato Otaka. That was a time when the development of land to the west of Shinjuku Station formerly occupied by a water purification plant was starting to become a widely discussed topic. This joint proposal was intended to be not so much an actual scheme for that area but a demonstration of the idea of group form. However, the proposal was not meant to confirm what I had discovered with respect to forms of dwelling in villages on my journey. At the time I was interested in the notion of an urban order based on a collection of elements and believed it offered an alternative to the order, based on enormous structures built on the scale of civil engineering works, that architects and utopians had been proposing since the start of the twentieth century.

The notion of starting with individual elements to arrive at a whole was not only elaborated in the idea of collective form but subsequently became a basic theme for my own architectural aesthetic and logic. This two-year journey was valuable in that it gave me an intuitive knowledge of the fact that ultimately, in an organic form such as a city, the urban order can only be maintained if the autonomy of individual buildings and districts is assured.

The early 1960s were a time when the architectural world was still exploring various issues of modern architecture which had been developed before the war. Yet at the same time doubts were starting to be expressed about the validity of the ideas of modern architecture with respect to the city, and new investigations were being initiated. The megastructure can be seen in the context of the time as an attempt, based on a faith in technology, to expand the realm of architectural possibility. In summer of 1960 I participated in a Team X conference in the south of France. Although the members took a humanist and regionalist approach and rejected megastructures, they were troubled by "the issue of great numbers," that is, the effectiveness of architects in dealing with the problem of housing large numbers of people.

In 1961 I returned to teaching at Washington University and, using notes I had previously made, wrote over the course of a year a paper describing the three paradigms of collective form that would subsequently become the first chapter of *Investigations in Collective Form*. I still remember typing the original sheets from which mimeographs were made. I sent copies of this "underground" publication to the members of Team X as well as American architects and urban designers with whom I had recently become acquainted. I received an unexpectedly large number of responses. People like Walter Gropius, Kevin Lynch, and Jacob Bakema took the time to send comments with their letters. One reason my paper met with such a response was that, as I have already mentioned, the early 1960s were a time when new explorations were at last being undertaken into architecture's place in the city and the relationship between the city and architecture. In addition my approach, which was to study the relationship between architecture and the city from the perspective of collections of buildings and quasi buildings, was different.

*Investigations in Collective Form* was published by Washington University in 1964. The first chapter may appear at first glance to present the three paradigms of collective form—compositional form, group form, and megaform—as opposing, antagonistic patterns. On the contrary the three patterns or modes are not mutually exclusive but can coexist in one configuration. They define the three basic relationships that always exist between individual elements and the whole. My lack of experience in actually designing buildings may have accounted for an oversight. I neglected to consider the existence of space as a medium, in either collective form or linkage. It was a premise of my argument that the elements of compositional form are architecturally more self-sufficient than those of

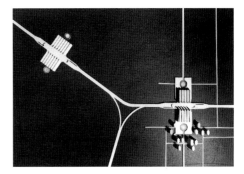

*Movement Systems in the City*, Boston, 1965

City room, *Movement Systems in the City*

Transportation Exchange, *Movement Systems in the City*

either group form or megaform, but I ought to have undertaken a more extended analysis of modes of exterior space and the interstices among elements within the composition. It was only later, in planning projects such as Hillside Terrace, Rissho University, and the Fujisawa campus of Keio University, that I gradually gained experience and learned that collective forms can depend on how such exterior spaces are created. Through experience I also discovered a more subtle technique. By emphasizing the autonomy of individual architectural elements and deliberately creating weak linkages between them, one enables those elements to become more distinct indices of time and place. I learned that both opposition and harmony in fact characterize relationships on many different levels and that their cumulative effect determines our actual image of the city.

The second chapter, which I wrote with Jerry Goldberg (then a research student at Washington University), was an essay on collections of elements from the perspective of linkage. We discussed the question of linkage on various levels. If each building, that is, each structural unit of the city, has its own life span, then different elements are apt to be replaced at different times. The relationship that ought to be created among elements of different ages is an issue of organic linkage among elements. The city can be seen as the sum total of countless events being generated simultaneously. When the architect or planner introduces something new under such circumstances, that action fits into certain operational categories. An attempt is made to discover the stance of the designer with respect to the city in the process and method of the particular operation. To put it another way, the historical context each individual carries with him is made apparent by such operations. This position recognizes that the city as a physical place and social system depends on the autonomy of individual elements and seeks ways in which each individual element may participate in the whole.

*Investigations in Collective Form*, which was published as a pamphlet, also had an appendix in which a number of urban design projects I was working on at the time were introduced. I understand that the undersized pamphlet with a red cover, though only about eighty pages long, continues to be widely read in the United States, particularly in universities.

In 1962 I moved from Washington University to the Graduate School of Design at Harvard University. There I stayed for the next few years until I opened an office in Japan in 1965. I taught with a group of people centered around Josep Lluís Sert in the newly established urban design program. During that period I worked with four students (Mario Corea, Eduardo Lozano, Gustavo Munizaga, and Jan Wampler) on certain collaborative projects. Boston, which adjoins Cambridge, was concentrated on the tip of a peninsula when it was first founded in the seventeenth century but has gradually expanded. Like a medieval European town, the area consid-

ered old Boston is covered with a network of narrow streets. By the 1950s a number of expressways leading into old Boston had been constructed, but a ring road that would eventually encompass Boston and Cambridge had not yet been completed. The subway and bus systems were fairly well developed for a metropolis of that size, but those means of transportation were not integrated into a network. Automobiles moving in and out of the old central district were one of the many problems that remained unresolved.

The project that I worked on with the four students was an attempt to integrate the already existing systems into an efficient network and to transform the urban area of old Boston into a primarily pedestrian-oriented district through the introduction of a number of new urban design elements.

I would like to discuss briefly this project because its approach to the relationship between the city and architecture is one that I have continued to take. First, the project tried to identify strategic transportation points in the modern city, working on the assumption, well-supported by empirical evidence, that heavy pedestrian traffic is generated by any transportation node. In addition to subway stations and important bus stops, there were transportation exchanges to be located where the inner ring road and the expressways intersected, and garages, to be constructed at major points in the central district. These were integrated into a network together with places frequented by pedestrians such as the river bank and parks. Second, new urban facilities were proposed such as the above-mentioned transportation exchanges as well as atriums called "city rooms" to be located at major gathering places and arcades called "city corridors" to be built above busy sidewalks.

This project was an attempt to consider the merits of a city organized as an open-ended system through strategic transportation points and the diverse movements of pedestrians generated by those points. The idea was to articulate a clear strategy for forming new linear and area domains in a city by gradually integrating each element into a network. Today there are many actual examples of atriums and arcades, but in the early 1960s those who advocated their deployment as pedestrian-oriented urban spaces were still in the minority. The thinking behind this project was antithetical to the approach favored by many urban designers and architects at the time, which was to alter the character of the urban structure completely through enormous construction projects that were in the nature of public works.

Our project also happened to be consistent with the notion that group form offered an alternative to megaform. At the same time there was an attempt to endow the transportation exchanges, which were garages to be directly linked at right angles to the ring road with mass transit facilities accommodated underneath, with the same scale and aesthetic as the highways.

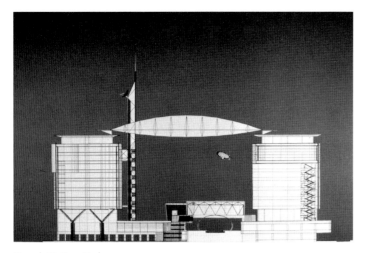

Yamada Station, Osaka

Recently we have been involved in the planning of a new transportation exchange near Yamada Station in Senri New Town, Osaka Prefecture. The content of the program and the scale may be different, but the idea remains what it was nearly thirty years ago: to discover an architectural form for the flow of urban transportation.

The waterfront project that Kenzo Tange worked on at Massachusetts Institute of Technology at about the same time, which was later developed into Tokyo Plan 1960, represented an urban intervention on the scale of public works. My project was more empirical and human-scaled. As I have already stated, my argument was autonomous elements—individuals in the case of social group, separate buildings in the case of architecture—were the basis for urban design, and that, endowed with new linkages, they could gradually develop into networks. The project represented a manifesto of my firm belief that the city and human society could adapt to the inevitable flow of time and the changes wrought by that flow only by adopting such an organic structure.

*Movement Systems in the City* was subsequently published as another pamphlet by Harvard University, this time with a contrasting black cover. These two pamphlets are signposts on my intellectual journey during the years spent primarily in the United States from the end of the 1950s until I opened an office in Tokyo in 1965. They show the development of my ideas regarding city architecture in my younger years.

The first and second phases of Hillside Terrace (1969–74) and the two-phased Kumagaya Campus for Rissho University (1967–72) are among the early works of my Tokyo office. Many years separate the Rissho University campus from the Fujisawa campus of Keio University. I was still in my late thirties and I felt quite fortunate to be given the opportunity to design several buildings on a single site. My strong interest in exterior spaces generated by a group of buildings can be traced in part to impressions gathered during a visit I made to India to see Le Corbusier and his project at Chandigarh. The great Le Corbusier was given the opportunity to design an ensemble of four buildings at the end of his architectural career. When I went to the project in early 1960, only the High Court and the Secretariat had been completed. Looking from the High Court toward the Secretariat, or from the Secretariat toward the High Court, one sensed the establishment of an intervening expanse of hot red earth, as if two electrons had formed a magnetic field or an electrical charge had leaped between two terminals. I was never to forget that a collective form has the capacity to dominate exterior space. At Hillside Terrace, Isar Büropark in a Munich suburb, and the Fujisawa campus of Keio University, I have found myself going back again and again to the question of the domination of exterior space by a collective form, though the scale has been different each time.

One does not physically experience urban space by simply gazing at buildings or looking at them from above. Space is experienced only through sequential movement. That being so, how the field is dominated becomes an important question. Space, like music, can be a source of elemental joy, something to which one can give up oneself entirely.

One's experience of time is another important issue. In the case of Hillside Terrace, time is represented by changes in the consciousness of the architect. The changes are acknowledged and put to use in the design. That is, time is clearly a parameter of design. Moreover, the collective form can include works by another architect. I have previously written in an essay on Hillside Terrace on the participation of Makoto Motokura, who designed the fourth phase. The buildings constructed in three earlier phases have a common thread and are related to one another, but his design introduces something new into the equation. I believe in the value of such an intervention. Groups of buildings generated in such a way may be the most desirable kind of collective form in a city.

Approaches to collective form: compositional form, megaform, group form, respectively

# COLLECTIVE FORM—THREE PARADIGMS

## Beginning

There is no more concerned observer of our changing society than the urban designer. Charged with giving form—with perceiving and contributing order—to agglomerates of building, highways, and green spaces in which men and women have increasingly come to work and live, they stand between technology and human need and seek to make the first a servant, for the second must be paramount in a civilized world.

For the moment, we are designers only, interested in technology and order insofar as these may be divorced from the political and the economic. Of course, the progenitors of any formal idea include politics and economics. The reason, in fact, for searching for new formal concepts in contemporary cities lies in the magnitude of relatively recent changes in urban problems. Our urban society is characterized by (1) coexistence and conflict of amazingly heterogeneous institutions and individuals, (2) unprecedented rapid and extensive transformations in the physical structure of society, (3) rapid communications methods, and (4) technological progress and its impact upon regional culture.

The force of these contemporary urban characteristics makes it impossible to visualize urban form as did Roman military chiefs, or Renaissance architects such as Sangallo and Michelangelo. Nor can we easily perceive a hierarchical order as did the original CIAM theorists in the quite recent past. We must now see our urban society as a dynamic field of interrelated forces. It is a set of mutually independent variables in a rapidly expanding infinite series. Any order introduced within the pattern of forces contributes to a state of dynamic equilibrium—an equilibrium that will change in character as time passes.

Our concern here is not the "master plan" but the "master program," since the latter term includes a time dimension. Given a set of goals the "master program" suggests several alternatives for achieving them, the use of one or another of which is decided by the passage of time and its effect on the ordering concept. As a physical correlation of the master program, there are "master forms" that differ from buildings in that they, too, respond to the dictates of time.

Our problem is this: do we have in urban design an adequate spatial language (an appropriate master form) with which we can create and organize space within the master program? Cities today tend to be visually and physically confused. They are monotonous patterns of static elements. They lack visual and physical character consonant with the functions and technology that compose them. They also lack elasticity and flexibility. Our cities must change as social and economic use dictate, and yet they must not be "temporary" in the worst visual sense. We lack an adequate visual language to cope with the superhuman scale of modern highway systems and with views from airplanes. The visual and physical concepts at our disposal have to do with single buildings, and with closed the compositional means for organizing them.

The wealth of our architectural heritage is immense. One cursory look at architectural history is sufficient to find that the whole development is characterized by an immense human desire to make buildings grand and perfect. True, they have often mirrored the strengths of their civilizations. They have produced the pyramids, the Parthenon, Gothic cathedrals, and the Seagram Building. This is still a prevailing attitude among many architects—the creation of something new and splendid in order to outdo others.

A theory of architecture has evolved through this one issue as to how one can create perfect single buildings. A striking fact against this phenomenon is that there is almost a complete absence of any coherent theory beyond that of single buildings. We have so long accustomed ourselves to conceiving of buildings as separate entities that we now suffer from an inadequacy of spatial language to make meaningful environments. This situation has prompted me to investigate the nature of "collective form." Collective form concerns groups of buildings and quasi buildings—the segments of our cities. Collective form is, however, not a collection of unrelated, separate buildings, but of buildings that have reasons to be together.

Cities, towns, and villages throughout the world do not lack in rich collections of collective form. Most of them have simply evolved; they have not been designed. This explains why today so many professionals, both architects and planners, often fail to make meaningful collective forms—meaningful to give the forms a forceful *raison d'être* in our society.

The following analysis has evolved through two questions: first, how collective form has been developed in history; and second, what are its possible implications for our current thinking in architecture and urban design.

The investigation of collective form is extensive, but promising. The first step is to analyze structural principles involved in making collective form. I have established three major approaches.

| | |
|---|---|
| Compositional Form | Compositional Approach |
| Megastructure/Megaform | Structural Approach |
| Group Form | Sequential Approach |

The first of these, the compositional approach, is a historical one. The second two are new, and are efforts toward finding master forms which satisfy the demands of contemporary urban growth and change.

Compositional form: Brasilia, Oscar Niemeyer

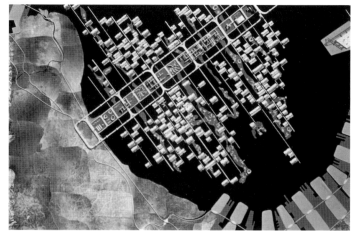

Megaform: a community for 25,000 people, Kenzo Tange

## Compositional Form

The compositional approach is a commonly accepted and practiced concept in the past and at present. The elements that comprise a collective form are conceived and determined separately. In other words, they are often individually tailored buildings. Proper functional, visual, and spatial (sometimes symbolic) relationships are established on a two-dimensional plane.

It is no surprise that this is the most understandable and used technique for architects in making collective form, because the process resembles one of making a building out of given components. It is a natural extension of the architectural approach. It is a static approach because the act of making a composition itself has a tendency to complete a formal statement.

Most contemporary large-scale urban designs fall into this category. Rockefeller Center, Chandigarh Government Center, and Brasilia are good examples of compositional urban design. The compositional approach is a familiar one, and it has received some treatment in works on architecture and planning. We will, therefore, let it stand on its own merit and introduce two less well-known approaches.

## The Megastructure

The megastructure is a large frame in which all the functions of a city or part of a city are housed. It has been made possible by present-day technology. In a sense, it is a human-made feature of the landscape. It is like the great hill on which Italian towns were built. Inherent in the megastructure concept, along with a certain static nature, is the suggestion that many and diverse functions may be beneficially concentrated in one place. A large frame implies some utility in combination and concentration of functions.

Urban designers are attracted to the megastructure concept because it offers a legitimate way to order massive grouped functions. One need only look at work in a recent Museum of Modern Art show on "Visionary Architecture" to sense the excitement generated among designers by megaform. While some of the ideas displayed in the show demonstrate virtuosity at the expense of human scale and human functional needs, others have a quality which suggests no divergence between compacted economic function and human use.

That utility is sometimes only apparent. We frequently confuse the potential that technology offers with a compulsion to "use it fully." Technological possibility can be useful only when it is a tool of civilized persons. Inhuman use of technological advance is all too frequently our curse. Optimum productivity does not even depend on mere concentration of activities and workers.

Paul Goodman says in *Communitas:*

We could centralize or decentralize, concentrate population or scatter it.... If we want to continue the trend away from the country, we can do it; but if we want to combine town and country values in an agri-industrial way of life, we can do that.... It is just this relaxing of necessity, this extraordinary flexibility and freedom of choice of our techniques that is baffling and frightening to people.... Technology is a sacred cow left strictly to (unknown) experts, as if the form of the industrial machine did not profoundly affect every person.... They think that it is more efficient to centralize, whereas it is usually more inefficient.[1]

Technology must not dictate choices to us in our cities. We must learn to select modes of action from among the possibilities technology presents in physical planning.

One of the most interesting developments of the megaform was done by Professor Kenzo Tange with M. I. T. graduate students when he was a visiting professor there. In a series of three articles in the September 1960 issue of *Japan Architect* Tange presented a proposal for a mass human scale form that includes a megaform and discrete, rapidly changeable functional units which fit within the larger framework.

Short-lived items are becoming more and more short-lived, and the cycle of change is shrinking at a corresponding rate. On the other hand, the accumulation of capital has made it possible to build in large-scale operations. Reformations of natural topography, dams, harbors, and highways are of a size and scope that involve long cycles of time, and these are the man-made works that tend to divide the overall system of the age. The two tendencies—toward shorter cycles and toward longer cycles—are both necessary to modern life and to humanity itself.[2]

Tange's megaform concept depends largely on the idea that change will occur less rapidly in some areas than it will in others, and that the designer will be able to ascertain which of the functions he is dealing with falls in the longer cycle of change and which in the shorter. The question is, can the designer successfully base his concept on the idea that, to give an example, transportation methods will change less rapidly than the idea of a desirable residence or retail outlet? Sometimes the impact and momentum of technology become so great that a change occurs in the basic skeleton of the social and physical structure. It is difficult to predict into which part of a pond a stone will be thrown and which way its ripples will spread. If the megaform becomes rapidly obsolete, as well it might, it will be a great weight about the neck of urban society.

Group form: a Greek village

Japanese linear village: a beautifully articulated spine of growth. Each of the units that is repeated along the street has similar elements: a large communal entry, house, courtyard, and fields. This kind of village is universal and frequently seen in the East.

On the other hand, the ideal is not a system in which the physical structure of the city is at the mercy of unpredictable change. The ideal is a kind of master form which can move into ever new states of equilibrium and yet maintain visual consistency and a sense of continuing order in the long run. This suggests that the megastructure composed of several independent systems that can expand or contract with the least disturbance to the others would be preferable to the one composed of a rigid hierarchical system. In other words, each system that contributes to the whole maintains its identity and longevity without being affected by the others, while at the same time engages in dynamic contact with the others. When an optimal relationship has been formed, an environmental control system can be made. The system that permits the greatest efficiency and flexibility with the smallest organizational structure is ideal. A basic operation is necessary to establish this optimal control mechanism. It is to select proper independent functional systems and to give them optimal interdependency through the provision of physical joints at critical points.

Although the megastructure concept has its problems as outlined above, it also has great promise for several fields:

1. *Environmental engineering.* Megastructure development necessitates collaboration between structural and civil engineers. Possibilities for large spans, space frames, light skin structures, prestressed concrete, highway aesthetics, and earth forming will be developed far beyond their present level. Large-scale climate control will be studied further. A new type of physical structure, environmental building, will emerge.

2. *Multifunctional structures.* We have, thus far, taken it for granted that a building is designed to fulfill one specific purpose. In spite of the fact that the concept of multifunctionalism must be approached with caution, it does offer useful possibilities. Within the megaform structure we can realize combinations such as those in Kisho Kurokawa's project, Agricultural City.

3. *Infrastructure as public investment.* Substantial public investment can be made in infrastructures (the skeleton of megastructures) in order to guide and stimulate public structures around them. This strategy can be further extended to a new three-dimensional concept of land use where public agencies will maintain the ownership and upkeep for both horizontal and vertical circulation systems.

## Group Form

Group form is the last of the three approaches in collective form. It is form that evolves from a system of generative elements in space. Some of the basic ideas of group form can be recognized in historical examples of

town buildings. Urban designers and architects have recently become interested in them because they appear to be useful and suggest examples for making large-scale forms. Medieval cities in Europe, towns on Greek islands, and villages in North Africa are a few examples. The spatial and massing quality of these towns is worth consideration.

Factors which determine the spatial organization of these towns are:

1. Consistent use of basic materials and construction methods as well as spontaneous but minor variations in physical expression;

2. Wise and often dramatic use of geography and topography;

3. Human scale preserved throughout the town (frequently in contrast to superhuman land forms); and

4. Sequential development of basic elements such as dwellings, open spaces between houses, and the repetitive use of visual elements such as walls, gates, towers, open water, and so forth. The idea of sequential development has recently been explicated by Professor Roger Montgomery of Washington University who sees a series of buildings or elements without apparent beginning or end as a contemporary compositional "theme" distinct from the closed composition of forms characterizing classical or axial "themes."

The sequential form, as seen in historical examples, developed over a period of time much longer than that in which contemporary cities have been built and rebuilt. In this sense, then, the efforts of contemporary urban designers are quite different from their historical counterparts, and the forms which they consciously evolve in a short time span must accordingly differ. The lesson is, however, a useful one. A further inquiry of the basic elements and particularly of the relationship between the elements and groups reveals interesting principles involved in making collective form.

In the past many Japanese villages developed along major country roads (as illustrated above). Houses are generally U-shaped and juxtaposed against one another perpendicular to the road (they are basically court-type row houses). The front part of the house is two stories high, and forms a tight continuous village facade together with other units. Behind it is an enclosed yard used for domestic work, drying crops, making straw, etc. A barn is located at the other end of the house, and faces an open country field. There exists unquestionably a clear structural relationship between the village and the houses, between village activities and individual family life, and between the movement of villagers and cows. Here the house unit is the generator of the village form, and vice versa. A unit can be added without changing the basic structure of the village. The depth and frontage of the unit, or the size of the court or barn, may differ from unit to unit. But there prevails an understanding of basic structural principles in making the village.

Another example is Dutch housing of the sixteenth century. The Dutch have a reputation for living in communal units. Volunteer cooperation has long existed by limiting their personal liberty through common obedience to self-made laws. Their houses reflect this spirit. Steen Eiler Rasmussen in his *Towns and Buildings* describes

> A stone-walled canal with building blocks above it on each side, covered with houses built closely together and separated from the canal by cobbled roadways. The narrow, gabled ends of the houses face the canal and behind the deep houses are gardens.... Outside the houses is a special area called, in Amsterdam, the "stoep", which is partly a pavement and partly a sort of threshold of the house.[3]

The *stoep* is actually part of the house, and the owner takes immense pride in maintaining it. It is also a social place where neighbors exchange gossip and children play. By raising the ground floor of the house, it gives privacy to the residence even with large glass panes in front, and also reduces the load on pilings under the house. There is again a unity between canals and trees, paved roadways and *stoeps*, and large glass windows and rear gardens. A set of relationships has emerged through long experience and the wisdom of the people.

Forms in group form have their own built-in links, whether expressed or latent, so that they may grow within the system. They define basic environmental space which also partakes of the quality of systematic linkage. Group form and its space are indeed prototype elements, and they are prototypes because of the implied system and linkage. The elements and growth patterns are reciprocal—both in design and in operation. The elements suggest a manner of growth, and that in turn demands further development of the elements in a kind of feedback process.

On the other hand, the elements in megaform do not exist without a skeleton. The skeleton guides growth and the elements depend on it. The elements of group form are often the essence of collectivity, a unifying force, functionally, socially, and spatially. It is worth noting that group form generally evolves from society rather than from powerful leadership. It is the village, the dwelling group, and the bazaar that are group forms in the sense we are using this term, and not the palace complex which is compositional in character.

Can we, then, create meaningful group forms in our society? The answer is not a simple one. It requires new concepts and attitudes of design. It also requires the participation of cities and their social institutions.

Remarks by two modern architects cast light on this definition of group form. The distinction between form and design was made by Louis Kahn in a speech at the World Design Conference in Tokyo in 1960. Kahn said on that occasion, "There is a need to distinguish 'form' from 'design.' Form implies what a building, whether it be a church, school, or house, would like to be, whereas the design is the circumstantial act evolving from this basic form, depending on site condition, budget limitation or client's idea, etc."[4] As soon as form is invented, it becomes the property of society. One might almost say that it was the property of society before its discovery. A design, on the other hand, belongs to its designer.

John Voelcker, in his CIAM Team X report, comments on a similar subject. Referring to Oscar Hansen's and Jerzy Soltan's work in Poland, he said, "In an open aesthetics, form is a master key not of any aesthetic significance in itself, though capable of reciprocating the constant change of life.... Open aesthetic is the living extension of functionalism."[5]

Both Kahn's "form" and Voelcker's "open aesthetic" describe a form that would be a catalyst that may become many forms rather than just a form for its own sake. Whereas they are speaking of it in an architectural idiom, we are interested in examining the form in a much larger context—collectivity in our physical environment. Nonetheless, both statements are significant in assuming that such a form can be created by architects today.

It is relatively easy for someone to invent a geometric form and call it a group form because such a form has the characteristic of being multiplied in a sequential manner. But this is meaningless unless the form derives from environmental needs. Geometry is only a tool of search for group form. One cannot seek group form in hexagons and circles. James Stirling, in his article "Regionalism and Modern Architecture" in *Architects' Year Book* 8, says:

> The application of orthogonal proportion and the obvious use of basic geometrical elements appears to be diminishing, and instead something of the variability found in nature is attempted. "Dynamic cellularism" is an architecture comprising several elements, repetitive or varied. The assemblage of units is more akin to patterns of crystal formations or biological divisions than to the static rigidity of a structural grid. The form of assemblage is in contrast to the definitive architecture and the containing periphery of, for example, a building such as the Unité.[6]

One finds the source of generative elements in dynamic human terms such as "gathering," "dispersal," or "stop." The human quality which determines form has to do with way of life, movement, and the relation of persons in society. If the function of urban design is the pattern of human activities expressed in city life, then the functional patterns are crystallized activity patterns. Le Corbusier limits generative human qualities to "air," "green," and "sun," while exponents of group form find a myriad of suggestive activities to add to that list.

The visual implications of such crystallized patterns of human activity become apparent. The way in which one activity changes to another as people move from work to shopping to dining suggests physical qualities that are used to express transformation in design rhythm, change, and contrast. Characteristic spaces may be named in accordance with the way in which human groups use them, that is, transitional space, inward space, outward space, etc. The addition of activities to physical qualities in a search for form determinants in the city suggests a new union between physical design and planning. The investigation of group form inevitably leads us to giving our attention to regionalism in collective scale.

Until recently our understanding of regional expressions had very much been confined to that of single buildings. But in an age of mass communication and technological facility, regional differences throughout the world are becoming less well-defined, and it is less easy to find distinctive expressions in building techniques and resultant forms.

If materials and methods of construction or modes of transportation are becoming ubiquitous, perhaps their combinations, especially in large urban complexes, now reflect the distinguishing characteristics of the people and the places in which they are structured and used according to value hierarchies. Thus it may be possible to find regionalism more in collective scale and less in single buildings. The primary regional character in urban landscape will probably be in the grain of the city. Both group form and megaform affect the urban milieu at precisely this level.

Homogenization of environment is not, as many people feel, the inevitable result of mass technology and communication. These very forces can produce entirely new products. With modern communication systems, one element (cultural product) is soon transmitted to other regions, and vice versa. While each region uses a set of similar elements, each region can express its own characteristics in certain combinations of these elements. Here regionalism arises not only from indigenous elements or products, but rather from the manner in which such elements are valued and expressed. This suggests a concept of open regionalism, which is in itself a dynamic process of selecting and integrating vital forces. However, these forces may conflict with inherent cultural values. Thus the genuine strength of different cultures can be tested and measured in this light. This is the thesis initially developed in collaboration Roger Montgomery.

In group form the possibility for creating grain elements, or regional qualities, exists. The reciprocal relation between the generative elements and the system can produce strongly regional effects. In megaform it is a large form that represents all the power of technique, and that may represent the best aspects of regional selectivity. In coming decades the investigation of regional expression in collective scale will be one of the most important and fascinating issues of architecture and planning.

Finally, these three approaches are models for thinking about possible ways to conceive large, complex forms. It is likely that in any final design form these three concepts could be combined or mixed.

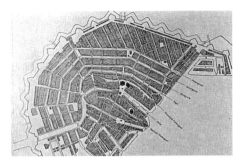

Nineteenth-century Amsterdam: canals flow between the buildings, establishing a pattern of movement and thus unifying the whole town in a way similar to Venice.

Orphanage, Amsterdam (Aldo van Eyck): the plan provides a place for every kind of activity and gentle transitions from one to another. An internal street has spaces along it to be used for gathering. The "street" gradually becomes more private, until each child has his or her own place to sleep and a cabinet for clothes and toys.

## LINKAGE IN COLLECTIVE FORM
written in collaboration with Jerry Goldberg

### Introduction

Investigation of collective form is important because it forces us to reexamine the entire theory and vocabulary of architecture, principally that of single buildings. For instance, the components of collective form, as conceived here, differ from the traditional elements of single structures.

1. *Wall:* any element that separates and modulates space horizontally. Walls are places where outward and inward forces interact, and the manner of the interactions defines the form and functions of the wall.

2. *Floor or roof:* any element that separates and modulates space vertically. In a broad sense, these terms include underground, ground, and water surfaces, and even elements floating in the air.

3. *Column:* architecturally a supporter of gravitational loads, but environmentally an element that transfers certain functions—people, goods, and other things.

4. *Unit:* a primary space in which some of the basics functions of human existence and society are contained and occur.

5. *Link:* "linking" and "dissolving linkage" are invariant activities in making collective form out of either discrete or associate elements. In operational terms there are a number of linkages—physically connected link, implying link, built-in link, and so forth.

Collective form also requires a new dimension in conceiving construction methods and structural and mechanical systems. The aesthetics of collective form necessitate new definitions of scale and proportion of buildings.

Above all, this entire essay questions the very act of design in our society; it contains no answers, but seeks to ask the right questions and to draw out further discussion.

### The Unity of Experience

Observation is the primary tool of the urban designer. What he sees in the city he can relate to his own experience. Fact and observer are combined to comprehend new problems and create new three-dimensional solutions. The whole group of articles on collective form is a means of ordering observation. What the categories of analysis are is not of great importance. They provide a framework within which we can present extremely important observable phenomena in cities. Only through seeing accurately can we locate the specific results of forces in the city—forces that sociologists, economists, and novelists have described in other terms.

We are fond of observing that our urban world is a complex one, that it changes with a rapidity beyond actual comprehension, and, finally, that it is a disjointed world. At times in our urban lives we relish the diversity and disjointedness of cities, and bask in the variety of them. Certainly cities have been the locus of humankind's most creative moments because of the varied experience they afford us.

But when a plethora of stimuli begins to divert us from receptive consciousness, the city renders us insensible. Then, in our inability to order experience, we merely suffer the city and long for some adequate means to comprehend it as a product of human creation—a product of intelligent, ordering forces. As the scientist is frustrated when the order or pattern of phenomena is too fleeting to observe or too complex to recognize with existing tools, so is the city dweller frustrated when human order cannot be found in the environment. At such moments when one sees only the results of mechanical and economic processes controlling the form and feeling of place, one feels estranged and excluded.

If urban design is to fulfill its role in making a contribution to the form of the city, it must do more than simply organize mechanical forces and make physical unity out of diversity. It must recognize the meaning of the order it seeks to manufacture: a humanly significant spatial order.

### Introduction to Linkage

Urban design is always concerned with the question of making comprehensible links between discrete things. Further, it is concerned with making an extremely large entity comprehensible by articulating its parts. The city is made of combinations of discrete forms and articulated large forms. It is a collective form—an agglomeration of past decisions (and abnegations of decisions) concerning the way in which things fit together or are linked. Linking and disclosing linkage (articulating the large entity) are integral activities in making collective form.

With regard to historical examples of collective form, we should refer to the work of Aldo van Eyck. He finds in vernacular building a substantial clue to the natural process of human association in urban situations. Vernacular unit and link evolve together and appear at the end as a perfectly coordinated physical entity—a village or town. But one need not go to completely vernacular situations to discover examples of a similar character. Builders of the cities we admire—that we sense are good environments—have generally been generations of men and women working over decades, even centuries. We perceive what they have done in our lim-

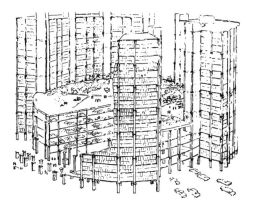

Gateway interchanges (Louis Kahn): the garage is a mediator between automobile and pedestrian movement, a symbol of arrival.

Plan for new city at Toulouse, France (Candellis and Woods): the constructed form serves as a continual three-dimensional link.

ited span of study. More importantly, we must build in our own environment in an abbreviated time.

One thing is certain: we have spent too little time observing the successes of our predecessors with an acute eye. Further, we probably do not approach particular parts of our cities with sufficient understanding to extrapolate what is useful, in human terms, from them. It is one thing to grunt ecstatically in the presence of a significant work. It is another to learn what it can offer for the future.

The specific subject of scrutiny here is linkage—in particular, the act of making linkage. In what follows, the business of putting things together is studied in detailed fashion. First, there are examples of historical linkage. Each place and each moment has had its characteristic way of making coherent physical form. We are interested in how and why particular links were used. In the end as designers we are concerned with making collective form. The examples that follow have been discovered in a framework of operational definitions. Looking at these examples, we must ask ourselves what the act of making a particular juncture among elements was, and how, theoretically, that act can be reproduced. This loosely operational framework is useful for purposes of analysis, but it does work for an entire survey of material.

It is perhaps a mistake to insulate types of links from one another by categorizing them. The activity we are discussing is, after all, a singular one—that of making a comprehensible and humanly evocative urban environment. It is one of the primary theses of this study that once a link is established for any reason, it takes on a complicated secondary system of meanings and uses. Consider the *stoep* in Amsterdam or Bologna's arcades. One can see the medieval street bridges over the Via Ritorta in Perugia as an example of a link that began as a simple means for reinforcing structurally weak walls. The bridges, which connect two buildings at the second-floor level, also serve to define "overhead" in the street and to reinforce the street spatially as a passageway. The bridges have all of these functions because they are repetitive along the street. It is no longer important which is the primary linkage and which the secondary.

What does this study of historical linkage suggest for the future? Certainly this—whatever we use to determine the form of urban linkage in urban design must come from a body of largely untapped information about cities as we know them. We are involved in an investigation of the morphological results of forces now present in cities. And this too is certain: the primary motive is to make unity from diversity. There is diversity in every unit of sufficient scale to admit more than one function, or one angle of vision.

That we have not previously adequately identified form-giving forces is perhaps due to the fact that they seem to defy formulation. At a particular scale of urban activity, they have more to do with movement through

space than with a standard vision of the shape of a space. Thus we have been notably remiss in our ability to conceive of shapes for paths of high-speed movement or commercial clusters or power lines. Each of these things seems to defy relation to a human collective scale—their functional and social aspects seem diametrically opposed. Yet the Romans succeeded in making enduring aqueducts and in the United States TVA dams integrate functional and symbolic characteristics.

If a garage can serve as an architectural stop between the moving world of a highway and the static world of a town center or shopping area, it can, if handled as Louis Kahn suggests, become a symbol of the collective and human aspect of what occurs in the town or the shops. Garages (or rapid transit stations) can be conceived as stops, as links between the highway (or train) and pedestrian movement. If designed with sufficient understanding, each can serve as a defining wall, or perhaps a built mountain, for the activity each links to the world of the highway.

Another thing that seems destined for future consideration is the realization of a wholly new concept of three-dimensional linkage. If we are successful at making unified and meaningful complexes of form and activity near the ground, we are notably unsuccessful in going into the air with linked functions. A high-rise tower (either for apartments or offices) provides us with little integrated experience of its form or of the excitement of rising through its many layers. Somehow, each deck of a tower or slab must be transparent to us, and each level of activity must be unique. Then, and only then, will we sense three-dimensional linkage. This type of linkage is necessary because we have to construct more high buildings as land in our cities becomes scarcer. And this is possible because of our building techniques and our love of communication. Antonio Sant'Elia gave some indication of what three-dimensional linkage might look like as early as 1913.

If we must learn to make use of our knowledge of short-range movement, movement through cities from point to point, we must also attach a more subtle time concept, one that deals with the constant cycle of decay in cities. An urban dwelling lasts 84 years on the average. If we allow all the old dwellings in a given area to become unsuitable for use at the same time, we are forced to declare extensive blight, clear hundreds of acres, and build new housing. There is, then, no link between such a cleared and renewed area and the city around it. People who, by choice or by force of economic circumstances, move into such developments feel isolation so keenly that they do not regard themselves as anything but "project" people. There is nothing less productive of cosmopolitan mixture, than raw renewal, that displaces, destroys, and replaces in such a mechanical way.

The cycle of decay can be a linking force in our cities. If recognized, it can provide an opportunity to replace old structures in an old environment with new structures, still in an old environment. Such diversity in

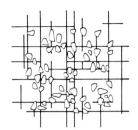

Mediation: connection with intermediate elements or implying medium (including composed open space)

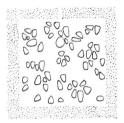

Definition: enclosing disparate structures with a sensible barrier; producing unity within the barrier and separating from what is outside

Repetition: giving each element a feature that is common to all in the group so that each is identifiable as a part of the same order

Sequential Path: placing activities that are performed in sequence in identifiable spatial relation to one another

age is itself a kind of linkage. It gives morphological demonstration of the ever-changing and diverse character of city life. It offers a new kind of choice to people in cities—the possibility that one can live in a historically significant place, but in a new house.

Our cities are fluid and mobile. But it is difficult to conceive of some of them as places, in the real sense of that word. How can an entity with no discernible beginning or end be a place? It is certainly more appropriate to think of a particular part of a city as a place. If it were possible to articulate each of the parts of the city more adequately, to give qualities of edge and node to now formless agglomerates, we would begin to make our large urban complexes at least understandable, if not ones with "image."

By the same argument, the rapidity with which the urban system expands suggests that there must be some means for linking newly established parts with parts not yet conceived. In short, there is a need for something that may be termed "open linkage." Such an idea is inherent in the linkage of group form. Links become integral parts of both unit and system, and suggest that the system can be expanded indefinitely and with variation.

### The City as Pattern of Events

Linkage is simply the glue of the city. It is the act by which we unite all the layers of activity and resulting physical form in the city. Insofar as linkage is successful, the city is a recognizable and humanly comprehensible entity. We are at home in it. We depend on understanding how events in a city are combined to make a living sequence, and we depend on understanding how we can get from place to place in the city. Each at its own level contributes to our ability to know and enjoy experience—social, temporal, and spatial linkage.

All of these kinds of linkage are described in physical terms in the analysis that follows. It is necessary to describe linkage in operational terms, to say what must be done to make a link. But each operation ends by suggesting a multitude of nonspatial facts. Ultimately, linking is assembling patterns of experience in cities.

### Operational Categories

There are five basic linking operations: to mediate, to define, to repeat, to make a sequential path, and to select. All of these terms need explanation using diagrams as well as text and presenting examples of each type of linkage as evidence that each exists or could exist. Keep in mind that each type of linkage may be done in physical fact (as a wall or bridge between two buildings) or by implication (as in the carefully balanced composition of buildings and spaces on a site). Physical links may be introduced into form as external elements, and the designer thus produces an a–a–a–a or

a–b–c–d pattern. On the other hand, they may appear as built-in links. That is of particular consequence in group form. There, integral link and unit are the basis of formal, functional, and structural results. Repetition and combination occur in accordance with the logic of the built-in link.

Implied links are those used to compose elements in the landscape. Using either quasi-mathematical standards, as in Italian Renaissance composition, or subjectively seeking combinations of void and solid that seem "right," designers produce (hopefully) compelling combinations. Space is an adhesive in compositional design. A paragon of this kind of composition should appear inevitable to all observers. (The question of inevitability does not arise in most cases of contemporary group form. Combinations of linkage and element can do no better than to express the process from which their growth in combination has come.) All the ways of implying linkage—by composing, by injecting transitional elements, by surrounding disparate things—depend largely on some kind of homogeneity. If elements in large-scale design are of the same order of magnitude (by virtue of mass, color, or surface quality), they become a "grain" or a texture. Elements of vastly different size are linked by implication only with difficulty. Transitional bits, or unifying surroundings, are frequently injected between them to make the implication strong and clear.

*To mediate:* to connect with intermediate elements or imply connection by spaces that demonstrate the cohesion of masses around them. An interesting thing about mediation is that once done, it is almost impossible for an observer to assign a single cause for it. Mediation accomplished by adequate physical means connotes multitudes of other transitions. It suggests that a link, properly conceived, changes with changing primary needs. The arcades of Bologna, for example, provide shelter from sun and rain and visual unity to the street.

Steen Eiler Rasmussen, in his article "The Dutch Contribution," says that the *stoep* is a place that is half house property, half public way. "The house itself cannot be built on it, but it may be used for the basement entrance or for steps up to the high ground floor. The steps are often quite monumental, carried out in blue-beige stone.... When not used to accommodate stairs or other projections, the stoep is raised a step above the road and covered with tiles or fine stonework."[7]

The *stoep* is a functional transition between the public way and the private house. It is conceptually the meeting of the family with the urban world, and it is visually a means by which one sees the streetscape as an entity. From house to street, it is a link by mediation, and from house to house along the street it is a link by repetition.

*To define:* to surround a site with a wall or any other physical barrier and thus set it off from its environs. The wall around a medieval town says that

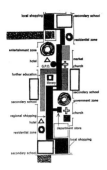

Hook New Town Center (London County Council): commercial, civic, and religious institutions are developed as mutually complementary activities. The town center is linked by the movement of people.

Plan of Miletus (attributed to Hippodamus): a town defined by the limits of the peninsula on which it stands.

Cittadella, Italy: Defense was the primary motivation for building walls around this medieval town, but they also unite the town by visually enclosing it.

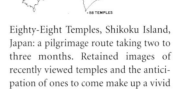

Eighty-Eight Temples, Shikoku Island, Japan: a pilgrimage route taking two to three months. Retained images of recently viewed temples and the anticipation of ones to come make up a vivid sequential path.

Montagnana, Italy: again defense is a primary reason for the selection of hillside site for the town.

all inside it belongs and is different from all outside. Putting a wall around elements implies a visual connection among them, even though they have nothing in common.

A wall may be many things, such as a loop of rapid transit tracks in the heart of Chicago, or a ring of parking structures in Louis Kahn's proposal for Philadelphia. Depending on its nature and location, a wall may be either oppressive and confining or pleasantly protective. Walls in African villages on the plains are a welcome relief from the endless vistas that otherwise occupy the inhabitants' gazes.

*To repeat:* to link by introducing one common factor in each of the dispersed parts of a design or existing situation. That common factor may be formal, material, functional, or historical.

Perhaps the best understood example of this kind of link occurs in Italian hill towns which may be identified by the hundreds of private defensive towers standing above the house tops. A more subtle example of repetition as a linking device is in what Kevin Lynch has called the "grain." If the plan of an urban place reveals clusters of buildings which have spaces between them of a common size and shape, we see such a cluster as just that—a cluster of elements relating to one another in a way different from the way those of other buildings in the vicinity do. They are an identifiable group in plan because they have a peculiar grain or pattern. On the ground one perceives the same unity because of the repetitive size of building and size of space between the masses of buildings. The only difference between this situation and the compositional means of linking by implication is that this repetition need not be a case of intent. Grain occurs in the historic buildup of an area because the use of the buildings is similar, the style of building in a given time is similar, and the amount of space deemed adequate between them is similar.

*To make a sequential path:* to arrange buildings or parts of multiuse buildings in a sequence of useful activity. Further, to reinforce such a path by any means necessary to propel persons along a general designated path. Finally, to design a path or reinforce a path in the natural landscape which will catalyze and give direction to new development along its course.

Designers make sequences of functions on paper, connect them with arrows, and establish the logic of the flow diagram. In some cases the three-dimensional realization of that diagram is a building in which each symbol has become a room and the arrows doors. The case we are interested in, however, is one in which each symbol is a place of the scale of a building. The arrows then become three-dimensional paths between buildings or progressions through the megaframe that contains quasi buildings. A large multifunctional structure may be described as a frame that contains many discrete quasi buildings (or monofunctional struc-

tures) and a transportation system for going from one function to another within the frame. Such a symbiotic entity is an example of a three-dimensional activity sequence.

The temporal sequence sometimes becomes so long that it overwhelms the visual aspects of an activity path. A two- or three-month temple pilgrimage on Shikoku Island can be seen as a kind of activity sequence—it is a linked experience. The after image of some 88 temples and rituals is a demonstrable residue of the activity.

*To select:* to establish unity in advance of the design process by choice of site. The designer may preselect a link for a large-scale project. That is, he may choose a piece of land for a town (or an element in the town) prominent enough so that it will both affect his design and be a unifying visual force when the project is built. Obvious examples of this kind of situation exist in towns like Miletus and Priene in Turkey. We frequently identify an area in a larger context by referring to some overriding topographical feature—such as at Russian Hill in San Francisco. Unfortunately, designers infrequently utilize the formal potential of land in contemporary America.

## Notes

1. Percival Goodman and Paul Goodman, *Communitas: Means of Livelihood and Ways of Life* (Chicago: University of Chicago Press, 1947), 2–3.

2. Kenzo Tange, "Kenchiku to Toshi ni Tsuite" (Regarding Architecture and the City), *Japan Architect* (September 1960): 51–63.

3. Steen Eiler Rasmussen, *Towns and Buildings* (Cambridge, MA: MIT Press, 1951), 81.

4. Louis Kahn, speech on the occasion of the World Design Conference, Tokyo, 1960.

5. John Voelcker, *CIAM Team X Report.*

6. James Stirling, "Regionalism and Modern Architecture," *Architects' Year Book* 8 (New York: Philosophical Library, 1957), 65.

7. Rasmussen, *Towns and Buildings*, 92.

# KEIO UNIVERSITY SHONAN FUJISAWA CAMPUS

Fujisawa, Kanagawa 1990–94

Entrance facade of central campus

Guardhouse at north campus entrance

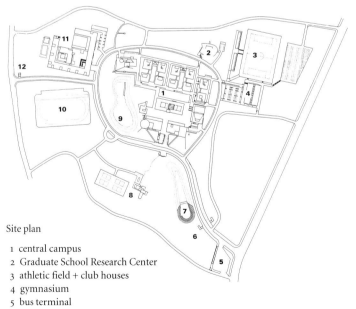

Site plan

1 central campus
2 Graduate School Research Center
3 athletic field + club houses
4 gymnasium
5 bus terminal
6 north guardhouse
7 outdoor theater
8 seminar house + tennis courts
9 pond
10 high school athletic field
11 middle & high school
12 south guardhouse

*Facing page:* Administration building arcade with media center beyond

*Right:* View from media center courtyard to esplanade stair

*Below:* Passage between media center and classroom buildings

*Below right:* Axonometric of central campus

1  administration building
2  main lecture hall
3  media center
4  student lounge
5  auditorium
6  lecture room buildings
7  research offices
8  student center

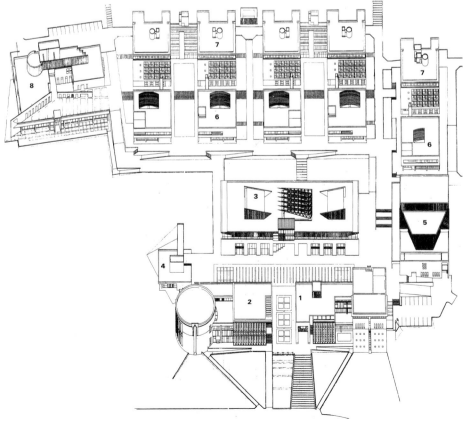

The grassy banks of a retaining pond on the south side of campus provide an informal outdoor space for studying and social activity.

In the late 1980s Keio University decided to establish in the Shonan district of Fujisawa, approximately 30 kilometers from Tokyo, a new campus centered around two new faculties: policy management and environmental information. For Japan's oldest private educational institution these new departments indicated a break from its traditional curriculum and a desire to reassess its educational philosophy, adjusting to what it perceived to be "the rapid and volatile nature of our times." The campus was constructed in four stages from 1990 to 1994, and at present there are in attendance about 4,000 undergraduate students, 200 graduate students, and 1,000 middle and high school students. Manifesting a new spirit of education in the information age, the Shonan Fujisawa Campus has already become the most celebrated institution of higher learning in postwar Japan.

The 30-hectare site is in a hilly area typical of the western part of the Tokyo metropolitan region. There are a number of gently sloping hills on the site, with a few evergreens interspersed on the *susuki* (Japanese pampas grass) covering the land. On clear days Mount Fuji is visible beyond the woods on the top of the hill to the west.

The site planning was initiated by establishing two domains: a center and a periphery. This was a way of giving the collection of buildings an identity, at the same time allowing the campus edge to merge gradually into the surrounding pastoral landscape. A loop road was constructed around a small rise in the middle of the site, thus defining a central domain within the loop and a peripheral domain without. By placing the central domain on visibly higher ground, we were not only consciously making reference to the hills of Mita and Hiyoshi campuses with which Keio University has been associated in the past, but also using the concept of visual domination to reinforce the notion of centrality.

The area enclosed by the loop measures 250 meters east to west and 330 meters north to south, and contained a pond and grove of trees which were preserved. The remaining area we divided into small domains of equal size by laying out a number of east-west and north-south axes. This approach corresponded to the university's request that facilities be dispersed as much as possible like houses in a village. By siting buildings along east-west and north-south axes, we were able to create

exterior spaces that are different in character, scale, and view. The architectural spaces of individual buildings were adapted to these exterior spaces, and glazed lobbies and circulation spaces were oriented toward exterior plazas to provide a high degree of spatial interpenetration.

There are two gates to the campus, one at the northern end and one at the southern, and by connecting the approaches from those gates to the loop road a network for pedestrian and vehicular circulation was created. At the point where visitors, having climbed a gently sloping road from the gatehouse, first reach the central hill within the loop road, the campus presents a strong frontal facade. Three buildings are arranged on the main approach as one walks up the hill: the main lecture hall and administration buildings, situated on either side of a terraced walkway, and the media center located beyond them. These three buildings define an elongated open space, which is the only plaza on campus, and at opposite ends of this space are the student center and the auditorium. This is the portion of the campus that is most formal from the point of view of composition.

Another distinctive exterior domain is the axial space created by the cluster of research and classroom buildings that extends north to south. At the south end is the terrace on top of the student center. Beyond the terrace can be seen the tall stair tower of the middle and high school complex (designed by architect Yoshio Taniguchi). In the intervals between lectures, this space fills with students, making it the most heavily trafficked area on campus.

A third domain is the area that includes the pond and woods. The terrace of the student center looks out on a grassy open space sloping down to the pond. One can sit on the terrace and gaze at the ducks swimming on the pond, engage in discussions with friends, or stretch out on the grass and read a book.

Outside the loop are the following facilities: a gymnasium, the university athletic field, the graduate research center, the middle and high schools associated with the university, a guest/seminar house located on top of another hill, and an outdoor theater. Each of the facilities on the periphery has been arranged to suit its own topographical context and, as is particularly the case with the graduate research center (pp. 110–119), designed as an architecturally independent entity.

*Above:* The seminar guest house sits on a separate hill facing the main campus and provides lodging and meeting space for visiting faculty and guests of the university.

*Facing page:* Passage between classroom and faculty office buildings

# ISAR BÜROPARK

Munich, Germany 1994
(in association with Schmidt-Schicketanz & Partner)

Isar Büropark juxtaposes a green landscape with a group of sleek glass surfaces reflecting the sky. The separate buildings are positioned to form a series of animated, semi-enclosed courtyards in a campus-type plan.

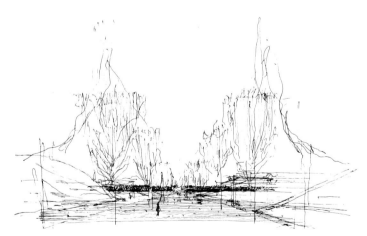

Sketch of tilting glass roof forms rising over an *allée* of trees. The Isar Forest is seen as a dark band on the horizon.

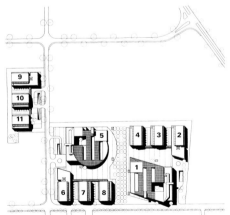

Site plan with numbered buildings

Landscape analysis drawings

**TERRAIN FORM**

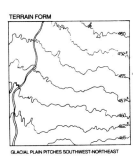

GLACIAL PLAIN PITCHES SOUTHWEST-NORTHEAST

**OLD SETTLEMENT**

19TH CENTURY SETTLEMENT REFLECTS THE TERRAIN FORM

**WATER FEATURE**

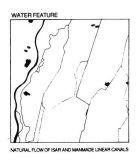

NATURAL FLOW OF ISAR AND MANMADE LINEAR CANALS

**EXISTING VEGETATION**

NATURAL FOREST OF ISAR AND MAN MADE LINEAR GREEN STRIPS

**NEW AIRPORT**

AIRPORT REVEALS THE MAJOR WIND DIRECTION AND NEW HI-SPEED TRAFFIC REFLECT ITS ORIENTATION

**NEW DEVELOPMENT**

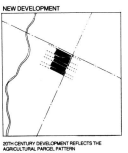

20TH CENTURY DEVELOPMENT REFLECTS THE AGRICULTURAL PARCEL PATTERN

**LAND PATTERN**

AGRICULTURAL PARCEL PATTERN PROTECTS AGAINST THE SURFACE WATER EROSION

**'ARMS OF ISAR'**

NEW OFFICE PARK WORKS AS A BRIDGE BETWEEN THE COMMUNITY AND ISAR FOREST

**POPURATION**

■ EXPANDED OFFICE PARK (THE WIDER DOMAIN OF THE COMPETITON)   40,000 PEOPLE
  20,000 PEOPLE
▨ EXISTING COMMUNITY   4,350 PEOPLE

**LAND USE AND INFRASTRUCTURE**

■ THE WIDER DOMAIN OF THE COMPETITION
■ EXPANDED OFFICE PARK
▨ PROPOSED BUFFER ZONE
— PROPOSED THOROUGHFARES

**PEDESTRIAN NETWORK**

**VEHICULAR NETWORK**

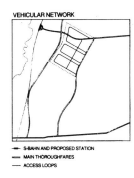

➤ S-BAHN AND PROPOSED STATION
═ MAIN THOROUGHFARES
— ACCESS LOOPS

**GREEN ZONE NETWORK**

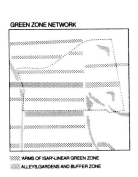

▨ 'ARMS OF ISAR'-LINEAR GREEN ZONE
▨ ALLEYS,GARDENS AND BUFFER ZONE

**PUBLIC FACILITIES**

SPORTS CLUB,HOTELS,FARM MARKET,EMPLOYEE CENTER,EXHIBITION CENTER AND FESTIVAL GROUND

**ATRIUMS AND GLASS CORRIDORS**

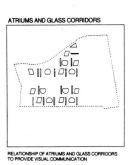

RELATIONSHIP OF ATRIUMS AND GLASS CORRIDORS TO PROVIDE VISUAL COMMUNICATION

**STREET SCAPE**

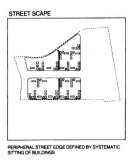

PERIPHERAL STREET EDGE DEFINED BY SYSTEMATIC SITTING OF BUILDINGS

Isar Büropark, our first project built in Europe, developed from a winning entry for an architecture and urban design competition dealing with the development of an office park district near Munich's new international airport. The design concept arose from a study of the landscape of the local area known as Hallbergmoos. By preserving and using to the fullest advantage the surrounding forests and meadows, a new type of working environment was created for high-technology industries, combining the exciting, urbane atmosphere of high-tech offices with more contemplative, leisurely, and rural qualities already in the site.

The site strategy was based on a study of relationships between land patterns and natural forces—whether this means the age-old layout of farming fields according to the slope of land and direction of watercourses or the inscription of airport runways according to the predominant winds. The grounds of the office park recollect the meadow ecology into which new interventions are introduced in juxtaposition—paving blocks, wooden boardwalks, crystalline office buildings whose roofs mirror the sky. Nearby Isar Forest is brought into the site by means of dense *allées* of maple trees crossing the complex. All of the office buildings are oriented toward these *allées*, and numerous footpaths offer alternative routes among offices, the town of Hallbergmoos, and the forest. The public areas of each building are oriented to face one another so as to increase visual communication and activate the park setting of the inner blocks.

The program provided for eleven office buildings divided into two types: two large buildings (5,000 square meters) for single "anchor" tenants and nine smaller buildings (500 square meters) for multiple tenants. In considering both types we wished to avoid linear ribbon-type buildings that provide homogeneous office units. Buildings for multiple tenants are characterized by smaller spatial units, articulated by floors in order to provide a clear sense of territory. Outdoor covered arcades unite the multitenant buildings and enhance a feeling of openness to the exterior park spaces. Large single-tenant buildings are designed around the idea of a central atrium enveloped in glass to create a sense of unity among the employees. The atrium's transparency allows for views of the surrounding trees and sky as well as the neighboring offices. The contrast of roof forms between the two large buildings—one circular, one parallelogram—produces a skyline silhouette that continually changes as one walks around the complex.

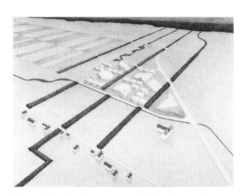

Competition landscape proposal, showing office complexes centered on *allées* of trees leading to the Isar Forest—the "arms of the Isar"

Lookout tower peering over the slanting glass roof of Haus 1

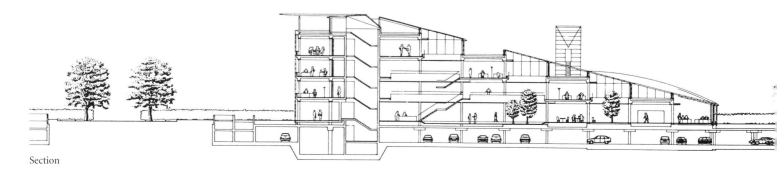

Section

View from Isar Büropark to the surrounding landscape. The striped patterns of the campus landscaping visually recall the banding of the surrounding agricultural lands.

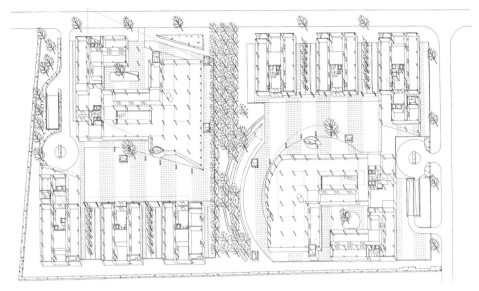

First phase campus seen in axonometric

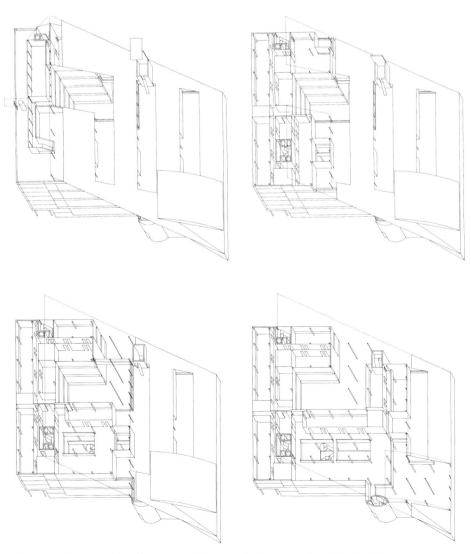

Haus 1 seen in axonometric: office spaces are interspersed with courtyards and interior atrium spaces.

Stair hall in Haus 5

West elevation

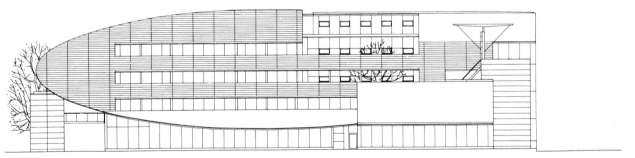

Haus 5, north elevation

The glass roofs sometimes seem to disappear into the sky.

# HILLSIDE TERRACE

Shibuya, Tokyo 1969–92

In the 1960s the site of Hillside Terrace was a strip of sloping forested land in a fashionable suburban area of Tokyo known as Daikanyama; on it were only a few wooden houses belonging to the Asakura family. As they saw Tokyo spreading outward and land values soaring, the owners decided they would need to develop their land in order to retain it. But they were not in a hurry and not looking for instant profits; rather they wanted to adapt the land gradually, to create a place where they could continue to live comfortably for generations. The owners invited our office to draw up a master plan for the development of residential and commercial space in several phases. The site was designated as a restricted residential zone with a 10-meter height limit and floor-area ratio of 150%. Nevertheless, it lay along a busy street connecting several important districts, and shops and restaurants at street level, though they required special zoning permission, seemed destined to succeed.

Despite the changes in planning and construction of the various phases, several themes have remained consistent throughout the design. Our first concern has been to maintain an intimate scale for interior and exterior spaces throughout. Second, we have been interested in the interaction of facade and street space, understanding the sidewalk as a place of activity. The broad, varying paths, platforms, and stairs provided in this zone play no small part in giving Hillside Terrace the spacious character that Tokyo residents might associate with its Western name. Common pedestrian areas act as transition spaces to shops grouped around them. At the same time a concern for the privacy and individuality of single apartments on the upper levels is essential in preserving the character of the Daikanyama site.

The various phases of the complex are unified by their attempt to synthesize modern construction with a more traditional Japanese planning strategy, one which respects the specific character and boundaries of the site as given. In this case we have been dealing with a rather historical piece of land — a small shrine perched on an ancient burial mound (*kofun*) in the site gives evidence of human habitation of this area as early as the seventh century, when Tokyo (then Edo) was no more than a small fishing village. Preserving the spirit of a place is almost implicit in the notion of incremental development, and it is much harder to achieve in building without this sense of change over time.

*Right:* 1995 photograph of Phase I (1969)

*Facing page:* 1995 photograph of Phase VI (1992)

For an architect the opportunity to do this kind of project does not come along that often; we were especially fortunate that our clients had a strong personal concern for the specific character of the development. Although it was not conceived primarily as a profit-making venture, the economic success of Hillside Terrace has brought the development an unexpected degree of popularity, which has changed the scope of the owners' aspirations for later phases.

**Phase I**

From the beginning designs for the Daikanyama site were based into my ongoing research on group form in different cultures. We were particularly interested in developing residences and shops whose public and private spaces would be closely interconnected, similar in a way to the small villages of the Mediterranean. We organized the long, narrow site along two axes: a raised pedestrian deck that runs parallel to the street, providing a mediating zone between the sidewalk and the shops; and a second, meandering axis toward the rear of the site, linking the basement shops with the sunken garden. Exterior stairs and passages were intended to give the buildings an active urban presence.

Only two buildings from this master plan were built in Phase I — those at the easternmost edge of the site. The corner building includes two floors of shops grouped around a transparent atrium space and two floors of apartments. The adjacent building houses a basement restaurant, one floor of shops, and maisonette apartments above. Maisonettes, at that time a new housing type for Japan, were envisioned as the prototype for future development of the street edge. The construction is exposed concrete, with large expanses of glass allowing a high degree of transparency throughout the public spaces.

Phase I: shops are located on the lower levels, with apartments above.

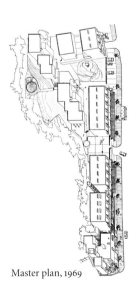

Master plan, 1969

Entrance of maisonette-type apartment

Phase I, second and third floors

1 entrance
2 living room
3 kitchen
4 bedroom
5 terrace
6 maid
7 office

Phase I in 1995

Transparent view through courtyard of Phase II

## Phase II

In the few years that had elapsed since the design and construction of Phase I, significant changes taking place in the city of Tokyo had an impact on the site. The explosion of development in nearby Shibuya meant a significant increase in traffic, noise, and pollution along the front street. Revisions to zoning laws did not permit further development of maisonette-type apartments. At the same time there were lessons to be learned from the performance of the first-phase buildings. In particular the raised pedestrian deck had not worked as intended; one shop owner had rented the entire first floor space, closed up entrances, and reoriented the shop toward the rear.

As a result the building form of Phase II evolved into something quite distinct from what had originally been envisioned. Concerns about the noise and pollution of the street suggested a scheme where shops and apartments would open onto an inner courtyard. The very narrow site directly adjacent to Phase I was left as much needed parking for the shops and Phase II was built farther to the west. Although the street facade presents a more solid edge, the interior passageways are characterized by greater freedom and transparency. Exterior stairs continue as figurative elements in the urban composition. Above street level are a floor of offices and apartments; the third floor is devoted to apartments and common spaces for various members of the Asakura family.

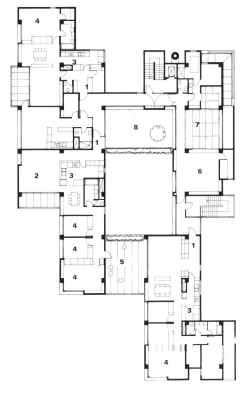

*Above:* View to a roof garden from the Asakura family's third-floor apartment.

*Right:* Phase II, third floor

1 entrance
2 living room
3 kitchen
4 bedroom
5 terrace
6 common room
7 *tatami* room
8 roof garden

*Facing page:* Entrance to the courtyard of Phase II. The street facade maintains the line of the street wall, yet elements such as the stairs and sign sculpture introduce a human scale.

Ancient *kofun* contained in Phase III's courtyard

Entrance lobby

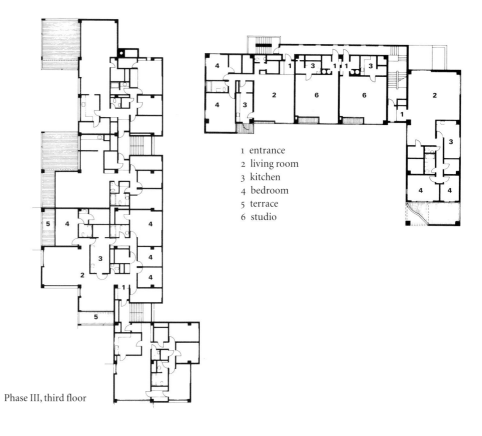

1 entrance
2 living room
3 kitchen
4 bedroom
5 terrace
6 studio

Phase III, third floor

Interior view from third-floor apartment, Phase III. A large zelkova tree sits on top of the ancient *kofun*.

## Phase III

The passage of four more years brought about changes to the Daikanyama site. The area had grown in popularity as a location for business and commerce, particularly for retail fashion. Several of the apartments in the earlier phases had been converted into offices. We anticipated this alternative use in designing the apartments and facades of Phase III. Encouraged by the success of the interior pedestrian court of the previous phase, we allowed the two new buildings to form a broader, more generous courtyard. In contrast to the original masterplan, which overlooked the potential value of the ancient *kofun* in the ensemble of buildings, here the mound is cradled within the space created by the new buildings, protected from the street, and set off as a place of symbolic importance within the entire complex.

The street facade is more controlled and abstract than before, and the palette of materials is more varied. Square ceramic tile, glass block, and both clear and translucent glass compose a facade that has an architectural interest of its own, independent of describing the interior spaces beyond. The *shoji*-inspired translucent panels provide a degree of privacy for the apartments while admitting softened daylight. Circulation spaces and stairs to the upper floors are now largely interiorized, reflecting a shift away from direct expression of movement on the exterior.

Courtyard entrance

Axonometric of southwest corner

## Royal Danish Embassy

During the planning stages of Phase III the Asakura family sold a parcel of land on the western end of their property to the Danish government for the building of a new embassy. The land sale carried with it the stipulation that Maki and Associates design the new building to ensure a harmonious relationship between the embassy and neighboring Hillside Terrace. For security reasons the Danish Embassy required high walls that would separate it from the street and adjacent properties. Nevertheless, we were able to achieve a feeling of continuity at the street facade by pushing the chancery up to the front property line where it functions as a wall protecting the inner court. Although the embassy is more ceremonial in form and material than the buildings of Hillside Terrace and is clad in salmon pink tile on the exterior to distinguish it from the neighboring buildings, we were able to maintain a similar spirit in scale and spatial configuration.

Interior of ambassador's residence looking out to garden. As one enters only a very short distance into the interior of the block, the commotion of Yamate Boulevard gives way to a quiet place of retreat.

The chancery of the Royal Danish Embassy follows the street edge-defining strategy of earlier Hillside Terrace phases and creates a sheltered forecourt to the ambassador's residence. After some negotiation we were able to shift the building a few meters from the property line in order to preserve a 300-year-old oak tree on the corner.

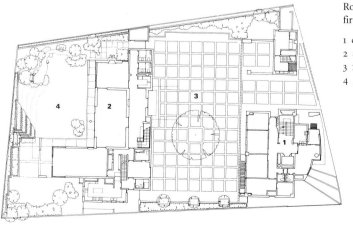

Royal Danish Embassy, first floor

1 chancery
2 ambassador's residence
3 forecourt
4 garden

## Phase IV

Several years after the completion of the third phase the Asakura family decided to develop two small properties adjacent to the Hillside Terrace site. Two buildings were desired to house flexible, atelier-type office space for Asakura Real Estate. Makoto Motokura, a former associate of this office who had worked on earlier phases of Hillside Terrace, was asked to design the fourth phase, known as the Hillside Terrace Annex. The two buildings, conceived as contrasting objectlike volumes, are raised above ground level to provide parking underneath. The opposition of a closed cylindrical volume with a flat wall of glass block creates a dynamic tension in the sloping backstreet space between them.

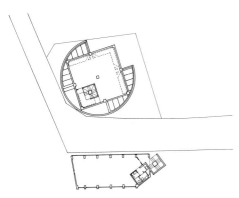

Phase IV, third floor

View of the closed cylindrical and translucent rectilinear volumes of Phase IV

## Phase V

In 1985 we were further invited to propose additional public meeting and exhibition space on the one remaining parcel of unbuilt land on the property: the parking lot between Phases I and II. We considered several schemes for a new building, but in order to preserve the spaciousness and scale of outdoor areas in Hillside Terrace, we finally decided that the best solution would be to maintain an open space at street level (thereafter named Hillside Plaza) and put a large meeting/exhibition space which would be used for fashion shows, public exhibitions, concerts, and parties underground. We repaved the lot and built two small pavilions aboveground — one for the parking attendant and one for stairs down to the exhibition room. A bronze signboard in front orients visitors to the complex.

The open space between Phases I and II were retained by locating Phase V's multipurpose event space below ground.

Phase V in use for exhibition

## Phase VI

In April 1990 the area around Hillside Terrace was rezoned as a class II residential area, which allows higher buildings and raises the allowable floor-area ratio to 200%. Under these new conditions we began the design of the sixth phase of Hillside Terrace on the last piece of land owned by the Asakuras: a site on the north side of the street across from Phase III and the Danish Embassy.

This latest phase comprises three buildings of varying heights. Each contains commercial spaces on the ground and basement floors, and offices and residences on the upper levels. The public spaces of Phase VI are the most elaborate yet and include an art gallery, a media activity center, a tea room, and an interior water court. Phase VI endeavors to retain the intimate scale of the previous buildings in several ways. Its three buildings are grouped around small courtyards; the front court on axis with the passage between Phase III and the Danish Embassy, connects Phase VI to the rest of Hillside Terrace across the street. Although the new buildings are taller (four and five stories) than the earlier ones, we have maintained the street scale by insisting on sharp, projecting eaves at a height of 10 meters and stepping back the volumes of upper floors. The fragmented massing of the large buildings reduces their apparent scale and gives a personal character to individual spaces within.

Perhaps the biggest change in this latest phase is that of constructional approach. Following our experimentation in other recent projects using perforated metals and composite curtain wall construction, we have dealt with issues of privacy and light in the new apartments through a layering of various light-transmitting materials.

View from the courtyard of Phase VI to Phase III

Entrance lobby of the southern building of Phase VI. The Royal Danish Embassy can be seen across the street.

Exhibition gallery and tea room

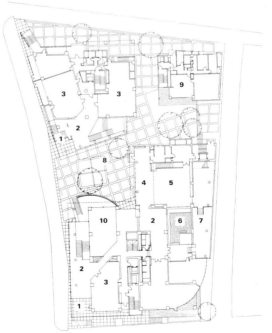

*Above:* Phase VI, first floor

| | |
|---|---|
| 1 entrance | 6 water court |
| 2 lobby | 7 gallery |
| 3 shop | 8 courtyard |
| 4 café | 9 residence |
| 5 forum | 10 void |

*Facing page:* Corner balcony detail, Phase VI

# (ONGOING) INVESTIGATIONS IN COLLECTIVE FORM:
# MAKI'S QUARTER OF A CENTURY AT HILLSIDE TERRACE

Alex Krieger, Professor of Urban Design, Director of Urban Design Program, Harvard Graduate School of Design

While lauded internationally for his architecture, Fumihiko Maki has always been an urbanist first. He has consistently sought to understand buildings as elements of larger settings, and to pursue urban design as an evolutionary process involving incremental rather than apocalyptic change. He assigns to much of his architecture the important role of making visible and, thus, asserting the value of urban life. A devout modernist, he has nonetheless remained committed to the most traditional role of architecture as place making; as a deliberate process of converting site to domain and of first giving form to what is public and therefore shared. All of these urbanistic inclinations lie apparent in the twenty-five-year history of the Hillside Terrace project.

In 1967 Hillside Terrace was a family-held strip of sloped and forested land in the path of expansion of a fashionable suburban neighborhood of Tokyo called Daikanyama. A small shrine on the site, sitting on an ancient *kofun* (sacred mound), offered evidence of habitation dating back to the seventh century. There was already an established bond between the Asakura family and their land. Over the course of the next quarter century, in several phases, the Asakura family commissioned Fumihiko Maki to transform their property into a complex of apartments, shops, offices, galleries, and public spaces that would prepare them and the site for the arrival of modern Tokyo while enabling them still to dwell on their

land. More than twelve members of the family, in several familial groups, still reside on the property.

The various phases of design and construction at Hillside Terrace were intertwined by the dual motivations to accommodate a site to the shifting demands of an expanding modern metropolis, yet maintain—or reinterpret—its spirit of place. It has been a process of reconciling the homogenizing tendencies of modernization and the instinct to protect a milieu. In describing the essence of a self-critical modern practice rooted to a locale, Kenneth Frampton wrote of the need "to mediate the impact of universal civilization with elements derived indirectly from the peculiarities of a particular place."[1] Maki has done this, and made use of the equally critical variable of time.

In an age of facsimile machines, Federal Express, e-mail, and MTV, it is possible to imagine that time has little bearing on design. We speak of instant cities. With our capacities for building rapidly and redundantly we create huge areas of development seemingly overnight, and refer to these as cities. Well, there are a few recent examples where sustained effort on the part of an individual architect, in the design of a collective environment, better portray the importance of temporality to place making. Maki's Hillside Terrace embodies what we still know to be true, despite our technological abilities to collapse time. That urbanity is only

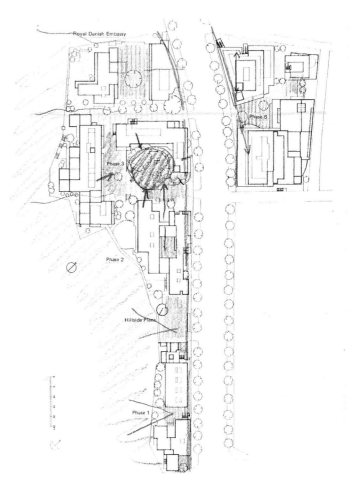

Diagram of views and axes within Hillside Terrace

achievable in increments and across time—a substantial passage of time.

Relying on a vision of urbanity and the gift of time, Maki has created a memorable aggregation of buildings and spaces oriented about, indeed, lending character to, a major urban artery. The achievement would be impressive anywhere, but it is especially remarkable for Tokyo, a city not recently known for its orderly growth patterns or urban continuities. Yet, it may also be said that the work is very much related to Tokyo. Maki has recently described his work as being about "unclear wholes containing clearly defined parts."[2] This may equally be said of modern Tokyo, whose countless districts and nuclei resist a singular impression. Maki's interest in overlapping orders and in the mosaic quality of "group form," as he is fond of calling it, produces at Hillside Terrace a complex order that is at once a microcosm and a fragment of its host metropolis. It is an achievement of contextualism. It is also an achievement of distilling a context.

For Maki modern Tokyo remains "a city without heaviness," where "fluctuation," "fluidity," and "lightness" prevail.[3] While others bemoan such phenomena as being antithetical to traditional urbanism, seeking instead to recapture the physical monumentality, order, and sense of stasis assumed to characterize the preindustrial city, Maki understands that qualities such as fluctuation and fluidity have long been synonymous with urban life. His career-long interest in urban form has not been centered on traditional urban imagery (where the interests of so many have recently been focused) but on how specific urban aggregations portray or, better yet, facilitate social interaction.

Maki's interest in urban design was first sharpened as a student in the 1950s and then as a young faculty member at the Harvard Graduate School of Design, working with people such as Eduard Sekler, Josep Lluís Sert, Jerzy Soltan, Jaquelin Tyrwhitt, and Shadrach Woods. Each of these individuals, as well as the international circle of colleagues revolving around the CIAM splinter group called Team X (of which Soltan and Woods were members), was fully committed to the modern cause, yet managed (unlike many of their immediate CIAM predecessors) to harbor high regard for the premodern traditions of urbanism.[4] This seemingly contradictory stance of championing modern architecture without dismissing the traditional city was an intellectual breakthrough.

They were not yet prepared in the 1950s and 1960s (unlike the postmodern polemicists of the 1970s) to directly use the forms of the traditional city, but by rediscovering time-honored urban qualities they began to mount a sustained critique against the kind of mechanized and bureaucratic urbanism that the post-World War II reconstruction efforts were yielding. That critique, with its reliance on words such as continuity,

Phase I in 1969

Phase I in 1995

mediation, network, linkage, connectivity, super grid, systemic order, megaform, superstructure, and megastructure, expressed a deep urge for a new kind of collective form. The paradox was that while accelerating urban growth seemed to require new models of consolidation and density, the city was actually disaggregating and losing form.

Frustrated with the fractured and rapidly dispersing modern metropolis, the generation out of which Maki emerged struggled to evoke a new holistic image, or shape, for the city. It is difficult today not to smile or feel bemused by the range of "floating cities," "walking cities," "flying cities," and "beehive cities" that sprang forth in the late 1950s and 1960s. Such evocations were simultaneously rejecting the city that modern technology produced while expressing a great optimism in the power of technology to reshape the city again. For the young Maki, having himself experimented with the megastructural muse, the path to a discipline of urban design would not depend exclusively on technological display.[5]

In 1964, three years before starting the initial work on Hillside Terrace, in essence before commencing his remarkable career as a practicing architect, Maki published a small, unassuming booklet (two extended essays, really) which set out to synthesize the prior, and first, decade of his research and teaching. It was entitled *Investigations in Collective Form.* Among its aims, as the title suggests, was to compel architects to transcend their obsession with the individual edifice. "We have so long accustomed ourselves to conceiving of buildings as separate entities," Maki wrote in the introduction, "that today we suffer from an inadequacy of spatial language to make meaningful environments."[6] The philosophical underpinnings for the soon-to-commence design effort at Hillside Terrace are largely to be found in this publication. Context, temporality, precedent, and the incremental build-up of partial and contingent orders each emerge as important variables in the creation of meaningful contemporary environments.

From his earliest writing, therefore, through the achievement of Hillside Terrace (and in much of his other work), Maki shows us the inseparability of architecture and urban design. He shows us that architecture is essential for good urban design. That concern for the city, an urbane view, is in fact essential for good architecture. He shows us that urban design is tangible, finite, physical, rooted, and not merely about policies and codes and social theories. He demonstrates that the optical sense is an essential instrument of making cities, as it is of architecture. He shows us the importance of persistence and patience and commitment to a milieu, not the breathless pursuit for instantaneous credibility. He shows us how to avoid the straitjacket of master planning without abandoning the need for planning. He challenges conventional wisdom about what makes good cities and, in so doing, excavates timeless principles about place making. Lastly, his work discredits one of our great recent myths: that modern architecture and cities are by nature antithetical. For this alone, all those who champion modern architecture and those who champion urbanity owe Fumihiko Maki a great debt.

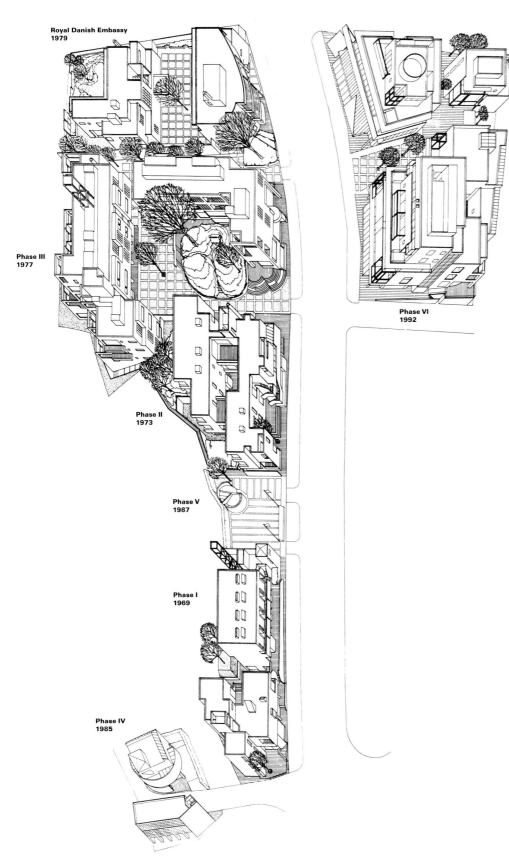

**Royal Danish Embassy**
**1979**

**Phase III**
**1977**

**Phase II**
**1973**

**Phase V**
**1987**

**Phase I**
**1969**

**Phase IV**
**1985**

**Phase VI**
**1992**

Master plan showing Phases I –VI, 1992

**Notes**

1. Kenneth Frampton, "Towards a Critical Regionalism: Six Points for an Architecture of Resistance," in Hal Foster, ed., *The Anti-Aesthetic* (Seattle: Bay Press, 1983): 21.

2. Mark Mulligan, "An Interview with Fumihiko Maki," *GSD News*, Harvard Graduate School of Design (Fall 1993): 55.

3. Fumihiko Maki, "The Roof at Fujisawa," *Perspecta: Yale Architectural Journal* 24 (1988): 106–121.

4. See in particular Alison and Peter Smithson, *Team X Primer* (London, 1965). John Passoneau and Roger Montgomery were two other important colleagues from Maki's teaching experience at Washington University in St. Louis.

5. As one of its founders Maki contributed both essays and conceptual designs to the initial issues of the journal *Metabolism*. The fifth edition of Sigfried Giedion's famed *Space, Time and Architecture* (Cambridge, Mass.: Harvard University Press, 1968), 841, includes a photograph and a brief but favorable description of one of Maki's megastructural projects.

6. Fumihiko Maki, *Investigations in Collective Form*, Washington University School of Architecture (June 1964): 5.

Aerial view of Phases I–VI

# PROJECT DATA

**Key**

**Project name**
1 Location
2 Site area
3 Building area
4 Total floor area
5 Structural system, number of floors
6 Structural engineer
7 Mechanical/electrical engineer
8 Other consultants (furniture, lighting, etc.)
9 Contractor
10 Completion date

**Spiral**
1 5-6-23 Minami Aoyama, Minato-ku, Tokyo
2 1,723m$^2$
3 1,462m$^2$
4 10,560m$^2$
5 steel-reinforced concrete (SRC), 9 stories + 2 basements
6 Kimura Structural Engineers
7 Sogo Consultants
8 Furniture: Maki and Associates + Kazuko Fujie Atelier
  Signage: Masayoshi Nakajo
  Sculpture: Aiko Miyawaki
  Carpets: Kei Miyazaki
9 Takenaka Corporation
10 October 1985

**National Museum of Modern Art, Kyoto**
1 Okazaki Park, Sakyo-ku, Kyoto
2 5,001m$^2$
3 2,142m$^2$
4 9,983m$^2$
5 reinforced concrete (RC) + steel frame, 4 stories + 1 basement
6 Kimura Structural Engineers
7 P. T. Morimura and Associates
8 Furniture: Kazuko Fujie Atelier
  Carpets: Kei Miyazaki
  Signage: Kijuro Yahagi
  Chandeliers: Hidetoshi Ohno
9 Takenaka Corporation
10 September 1986

**Tepia**
1 Kita Aoyama, Minato-ku, Tokyo
2 6,077m$^2$
3 2,324m$^2$
4 13,810m$^2$
5 SRC, 4 stories + 2 basements
6 Kimura Structural Engineers
7 Sogo Consultants
8 Furniture: Kazuko Fujie Atelier
  Carpets: Kei Miyazaki
  Signage: Kijuro Yahagi
9 Joint venture of Kajima, Shimizu, Hazama-gumi
10 April 1989

**Center for the Arts Yerba Buena Gardens**
Collaborating architects: Robinson Mills + Williams
1 701 Mission Street, San Francisco, California
2 4,994m$^2$
3 3,456m$^2$
4 5,338m$^2$
5 steel moment frame, 2 stories
6 Structural Design Engineers
7 SJ Engineers/FW Associates
8 Theatrical and lighting: S. Leonard Auerbach & Associates
  Graphics: Laura Hogan Design
  Bench: Kazuko Fujie Atelier
9 Turner Construction Company, Construction Manager
  Sumitomo Construction America, Contractor
10 October 1993

**Iwasaki Art Museum**
1 Ibusuki-shi, Kagoshima Prefecture
2 9,805m$^2$
3 1,114m$^2$
4 1,347m$^2$
5 RC, 1 story + 1 basement
6 Kimura Structural Engineers
7 Sogo Consultants
9 Hazama-gumi
10 December 1978

**Iwasaki Craft Museum**
1 Ibusuki-shi, Kagoshima Prefecture
2 9,805m$^2$
3 646m$^2$
4 1,182m$^2$
5 RC, 2 stories + 1 basement
6 Hanawa Structural Engineers
7 Sogo Consultants
9 Hazama-gumi
10 March 1987

**YKK Guest House**
1 3-418 Maezawa-dani, Kurobe-shi, Toyama
  Prefecture
2 56,124m$^2$
3 754m$^2$
4 1,695m$^2$
5 RC, 3 stories + 1 basement
6 Hanawa Structural Engineers
7 Sogo Consultants
8 Furniture: Endo Planning + Kazuko Fujie
  Atelier
9 Shimizu Corporation
10 September 1982

**Tokyo Church of Christ**
1 1-30-17 Tomigaya, Shibuya-ku, Tokyo
2 1,244m$^2$
3 947m$^2$
4 2,242m2
5 SRC + steel (roof), 3 stories + 1 basement
6 Kimura Structural Engineers
7 Sogo Consultants
9 Takenaka Corporation
10 September 1995

**Children's House**
Collaborating architects: Krakow Technical
University
1 Oswiecim, Poland
2 625m$^2$
3 127m$^2$
4 215m$^2$
5 RC + masonry infill, wood roof, 3 stories + 1
  basement

**Floating Pavilion**
1 Groningen, Netherlands
3 163m$^2$
5 steel structure on reinforced concrete barge
6 SDG

**Kirishima International Concert Hall**
1 3-311-29 Takachiho, Makizono-cho,
  Kagoshima Prefecture
2 44,800m$^2$
3 3,190m$^2$
4 4,904m$^2$
5 RC, steel frame (amphitheater), 2 stories + 1
  basement
6 SDG
7 Sogo Consultants
8 Acoustics: Yoichi Ando
  Lighting/Stage: Nagata Acoustics
  Landscape: Equipe Espace
9 Takenaka Corporation
10 June 1994

**Graduate School Research Center**
Keio University Shonan Fujisawa Campus
1 5-322 Endo, Fujisawa-shi, Kanagawa
  Prefecture
2 313,009m$^2$
3 1,299m$^2$
4 3,670m$^2$
5 RC, 4 stories
6 Kimura Structural Engineers
7 P. T. Morimura and Associates
8 Furniture: Endo Planning
  Signage: Edge Design Office
  Landscape: Equipe Espace
9 Tokyu Construction
10 February 1994

**Tsukuba University Central Building**

1 Shinji-gun, Ibaraki Prefecture
3 4,524m$^2$
4 18,026m$^2$
5 SRC + steel frame, 6 stories + 1 basement
6 Kimura Structural Engineers
7 Sakurai Consultants
9 Asanuma-gumi
10 September 1974

**Osaka Prefectural Sports Center**

1 Takaishi, Osaka
2 23,606m$^2$
3 10,092m$^2$
4 11,930m$^2$
5 RC + steel frame, 2 stories + 1 basement
6 Aoki Structural Engineers
7 Sakurai Consultants
9 Zenitaka-gumi
10 June 1972

**National Aquarium, Okinawa**

1 Motobu-cho, Kunisaki-gun, Okinawa
 Prefecture
2 28,100m$^2$
3 6,058m$^2$
4 7,700m$^2$
5 SRC, steel, precast concrete frame, 3 stories +
 1 basement
6 Kimura Structural Engineers
7 P. T. Morimura and Associates
9 Joint venture of Kajima Corporation and
 others
10 July 1975

**Fujisawa Municipal Gymnasium**

1 Endo-mukohara, Fujisawa-shi, Kanagawa
 Prefecture
2 64,105m$^2$
3 6,738m$^2$
4 11,100m$^2$
5 RC, SRC, steel (roof), 3 stories + 1 basement
6 Kimura Structural Engineers
7 P. T. Morimura and Associates
8 Landscape: Parks Bureau, City of Fujisawa
 Signage: Maki and Associates + Akihiro
 Nagao
9 Hazama-gumi
10 September 1984

**Tokyo Metropolitan Gymnasium**

1 Sendagaya, Shibuya-ku, Tokyo
2 45,800m$^2$
3 24,100m$^2$
4 43,971m$^2$
5 RC, SRC, steel (roofs), 3 stories + 2
 basements
6 Kimura Structural Engineers
7 Sogo Consultants
8 Landscape: Equipe Espace
 Counter: Kazuko Fujie Atelier
 Acoustics: NHK Technical Research Center
 + Yamaha Acoustic Research Center
9 Joint venture of Shimizu, Tokyu, and others
10 March 1990

**Makuhari Messe**

1 Nakase, Makuhari New Town, Chiba
 Prefecture
2 173,191m$^2$
3 105,144m$^2$
4 131,043m$^2$
5 RC + steel, 4 stories + 1 basement
6 Kimura Structural Engineers + SDG
7 Sogo Consultants
8 Landscape: Equipe Espace
 Signage: GK Sekkei
 Special exhibition interior: Kazuko Fujie
 Atelier
 Carpets: Kei Miyazaki
 Acoustics: NHK Engineering Service
 Lighting/Stage: Theatrical Engineering
 Research Center
9 Joint venture of Shimizu, Kajima, Takenaka,
 Toshima, Mitsui (Exhibition Hall);
 Obayashi, Asahi (Event Hall); Taisei, Shin-
 Nippon (Conference Center)
10 September 1989

**Makuhari Messe, Phase II**

1 Nakase, Makuhari New Town, Chiba
 Prefecture
2 43,960m$^2$
3 30,572m$^2$
4 33,413m$^2$
5 SRC + steel (roof structure), 2 stories
6 SDG
7 Sogo Consultants
8 Landscape: Equipe Espace
9 Joint venture of Shimizu, Obayashi, Mitsui
10 September 1997 (projected)

**Keio University Shonan Fujisawa Campus**
1 Endo, Fujisawa, Kanagawa Prefecture
2 313,009m$^2$
3 17,226m$^2$
4 42,882m$^2$
5 RC, steel (gymnasium roof), 4 stories +
  1 basement
6 Kimura Structural Engineers, SDG, and
  Hanawa Structural Engineers
7 P. T. Morimura and Associates
8 Acoustics: Nagata Acoustics
  Landscape: Maki and Associates + Equipe
  Espace
  Furniture: Maki and Associates + Endo
  Planning
  Signage: Maki and Associates + Akihiro
  Nagao
9 Divided among Tokyu, Shimizu, Kajima,
  Taisei, Ando, Obayashi, Zenitaka, Nippon
  Kokudo Kaihatsu, Takenaka, Fujita, Mitsui,
  Toda
10 February 1994

**Isar Büropark**
Collaborating architects: Schmidt-Schicketanz
& Partner
1 Hallbergmoos, near Munich, Germany
2 38,274m$^2$
3 14,357m$^2$
4 68,366m$^2$
5 RC, steel (roof), 5 stories + 1 basement
6 Schmidt-Stump & Frühauf
8 Landscape: Sasaki Environment Design +
  Cordes & Partner
  Facade Engineer: Fuchs Ing.-Büro
9 Philipp Holzmann-Held & Francke Bau AG
10 May 1995

**Hillside Terrace, Phases I–III**
1 Sarugaku-cho, Shibuya-ku, Tokyo
2 7,320m$^2$
3 2,682m$^2$
4 9,263m$^2$
5 RC, 3 stories + 1 basement
6 Yamaki Structural Engineers (I + II); Aoki
  Structural Engineers (III)
7 Sakurai Consultants (I + II); Sogo
  Consultants (III)
8 Furniture: Maki and Associates + Endo
  Planning
  Signage: Kei Kuritsu, ASPI, Makoto
  Motokura
9 Takenaka Corporation
10 October 1969 (I); May 1973 (II); December
  1977 (III)

**Royal Danish Embassy**
1 Sarugaku-cho, Shibuya-ku, Tokyo
2 1,972m$^2$
3 766m$^2$
4 1,896m$^2$
5 RC, 3 stories + 1 basement
6 Aoki Structural Engineers
7 Sogo Consultants
9 Takenaka Corporation
10 October 1979

**Hillside Terrace, Phase V**
1 Sarugaku-cho, Shibuya-ku, Tokyo
2 679m$^2$
3 90m$^2$
4 621m$^2$
5 RC, 1 story + 2 basements
6 Hanawa Structural Engineers
7 Sogo Consultants
9 Takenaka Corporation
10 June 1985

**Hillside Terrace, Phase VI**
1 Sarugaku-cho, Shibuya-ku, Tokyo
2 3,302m$^2$
3 2,233m$^2$
4 8,362m$^2$
5 RC, 6 stories + 2 basements
6 Aoki Structural Engineers
7 Sogo Consultants
8 Bench: Kazuko Fujie Atelier
9 Takenaka Corporation
10 March 1992

# PROJECT CHRONOLOGY

## 1960–1996

1960
Steinberg Hall at Washington University
St. Louis, USA

1960
Shinjuku Terminal Redevelopment Project
Shinjuku-ku, Tokyo

1961
Competition for Diamond Heights Housing Development
San Francisco, USA

1962
Nagoya University Toyoda Memorial Hall
Nagoya

1962
Chiba University Memorial Auditorium
Chiba

1963
Competition for Kyoto International Congress Hall
Kyoto

1965
Movement Systems in the City
Boston, USA

1968
Rissho University Kumagaya Campus
Kumagaya, Saitama

1968
Golgi Structures

1968
International Competition for UNIDO & IAEA
Vienna, Austria

1969–92
Hillside Terrace Apartment Complex, Phases I–VI
Shibuya-ku, Tokyo

1969
Competition for the Supreme Court
Tokyo

Toyoda Memorial Hall, Nagoya University

Rissho University

1969
Mogusa Community Center
Tokyo

1969
Senri Civic Center Building
Senri, Osaka

1970
Senboku Archeological Museum
Senboku, Osaka

1970
Park House Shirogane
Shinagawa-ku, Tokyo

1971
Kanazawa Ward Offices
Kanazawa, Yokohama

1972
Redevelopment Plan for Downtown Santiago
Santiago, Chile

1972
St. Mary's International School
Setagaya-ku, Tokyo

1972
Kato Gakuen Elementary School
Numazu, Shizuoka

1972
Osaka Prefectural Sports Center
Takaishi, Osaka

1973
Hiroo Homes & Towers
Minato-ku, Tokyo

1974
Tsukuba University Central Building
Tsukuba, Ibaraki

1974
Tsukuba Academic New Town
Tsukuba, Ibaraki

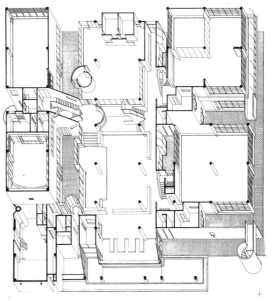

Kato Gakuen Elementary School

1974
Noba Kindergarten
Yokohama, Kanagawa

1974
Toyota Kuragaike Memorial Hall
Toyota, Aichi

1975
Public Housing Project
Lima, Peru

1975
Japanese Embassy
Brasilia, Brazil

1975
Marine Life Park for Expo '75
Okinawa

1976
Austrian Embassy
Minato-ku, Tokyo

1977
Competition for Okinawa Town Hall
Okinawa

1978
Competition for Gunma Prefecture Women's College
Gunma

1978
Namiki Elementary School
Yokohama, Kanagawa

1978
Maki Residence
Shinagawa-ku, Tokyo

1979
Windsor House
Shinagawa-ku, Tokyo

1979
Iwasaki Art Museum
Ibusuki, Kagoshima

Toyota Kuragaike Memorial Hall

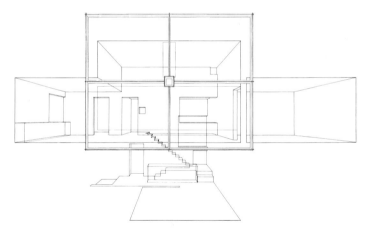

Maki Residence

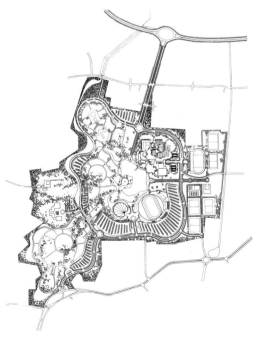

Kota Kinabalu Sports Center, Malaysia

1979
Royal Danish Embassy
Shibuya-ku, Tokyo

1979
Lounge in Jun Ashida Building
Shibuya-ku, Tokyo

1980
Kawawa Lower Secondary School
Yokohama, Kanagawa

1980
Residence in Takanawa
Minato-ku, Tokyo

1981
Kyoto Craft Center ABL
Higashiyama-ku, Kyoto

1981
Mitsubishi Bank, Hiroo Branch
Minato-ku, Tokyo

1981
Toranomon NN Building
Minato-ku, Tokyo

1981
Keio University Library, Mita Campus
Minato-ku, Tokyo

1982
Renovation of Former Keio University Library, Mita Campus
Minato-ku, Tokyo

1982
Kota Kinabalu Sports Center
Sabah, Malaysia

1982
YKK Guest House
Kurobe, Toyama

1983
Dentsu Osaka Office
Kita-ku, Osaka

Keio University Library

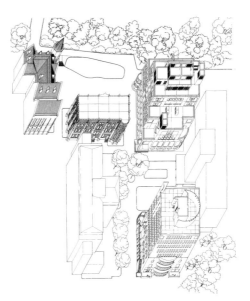

Keio University Library and Graduate Center, Mita Campus

1983
Residence in Shiroganedai
Minato-ku, Tokyo

1984
Cedar Stone Villa
Shibuya-ku, Tokyo

1984
Garden Plaza Hiroo
Minato-ku, Tokyo

1984
Minami Osawa Housing Project
Tama New Town, Tokyo

1984
Fujisawa Municipal Gymnasium
Fujisawa, Kanagawa

1985
Spiral
Minato-ku, Tokyo

1985
Keio University Graduate School, Mita Campus
Minato-ku, Tokyo

1985
Keio University Hiyoshi Library
Yokohama, Kanagawa

1985
West Plaza at Yokohama Central Station
Yokohama, Kanagawa

1985
International Pavilions for Tsukuba Expo '85
Tsukuba, Ibaraki

1986
National Museum of Modern Art, Kyoto
Sakyo-ku, Kyoto

1987
Competition for Vienna Messepalast
Vienna, Austria

International Pavilion for Tsukuba Expo '85

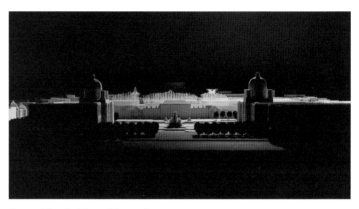

Competition for Vienna Messepalast

1987
Iwasaki Art Museum Annex
Ibusuki, Kagoshima

1988
Tsuda Hall
Shibuya-ku, Tokyo

1989
Dai-Tokyo Fire & Marine Insurance Shinjuku Building
Shibuya-ku, Tokyo

1989
Toyama Shimin Plaza
Toyama, Toyama

1989
Tepia
Minato-ku, Tokyo

1989
Competition for the Zeebrugge Sea Ferry Terminal
Zeebrugge, Belgium

1989
Competition for Bibliothèque Nationale de France
Paris, France

1989
Nippon Convention Center (Makuhari Messe)
Makuhari, Chiba

1990
Tokyo Metropolitan Gymnasium
Shibuya-ku, Tokyo

1990
Competition for Palazzo del Cinema
Venice, Italy

1990
Competition for Museum of Contemporary Art
Stuttgart, Germany

1990–
Children's House
Oswiecim, Poland

Tsuda Hall

1990–94
Keio University Shonan Fujisawa Campus
Fujisawa, Kanagawa

1991
Competition for Kyoto Symphony Hall
Sakyo-ku, Kyoto

1991–
Kitanaka Redevelopment
Yokohama, Kanagawa

1991–
Frankfurt am Main Center
Frankfurt, Germany

1992
Competition for Swimming/Diving Hall, Velodrome for Olympics 2000
Berlin, Germany

1993
Competition for Salzburg Congress Center
Salzburg, Austria

1993
Nakatsu Obata Memorial Library
Nakatsu, Oita

1993
Sandoz Tsukuba Research Institute
Tsukuba, Ibaraki

1993
YKK R & D Center
Sumida-ku, Tokyo

1993
Center for the Arts Yerba Buena Gardens
San Francisco, USA

1994
Graduate School Research Center, Keio University Shonan Fujisawa Campus
Fujisawa, Kanagawa

1994
Seminar Guest House, Keio University Shonan Fujisawa Campus
Fujisawa, Kanagawa

Frankfurt am Main Center

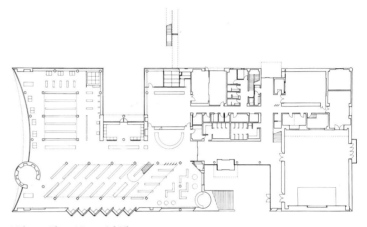

Nakatsu Obata Memorial Library

YKK R & D Center

1994
Kirishima International Concert Hall
Makizono, Kagoshima

1994–
Project Alameda Urbana
Mexico City, Mexico

1995
Isar Büropark
Munich, Germany

1995
Floating Pavilion
Groningen, Netherlands

1995
Tokyo Church of Christ
Shibuya-ku, Tokyo

1996
Kaze-no-Oka Crematorium
Nakatsu, Oita

1996
Fukuoka University Student Center
Jonan-ku, Fukuoka

1996
Kanagawa University Auditorium
Yokohama, Kanagawa

1997
District Community & Care Center
Yokohama, Kanagawa

1997
Natori Performing Arts Center
Natori, Miyagi

1998
Nippon Convention Center (Makuhari Messe), Phase II
Makuhari, Chiba

1998
Bürocenter Grafenberger Allee
Düsseldorf, Germany

2000
Asahi Television Headquarters & Studios
Minato-ku, Tokyo

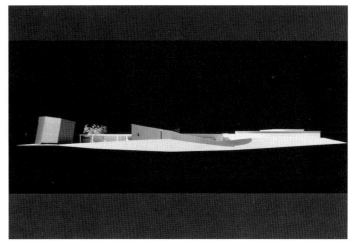

Kaze-no-Oka Crematorium

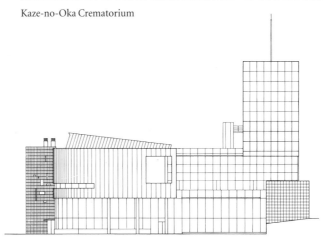

Student Center, Fukuoka University

# BIOGRAPHY

Born 1928, Tokyo

## Education

| | |
|---|---|
| 1952 | Bachelor of Architecture, University of Tokyo |
| 1953 | Master of Architecture, Cranbrook Academy of Art |
| 1954 | Master of Architecture, Graduate School of Design, Harvard University |

## Professional Career

| | |
|---|---|
| 1954–55 | Designer, Skidmore Owings and Merrill, New York, New York |
| 1955–58 | Designer, Sert Jackson and Associates, Cambridge, Massachusetts |
| 1956–58 | Associate, Campus Planning Office, Washington University, St. Louis, Missouri |
| 1958–65 | Consultant for a number of offices in the United States and Japan |
| 1965– | Principal, Maki and Associates, Tokyo |
| 1987–90 | Member, International Committee of Japan Institute of Architects |

## Professional Affiliations

Registered Architect, Japan
Member, Japan Institute of Architects
Honorary Fellow, American Institute of Architects
Honorary Fellow, Royal Institute of British Architects
Honorary Fellow, Czech Institute of Architects

## Teaching and Research

| | |
|---|---|
| 1956–58 | Assistant Professor, Washington University |
| 1958–60 | Graham Foundation Fellow |
| 1960–62 | Associate Professor, Washington University |
| 1962–65 | Associate Professor, GSD, Harvard University |
| 1965–67 | Visiting Critic, GSD, Harvard University |
| 1969–70 | Visiting Critic, University of California, Berkeley |
| 1971 | Visiting Critic, University of California, Los Angeles |
| 1976 | Visiting Lecturer, JDR III Fund Fellow, Columbia University |
| 1976 | Visiting Critic, University of California, Los Angeles |
| 1977 | Visiting Lecturer, Technical University of Vienna |
| 1983 | Elliot Noyse Visiting Professor, Harvard University |
| 1985 | Overseeing Assessor, Hong Kong University |
| 1985 | Visiting Critic, Columbia University |
| 1968–79 | Visiting Lecturer, Department of Urban Engineering, University of Tokyo |
| 1979–89 | Professor, Department of Architecture, University of Tokyo |
| 1993–95 | Visiting Lecturer, Keio University, School of Environmental Information |

## Domestic Awards

| | |
|---|---|
| 1963 | Japan Institute of Architecture (for Toyoda Memorial Hall) |
| 1969 | Mainichi Art Prize (for Rissho University Kumagaya Campus) |
| 1973 | The 24th Art Prize from Ministry of Education (for Hillside Terrace) |
| 1980 | Japan Art Prize (for Hillside Terrace) |
| 1985 | Japan Institute of Architecture (for Fujisawa Municipal Gymnasium) |
| 1991 | International Design Award, Osaka |
| 1993 | Asahi Prize |

## International Awards

| | |
|---|---|
| 1987 | Honorary Doctor's Degree in Art and Architecture, Washington University |
| 1987 | Reynolds Memorial Award (for Spiral Building) |
| 1988 | Wolf Prize, Israel |
| 1988 | Chicago Architecture Award |
| 1990 | Thomas Jefferson Medal in Architecture, Charlottesville, Virginia |
| 1993 | Pritzker Architecture Prize |
| 1993 | Gold Medal, International Union of Architects (UIA) |
| 1993 | Prince of Wales Prize in Urban Design, Harvard University (for Hillside Terrace) |
| 1993 | Quaternario '93 International Award for Innovative Technology in Architecture (for Makuhari Messe) |
| 1994 | Asia-Pacific Distinguished Architectural Scholar Award, Honolulu, Hawaii |
| 1995 | Concrete Architecture Prize, Swedish Concrete Institute |

## Project Prizes

| | |
|---|---|
| 1958 | P/A Award Program, Citation for Meditation Chapel, Washington University |
| 1963 | Finalist, National Competition for Diamond Heights Housing, San Francisco, California |
| 1969 | First Prize (one of three), International Competition for Low Cost Housing, Lima, Peru |
| 1986 | First Prize, Makuhari Messe Competition, Chiba, Japan |
| 1990 | First Prize, Büropark Hallbergmoos Competition, Munich, Germany |
| 1991 | First Prize, Bürozentrum Hemmerichsweg Competition, Frankfurt, Germany |
| 1993 | First Prize, Bürocenter Grafenberger Allee, Düsseldorf, Germany |
| 1993 | Second Prize, Salzburg Congress Center, Austria |

## Juror

## Recent Major Public Lectures Abroad

## Exhibitions

# FUMIHIKO MAKI—SELECTED BIBLIOGRAPHY

1960    *Metabolism 1960*, Bijutsu Shuppansha, Tokyo

1964    *Investigations in Collective Form*, Washington University, St. Louis

1965    *Movement Systems in the City*, Graduate School of Design, Harvard University, Cambridge
        "Some Thoughts on Collective Form" (co-author) in *Structure in Art and Science*, edited by Gyorgy
          Kepes, George Brazilier, New York
        Japanese translation of *Communitas* by Paul and Percival Goodman, Shokokusha, Tokyo

1978    *Fumihiko Maki 1: 1965-78*, Contemporary Architects Series, Kajima Publishing Co., Tokyo

1979    *Miegakuresuru Toshi: A Morphological Analysis of the City of Edo-Tokyo*, Kajima Publishing Co.,
        Tokyo

1986    *Fumihiko Maki 2: 1979-86*, Contemporary Architects Series, Kajima Publishing Co., Tokyo

1987    *Design Methodology in Technology and Science* (co-author), Tokyo University Press, Tokyo
        *Fumihiko Maki: Une Poétique de la Fragmentation* by Serge Salat, Electa Moniteur, Paris

1989    *Fragmentary Figures: The Collected Architectural Drawings of Fumihiko Maki*, Kyurudo, Tokyo

1992    *Kioku no Keizo: A Collection of Essays*, Kajima Publishing Co., Tokyo

1993    *Fumihiko Maki 3: 1986-92*, Contemporary Architects Series, Kajima Publishing Co., Tokyo

# MAKI AND ASSOCIATES
## STAFF LIST 1965–1996

| Name | Years |
|---|---|
| Jun Aoki | 1980–1991 |
| Kohsuke Arai | 1993– |
| Fabian Berthold | 1993–1995 |
| Masahiro Chiba | 1992– |
| Steve Dayton | 1987–1989 |
| Seiichi Endo | 1965–1968 |
| Tomoyoshi Fukunaga | 1967– |
| Kenji Fukuzawa | 1965–1972 |
| Takayuki Fumoto | 1992–1996 |
| Reiko Habe | 1968–1970 |
| Toshio Hachiya | 1983– |
| Paul Harney | 1991–1993 |
| Tatsutomo Hasegawa | 1995– |
| Yutaka Hirota | 1977–1987 |
| Shigeki Honda | 1993– |
| Hideaki Hoshina | 1972–1977 |
| Masao Ichikawa | 1990–1993 |
| Yasushi Ikeda | 1987–1995 |
| Jun Imaizumi | 1995– |
| Naoki Kadowaki | 1990–1995 |
| Gary Kamemoto | 1984– |
| Naruya Kamihara | 1976–1993 |
| Hirochika Kashima | 1984– |
| Noriko Kawamura | 1986–1995 |
| Kohta Kawasaki | 1995– |
| Yoko Kobayashi | 1972–1977 |
| Akiko Kokubun | 1988– |
| Yoshiki Kondo | 1992– |
| Hiromi Kouda | 1991– |
| Minoru Kudaka | 1991–1994 |
| Masaaki Kurihara | 1991– |
| Akira Kuryu | 1973–1979 |
| Takao Masuda | 1987– |
| Lawrence Matott | 1988–1990 |
| Shigekazu Miyamoto | 1988–1993 |
| Hiroshi Miyazaki | 1979–1989 |
| Kei Mizui | 1982– |
| Tetsuya Mori | 1987–1995 |
| Toshihide Mori | 1974–1990 |
| Makoto Motokura | 1971–1976 |
| Geoffrey Moussas | 1994– |
| Mark Mulligan | 1990–1996 |
| Akira Murai | 1965–1968 |

| Name | Years |
|---|---|
| Koichi Nagashima | 1966–1969, 1972–1977 |
| Koichi Naito | 1965–1968 |
| Ben Nakamura | 1969–1977 |
| Kenichi Nakamura | 1984–1991, 1993– |
| Tsuneaki Nakano | 1974–1984 |
| Yasuo Nakata | 1991– |
| Katsuhiko Nishida | 1971–1990 |
| Hidetoshi Ohno | 1976–1983 |
| Seiji Okamoto | 1970–1984 |
| Shuji Oki | 1987– |
| Masahiro Ono | 1965–1973 |
| Tohru Onuma | 1991– |
| Fumiko Ozaki | 1974–1976 |
| Kazunori Ozaki | 1970–1992 |
| Tamotsu Ozaki | 1965–1970 |
| Akira Ozawa | 1967–1975, 1977–1980 |
| Goro Saigo | 1970–1976 |
| Osamu Sassa | 1994– |
| Fumito Sato | 1981– |
| Kiyohide Sawaoka | 1980–1992 |
| Morikazu Shibuya | 1966–1985 |
| Iwao Shida | 1965– |
| Tomoya Sugiura | 1994– |
| Makoto Takashina | 1970–1974 |
| Tokihiko Takatani | 1976–1989 |
| Norio Takata | 1978–1990 |
| Koichi Tanaka | 1986–1993 |
| Kazuo Teramoto | 1972–1978 |
| Atsushi Tokushige | 1992– |
| Reiko Tomuro | 1983–1996 |
| Akira Uenishi | 1984– |
| Yoshitaka Wada | 1987– |
| Yukitoshi Wakatsuki | 1973– |
| Eiji Watanabe | 1973–1992 |
| Hiroshi Watanabe | 1971–1977 |
| Jun Watanabe | 1985–1990 |
| Yasuo Watanabe | 1966–1971 |
| Keisuke Yamamoto | 1974–1989 |
| Yuzo Yamanaka | 1978– |
| Satoru Yamashiro | 1995– |
| Norio Yokota | 1989– |
| Masaaki Yoshizaki | 1987– |
| Seiichi Yukutomi | 1970–1975 |

# PHOTO CREDITS

Maki and Associates wishes to extend its deepest gratitude to the following persons for allowing their photographs to be reprinted in this book:

Richard Barnes: 47, 51
Fabian Berthold: 110 (top)
Botond Bognar: 124 (lower left), 125 (left and middle), 127, 130, 131
Katsuaki Furudate: 9
Toshiharu Kitajima: 6 (top), 8 (bottom), 10–11, 15–17, 20, 23, 25–27, 28 (bottom), 29-31, 32 (top), 34–35, 37, 41, 60-62, 71–75, 84 (top), 86–87, 99, 100 (top), 113, 106–107, 109, 112, 114, 116 (top), 166 (bottom), 171 (top), 175–178, 187, 190–193, 194 (bottom), 197, 199–201, 220, 224, 250 (top), 264, 266
Koji Kobayashi: 161
Satoru Mishima (Nikkei Business Publications, Inc.): 12, 165
Ryuji Miyamoto: 245 (top)
Kaneaki Monma: 144 (top), 145–147, 242, 243 (top), 244
Osamu Murai: 56, 59, 65–69, 137–138, 141–143
Office Age: 110, 116 (bottom)
Taisuke Ogawa: 184–185
Tomio Ohashi: 4 (top), 19, 123 (left)
Paul Peck: 42–46, 48
Hiroyasu Sakaguchi: 84 (bottom)
Shinkenchiku-sha: 6 (bottom), 8 (top), 18, 21 (top, bottom),22, 28 (top), 38–39, 49, 53, 63, 76–77, 89, 115 (right), 135, 148, 151, 155–158, 162 (top), 166 (top), 171 (bottom), 195, 198 (left), 218–219, 221, 222 (top), 223, 225–226, 229–231, 233, 234 (top), 235, 238 (top), 241, 246–247, 248 (bottom), 249, 251, 254, 255, 267
Shokoku-sha: 123 (lower right), 238 (bottom)
John Stoel: 197
Judith Turner: 153
Tohru Waki (Shokoku-sha): 140, 156, 170, 176, 180–181
Kijuro Yahagi: Photo Essay (i–xi) and 3, 4 (bottom), 5, 13, 24, 32 (bottom), 33, 55, 58, 100 (bottom), 101, 104–105, 108, 111, 113, 118, 150, 152, 160, 163, 168–169, 172–173, 179, 188, 196 (left), 236–237, 239–240

The *ukiyo-e* image on 128 was first published in Japan by Shueisha, Inc.

The aerial photograph of a Japanese village on 211 is reprinted from *Japan from the Air* by Susumu Higachi.

The nineteenthth-century image of Amsterdam on 214 is reprinted from *Towns and Buildings* by Steen Eiler Rasmussen.

The plan of Hook New Town Center on 217 is reprinted from *Planning a New Town* by the London County Council.

All other photographs and images are the property of Maki and Associates.